Sunset

Easy Basics

for Good Cooking

BY THE EDITORS OF SUNSET BOOKS AND SUNSET MAGAZINE

Lane Publishing Co. • Menlo Park, California

Welcome to good cooking...

If you have a special liking for good food, this book is for you—even if you've never done much beyond boiling water. Or if you are a person with years of cooking experience, but want to stretch your skills, want to explore the whys and hows of great chefs' expertise, this is your book, too.

An art as well as a science, good cooking rests on basic principles and skills that have been refined over many centuries by food-lovers throughout the world. These skills are spelled out here, in clear, easy steps—many of them in drawings or photo sequences.

Plunge in and have fun—your family, friends, and you yourself will relish the results while you build your new reputation as a terrific cook.

Preparing this book was a team effort by many people, and to all of them, we say thanks.

For her inspiration and knowledge of basic good cooking, we extend a special thank-you to Pam Wischkaemper. We also extend thanks to Patti Nikolić for her assistance in our many testing sessions, and to Charles O'Donnell, Egon Handel, Arturo Lionetti, and Shirley and Will Huffstutler for their expertise in special fields.

For sharing the kitchenware and decorative accessories used in our photographs, our appreciation goes to Allied Arts Traditional Shop, Good Cooks & Co., House of Today, Menlo Park Hardware, Taylor & Ng, The Cotton Works, William Ober Co., and Williams-Sonoma Kitchenware.

Research & Text
Janeth Johnson Nix
Elaine R. Woodard

Coordinating Editor
Cornelia Fogle

Staff Editor
Susan Warton

Contributing Editor
Joan Griffiths

Managing Editors
Elizabeth Livingston Hogan
Holly Lyman Antolini

Design: **Joe di Chiarro**
Photography: **Darrow M. Watt**
Photo Editor: **Lynne B. Morrall**
Illustrations: **Sally Shimizu**

Cover: Photograph by **Cunkel & Turner.** Cover design by **Williams & Ziller.**

Editor, Sunset Books: David E. Clark
May 1988

CONTENTS

GETTING STARTED

Welcome to fun, satisfaction, and unmatched achievement. Welcome to good cooking. With your kitchen as workshop, fresh ingredients as raw material, and this book as your guide, you're all set to embark on creative adventures with immediate and great-tasting rewards. None but the culinary arts can promise quite such a bonus to you and your lucky family, you and your grateful guests.

This is no armchair book; it's one to experience as you read. With recipes serving as detailed cooking lessons, the text spells out all the fundamentals of basic good cooking. You'll find—thoroughly explained—every basic technique you need, techniques that will help you follow recipes in other cook books besides this one, and will take you to table with memorable family favorites—as well as company classics.

By doing and tasting, you'll come to know the principles of good cooking. You'll learn which aspects of cooking allow freedom to bend the rules, to experiment, and which techniques depend on scientific precision.

Even if you've never ventured much beyond heating a frozen dinner, this book can lead you to feats you've always thought of as intimidating or impossible—a puffy soufflé, for example, or a perfectly poached egg, or a holiday turkey, plump with savory stuffing and roasted to perfection.

Novice cooks often worry that this sort of "from-scratch" goodness will mean hours of steamy toil, masses of hard-to-find ingredients, and more masses of dishes to wash later. You can forget any such qualms. We've streamlined our material to suit the busy schedule of today's cook who, as likely as not, works at a job until 5 or 6 in the evening. We've used only widely available ingredients, and there are no long lists to shop for. Some of the difficult, highly sophisticated dishes we've simply left out—there are plenty of *haute cuisine* books that offer them.

And, anyway, expert cooks tend to agree that the best-tasting dishes are the simple ones, created with fresh ingredients and skillful techniques. Follow our directions with care and you needn't fear disappointment or failure; each recipe will yield exquisite success. Many techniques are presented in numbered steps accompanied by photographs or illustrations. You'll also find special tips and short-cuts interspersed throughout. And to help you orchestrate the full show, we advise you on how to create interesting and balanced menus, as well as how to shop wisely and store food to retain its freshness.

The upcoming pages take you on a quick tour of the good cook's basic equipment. Just like the freshness of ingredients, the proper pan—whether that means its size or shape or quality of heat distribution—matters a great deal in your achieving delicious results and avoiding mishaps.

So—dive in and have fun developing your new reputation as the best cook in town.

Measuring

There's no getting around it—measurement is critical. To achieve consistent results each time you make a recipe, you must measure accurately.

Measure liquids in standard glass or clear plastic measuring cups designed for liquids.

Measure dry or solid ingredients in metal or plastic cups that hold the exact capacity specified in a recipe. Don't shake or pack dry ingredients down—spoon them in, piling the cup high and light; then level off. (Brown sugar is an exception.)

MEASURING EQUIPMENT

Standard cups for liquid measuring come in 1, 2, and 4-cup sizes with pouring spout. Measurement marks are on the sides.

Standard cups for dry measuring come in sets that include ¼ cup, ⅓ cup, ½ cup, and 1 cup.

Standard measuring spoons in sets of four include ¼, ½, and 1-teaspoon measures, plus 1 tablespoon. Use for liquid and dry ingredients.

HOW TO MEASURE INGREDIENTS

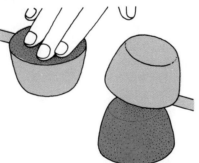

Liquid. For accurate measuring, place cup on level surface, pour in ingredient, read markings on cup at eye level.

Brown sugar. With fingers, pack firmly into cup until even with rim. When inverted, brown sugar will hold its shape.

Dry. Gently spoon ingredient into cup, piling high; level off with metal spatula or straight-sided knife.

Solid shortening. With rubber spatula, pack into cup; run spatula through shortening to release air; pack again and level off.

Butter or margarine. From 8-tablespoon stick, cut desired amount; from tub margarine (*not whipped*), spoon out and level off.

Shredded cheese. Lightly place shreds in dry measuring cup until even with rim—do not pack into cup.

Selecting cookware

A cook's fundamental armory of pots and pans needn't be as extensive as the gleaming displays in the local department store may suggest. It's much wiser to collect quality tools piece by piece rather than to invest in a decorative set of matching cookware. No matter what you choose, though, buy the best you can afford. A good, strong pan with a riveted handle and thick bottom will perform beautifully for a lifetime. Thin, inexpensive cookware is likely to dent, break, or develop "hot spots" (causing food to burn) within a few months. Make sure your pans have tight-fitting lids, sturdy insulated handles and knobs, and straight sides that curve gently at the bottom so there are no "corners" inaccessible to a spoon or wire whisk.

Below is a brief survey of cookware, each with its virtues and a few failings as well.

Aluminum. Good heat conductor (important for browning meat and sautéing), lightweight, and relatively inexpensive. Tends to react chemically with acidic foods (artichokes, citrus fruits, spinach, tomatoes, wine-laced sauces), causing slight metallic flavor and surface pitting of metal.

Cast iron. Evenly distributes and retains heat, extremely durable; heaviest metal used in cooking, yet inexpensive. Season before using; see manufacturer's directions. Prone to rust—must be dried thoroughly.

Copper. Superb heat conductor, most popular for sensitive temperature control and foods requiring exact timing; weight varies. Some are ultra expensive (a medium-size frying pan can cost $75); thin, less expensive pans are attractive, but best reserved for baking or serving. Because copper reacts chemically with all foods and moisture and can cause unpleasant tastes (even toxicity), copper pans are always lined—usually with tin. This lining will eventually need replacement (also expensive). Must be polished with special cleaners after each use.

Nonmetal coating. Porcelain (usually bright in color, and frequently mislabeled "enamel") is sometimes bonded to iron, aluminum, or steel; weights vary. Porcelain bonded to iron evenly distributes and retains heat, but when bonded to aluminum or steel, heat conduction is spotty. Porcelain won't react with foods; it's easy to clean and resists scratching and staining (use nonmetal utensils), but may chip. Colorful acrylic or polymide are also available—less expensive than porcelain, but more prone to fading and discoloration.

Stainless steel. Conducts heat unevenly, so food may scorch if pan is placed on very hot burner; best used for cooking liquids. Doesn't react to foods; lightweight, durable. Remains bright and tarnish free, but is dulled by water spots if not dried carefully. Moderately expensive.

Glass and ceramic. Both types conduct and retain heat well. When baking breads, pies, and cakes in glass, reduce specified oven temperature by 25°, because glass absorbs so much heat. Most glass and ceramic bakeware can travel directly from freezer to oven to table (check manufacturer's instructions).

POTS & PANS

3-quart pan

2-quart pan

1-quart pan

Frying pan with lid

Stock pot

Omelet pan

Double boiler

Dutch oven

Cast-iron frying pan

Bakeware & baking accessories

Always use a pan or dish in the size that's called for in a recipe. If the size isn't marked on the utensil, measure the width, length, and depth from the inside top edges, or check its capacity by measuring the amount of water it holds. An 8 by 8-inch pan holds 1½ quarts; a 9 by 9-inch pan or a 7 by 11-inch pan, 2 quarts; and a 9 by 13-inch pan, 3 quarts.

For cakes and cookies, use shiny aluminum, tin, or stainless steel pans with smooth seams (for ease in cleaning); these distribute heat evenly and give baked goods a golden brown surface. For pies, use glass, ceramic, or dull metal pans, all of which absorb heat and brown the crust.

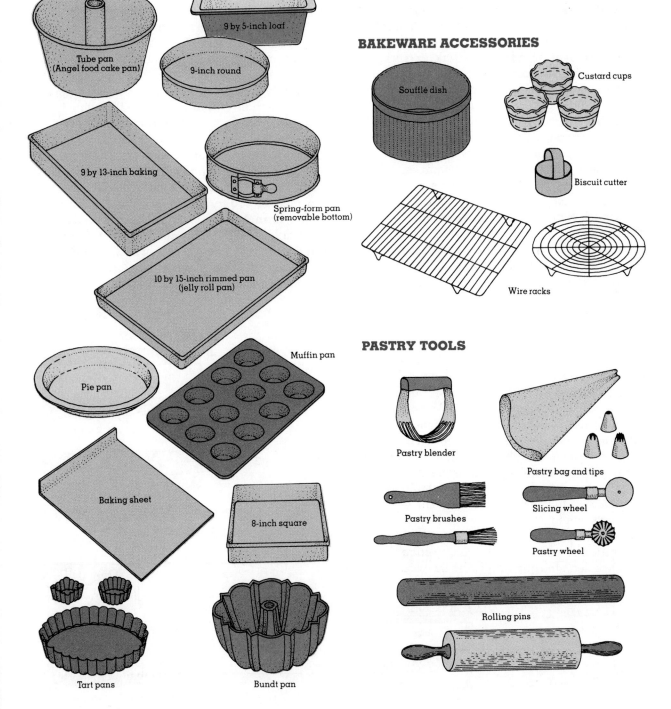

BAKEWARE

Tube pan
(Angel food cake pan)

9 by 5-inch loaf

9-inch round

9 by 13-inch baking

Spring-form pan
(removable bottom)

10 by 15-inch rimmed pan
(jelly roll pan)

Pie pan

Muffin pan

Baking sheet

8-inch square

Tart pans

Bundt pan

BAKEWARE ACCESSORIES

Soufflé dish

Custard cups

Biscuit cutter

Wire racks

PASTRY TOOLS

Pastry blender

Pastry bag and tips

Pastry brushes

Slicing wheel

Pastry wheel

Rolling pins

Knives: The basic cutting tools

It's surprising how often a kitchen is well equipped in almost every respect except knives—possibly because the cook hasn't yet discovered how expertly a really good knife performs.

A knife's performance depends on the quality of its steel and the excellence of its "grind" (cutting edge). To take and hold a keen edge, a blade must be made of a high carbon content steel. Carbon content determines the hardness of a blade—and hardness is essential for a sharp edge.

A carbon steel knife, therefore, would seem to be the best choice, but there is one disadvantage—this material tends to turn dark, and it will rust if you don't dry it carefully after washing. Stainless steel, a combination of carbon steel and chromium, has noncorrosive properties, so it stays shiny. But most stainless steel has a low carbon content and will not keep a sharp edge. You can find high carbon stainless, which takes a good edge, but it's more difficult to sharpen.

The pros and cons of carbon and stainless balance each other fairly well—you'll probably put as much effort into keeping a carbon steel knife clean as you would put into keeping a stainless steel knife sharp, and if frequently sharpened, the stainless will probably give just as good a cutting edge as the carbon.

Chrome-plated knives look similar to stainless steel, but they don't give anything like the same service. In time, the chromium finish wears off, and the edge is likely to rust.

Test for quality. Usually a knife's price is directly related to its quality. But there are other tests. Grip the handle to be sure the knife is well balanced, with the center of gravity near the handle (especially important in large knives). Look for a "full tang"—an extension of the blade that runs the full length of the handle. This metal extension may not be visible, but three rivets in the handle usually indicate a full tang (watch out for knives with fake rivets hiding a tang of only 2 inches or so). The best knives taper from the heel to the tip, and from the top of the blade to the cutting edge. The bolster protects the grip hand from the blade.

Proper care of knives. Keep your knives in their own protected place—not in a drawer of miscellany where edges will be dulled by knocking against other tools. Hang them on a magnetic rack, or keep them in a grooved block of wood. To preserve their handles, never soak knives in dishwater, and absolutely never subject them to a dishwasher. The water may dry and warp wooden handles, causing the tang to loosen. The best way to care for knives is simply to wash them quickly and dry them immediately. It's perfectly safe to scour carbon knives with abrasives—this actually helps to keep them sharp.

Basic knives. Listed below are seven knife types that can handle virtually any kitchen cutting job you're likely to encounter: **paring knife,** for peeling, seeding, and pitting; **utility knife,** for slicing tomatoes and fruit; **boning knife,** for boning meat, fish, or chicken; **slicing knife,** for thinly slicing large cuts of meat; **butcher knife,** for cutting up raw meat or poultry and large foods like watermelon; **French knife,** for chopping and mincing vegetables and for many other uses; and a **serrated knife,** for cutting bread or such baked goods as angel food cakes. A **steel** keeps your knife in condition (see page 77).

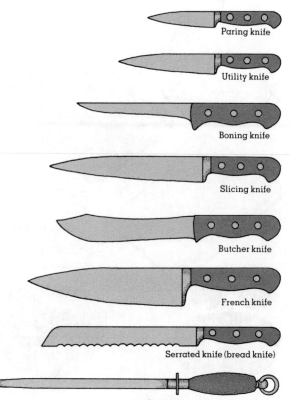

Paring knife

Utility knife

Boning knife

Slicing knife

Butcher knife

French knife

Serrated knife (bread knife)

Steel (see page 77 on how to use)

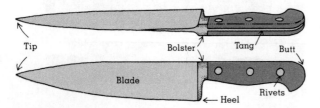

Tip

Bolster Tang Butt

Blade

Rivets

← Heel

Useful kitchen equipment

Metal spatulas

Wooden spoons

Rubber spatulas

Sifter

Rotary beater

Wire whisks

Utility spoon

Slotted spoon

Ladle

Mixing bowls

Bulb baster

Kitchen scissors

2-tined kitchen fork

Wide metal spatula

Bottle opener

Can opener

Tongs

Nonmetal spatula

Strainer

Colander

Vegetable steamer

Funnel

Garlic press

Grater

Vegetable peeler

Mallet

Meat thermometer

Helpful electrical equipment

Electric blender

Food processor

Electric mixer

A glossary of cooking terms

Acidulated water: Water to which vinegar or lemon juice has been added to prevent discoloration and darkening of certain foods.

Al dente: Italian term used to describe pasta cooked until tender but slightly firm to the bite.

Au jus: French term meaning served in natural unthickened meat juices (from roasting).

Bake: To cook, covered or uncovered, by dry heat (usually in an oven). When applied to meats and poultry cooked uncovered, the process is called roasting.

Bake blind: To bake a pastry shell empty, without a filling. See page 110.

Baking powder: See page 144.

Baking soda: See page 144.

Baste: To brush or spoon pan drippings or other fat or liquid over food as it cooks, to keep the surface moist and add flavor.

Batter: A liquid mixture (containing flour and other ingredients) that can be poured or dropped from a spoon. Also, a coating for fried foods.

Beat: To stir or mix rapidly, adding air with a quick, even, circular motion to make a mixture smooth, lighter, or fluffier. When using a spoon or wire whisk, lift mixture up and over with each stroke.

Blanch: To immerse food briefly in boiling water, either to help loosen the skin or to precook briefly to set color and flavor. See page 125.

Blend: To thoroughly combine two or more ingredients until smooth and uniform in texture, color, and flavor.

Boil: To cook liquid rapidly so that bubbles constantly rise and break on the surface. To cook food in boiling liquid.

Bone: To remove bones from meat, poultry, or fish.

Boned & rolled: Term applied to certain meat cuts that are boned, rolled, and tied for roasting.

Bouquet garni: Bundle of several herbs tied into cheesecloth used to flavor soups and stews.

Braise: To cook slowly in a small amount of liquid in a covered pan. Food may or may not be browned first in a small amount of fat.

Bread: To coat with bread or cracker crumbs before cooking, usually after first dipping food into beaten egg or other liquid so crumbs will adhere.

Broil: To cook by direct heat in the broiler of an electric or gas range.

Broth: Liquid in which meat, poultry, fish, or vegetables, or a combination of these, have been cooked; a stock.

Brown: To cook in a small amount of fat, until browned on all sides, giving food an appetizing color and, in meats, sealing in natural juices.

Caramelize: To melt sugar over low heat, without scorching or burning, until it turns golden brown and develops characteristic flavor. To cook onions until sweet and golden.

Chill: To refrigerate food or let stand in ice or ice water until cold.

Chop: To cut food into small pieces.

Coat: To cover a food with a surface layer of another ingredient, such as beaten egg or flour, by sprinkling, dipping, or rolling.

Coat a spoon: Stage reached by a thickened liquid mixture when it leaves a thin film on the back of a metal spoon.

Combine: To stir together two or more ingredients until blended.

Condiment: A sauce, relish, or spice used to season food at the table.

Core: To remove the center of a fruit or vegetable.

Cream: To beat with a spoon or an electric mixer until soft, smooth, and fluffy, as in blending butter and sugar.

Crêpe: See page 154.

Cube: To cut into small cubes (about ½ inch). In meats, to tenderize by pounding with a special tool that imprints a small checkered pattern on the surface, breaking tough fibers to increase tenderness.

Curdled: Separated into a liquid containing small solid particles (caused by overcooking or too much heat or agitation).

Cut in: To distribute solid fat into dry ingredients with a pastry blender (or two knives, scissor-fashion) until particles are desired size.

Dash: A very small amount, less than ⅛ teaspoon.

Deglaze: To loosen drippings from bottom of roasting or frying pan by adding wine, stock, or other liquid.

Degrease: To skim fat from surface of a liquid.

Dice: To cut into very small pieces (about ⅛ to ¼ inch).

Dot: To scatter bits of an ingredient, such as butter, over surface of food.

Dough: A thick pliable mixture of flour and liquid ingredients, firm enough to be kneaded or shaped with the hands.

Dredge: To coat or cover food lightly but completely with flour, sugar, or other fine substance.

Drippings: Melted fat and juices given off by meat and poultry as it cooks.

Drizzle: To pour melted fat, sugar syrup, or other liquid in a fine stream, making a zigzag pattern over food surface.

Dust: To sprinkle lightly with flour (then shake off excess), or with sugar (for cakes).

Emulsion: A liquid mixture in which fatty particles are suspended.

Entrée: The main dish of a meal.

Fat: Generic term for butter, margarine, lard, vegetable shortening; also the rendered drippings of meat, fowl.

Fillet: A piece of meat or fish that is boneless or has had all bones removed.

Fines herbes: Equal amounts of fresh or dried parsley, tarragon, chervil, and chives.

Flake: To lightly break into small, thin pieces, with tines of a fork.

Floret: A small flower, one of a cluster of composite flowers, as in broccoli or cauliflower.

Flute: To make decorative indentations around edge of pastry, vegetable, or fruit.

Fold in: To gently combine a light, delicate, aerated substance, such as whipped cream or beaten egg whites, into a heavier mixture.

Freeze: To chill rapidly at 0° until solid.

Fry: To cook in hot fat—pan-frying in a skillet (very little fat) or deep-frying in a heavy pan (food immersed in fat).

Garnish: To decorate a completed dish, making it more attractive.

Gel: To congeal, becoming firm enough to retain shape of container.

Glaze: To coat with smooth mixture, giving food a sheen.

Gluten: Protein part of wheat or other cereal that gives flour its properties—essential in bread making.

Grate: To rub solid food against a metal object that has sharp-edged holes, reducing food to thin shreds.

Grease: To rub fat or oil on surface of utensil to prevent food from sticking.

Grill: To cook on a rack over direct heat—gas, electricity, or charcoal; to broil on a grill.

Hull: To remove stems and hulls (as from strawberries).

Julienne: Matchstick pieces of vegetables, fruits, or cooked meats.

Knead: To work dough with hands in a fold-and-press motion.

Line: To cover inside or bottom of baking dish or pan with parchment paper, wax paper, or crumbs before adding food.

Marinade: A seasoned liquid, usually containing acid, such as vinegar or wine, in which food soaks, tenderizing it and enhancing its flavor.

Marinate: To soak in a marinade.

Mash: To crush to a pulpy, soft mixture.

Mask: To cover completely with a sauce, aspic, jelly, mayonnaise, or cream.

Meringue: Stiffly beaten egg whites combined with sugar.

Mince: To cut or chop into very fine particles.

Pan-broil: To cook, uncovered, in an ungreased or lightly greased frying pan, pouring off fat as it accumulates. Sometimes pan is salted or rubbed with a piece of fat from the meat.

Pan-fry: To cook in a frying pan in a small amount of fat.

Parboil: To boil until partially cooked; remainder of cooking is done by another method.

Pare: To remove outer skin.

Peel: To strip, cut off, or pull away skin or rind.

Pit: To remove seed from whole fruits—such as apricot, avocado, cherry.

Poach: To cook in a simmering liquid, so gently that food retains its shape.

Pot roasting: To cook a large piece of meat by braising.

Precook: To cook food partially or completely before final cooking or reheating.

Preheat: To heat oven or griddle to desired temperature before beginning to cook (done when temperature is critical or cooking time is short).

Punch down: To deflate a risen yeast dough by pushing it down with fist to expel air.

Purée: To sieve or whirl food into a smooth, thick mixture.

Reduce: To decrease quantity and concentrate flavor of a liquid by rapid boiling in an uncovered pan.

Refresh: To plunge a food that is hot from cooking into cold water, halting the cooking process.

Roast: To cook meat or poultry, uncovered, by dry heat (usually in an oven); also, a cut of meat cooked by this method.

Roux: Mixture of melted fat and flour, cooked until bubbly to remove the raw starch taste of flour; used to thicken soups and sauces.

Salad oil: Vegetable oil.

Scald: To heat milk just below the boiling point (when tiny bubbles appear around edge of pan).

Score: To cut shallow grooves or slits through outer layer of food to increase tenderness, to prevent edge fat of meat from curling, or to make decorative top before roasting certain meats.

Sear: To brown meat briefly over high heat to seal in juices.

Shortening, solid: A white, solid fat made from refined vegetable oil that has been partially hydrogenated, chilled, and whipped.

Shred: To cut or grate into thin, irregular strips.

Simmer: To cook in liquid over low heat just below the boiling point (bubbles form slowly and burst before reaching the surface).

Skim: To remove fat or scum from the surface of a liquid with a spoon or bulb baster.

Steam: To cook in water vapors, on a rack or in a steam basket, in a covered pan above boiling water.

Stew: To cook food slowly in simmering liquid in a covered pot.

Stir: Using a spoon or whisk in a broad, circular motion, to mix ingredients without beating, or to prevent them from sticking.

Stir-fry: To cook sliced food quickly in a small amount of fat over high heat, stirring constantly.

Tart: A shallow open-faced pie with a filling.

Tent: To cover meat or poultry loosely with a piece of foil.

Texture: The structural quality of a food—roughness, smoothness, graininess, or creaminess.

Toss: To mix lightly but rapidly by lifting and turning ingredients with two forks or spoons.

Truss: To secure poultry or meat with skewers or string so that it will retain its shape during cooking.

Whip: To beat rapidly with a wire whisk, or electric mixer, incorporating air to lighten a mixture and increase its volume.

Whisk: To beat with a wire whisk until blended and smooth.

Yeast: See page 157.

Zest: Outer colored peel of citrus fruits. See page 184.

Putting it all together

"What a marvelous meal!" "May I have your muffin recipe?" "Let's have this again tomorrow night." Compliments like these are a cook's sweet sounds of success. To earn them takes not only careful cooking, but plenty of planning, as well. It means spending time with paper, pencil, and recipe selections. It definitely means organized shopping lists. But the rewards are delicious, indeed ... well worth the effort.

Planning your menu

Focus first on meeting daily nutritional needs, rather than devising single meals without considering what else is eaten in the same day. To build in variety and avoid waste, plan for several days at a time. It saves hours and energy (and usually dollars, as well) to go grocery shopping weekly rather than daily, and appealing leftover meals are easier to achieve with a little forethought— that's how Sunday's succulent roast leg of lamb becomes Tuesday's savory lamb curry.

Nutrition experts recommend the following guidelines for a healthy daily balance of foods: two or more servings from the meat group (meats, fish, poultry, eggs, and cheese, with dry beans, peas, and nuts as alternates); four or more servings from the vegetable and fruit group (dark green and yellow vegetables, including citrus fruit daily); four servings from the bread and cereal group (enriched or whole grain breads, pasta, or cereals), and milk from the dairy group (three or more glasses for children, four or more for teenagers, two for adults). Cheese and ice cream can substitute for part of the milk.

A good cook is both practical and selective, designing menus around what's fresh and in season. Asparagus or strawberries won't do in a December menu; even if you paid a premium price for flown-in specimens at a gourmet grocery, the flavor and texture still wouldn't measure up to springtime standards. Good cooking is less likely to result from spontaneous splurging than from appreciating what's in season.

Provide an interesting variety of color, flavor, shape, temperature, and texture in the foods you arrange together in a menu. An extreme example of what *not* to serve at one meal might be steamed cauliflower, white fish with white sauce, and mashed potatoes—everything colorless and soft to the palate, in a combination that's bland and boring. But if you serve the white-sauced fish with a brown rice pilaf and add a chilled and colorful green bean and tomato salad, the menu becomes more exciting.

Combine something crisp, something chewy, and something soft, and provide foods both hot and cold. As a cool counterpoint to robustly seasoned chili, you might serve a crisp garden salad and crusty bread. For most of us, one spicy food at a time is enough, and several sweet dishes in the same menu would be too much.

Balance dessert choices against the kind of food they follow. After a hearty beef stew with whole wheat bread, fresh fruit tastes refreshingly light. But you can follow a light meal—maybe soup and salad—with something outrageously rich—like a favorite chocolate cake.

Selecting your recipes

It's easy to wind up with a three-ring circus on your hands at serving time. Imagine the juggling act of mashing potatoes, coping with gravy, and pan-frying veal cutlets—all last-minute cooking tasks. Consider, too, whether two recipes in a menu call for oven cooking—such combinations can be fuel efficient, but only if both bake at the same temperature. Don't hope to serve (without burning—or without two ovens) a chicken that roasts at 350° with biscuits that bake at 425°.

For a smoother kitchen schedule, plan at least two menu items to make ahead of time—perhaps a potato casserole that can bake alongside the roasting chicken. Many salads and desserts offer such make-ahead convenience. Guard against choosing three recipes that demand an hour of exacting preparation apiece. Lavish your time on a complicated and slow-cooking entrée (such as stuffed pork chops), and limit the remaining menu to simpler fare.

Most cooks find it's safest to try only one new recipe at a time, too. If you're eager to serve something new to guests, you may want to give the recipe a dress rehearsal.

Planning your time

Scheduling a meal for smooth serving—with everything ready at once—can be tricky. But freedom from last-minute panic is well worth the planning it requires.

Base your schedule on the time you'll serve the meal, and then work backward from serving time, creating a step-by-step plan. Use written notes, if it helps. Allow time for setting the table and assembling serving dishes, as well as for food preparation and actual serving.

We all work at a different pace, so experience is the best guide. Everything speeds up a bit once you know a recipe well and have become comfortable with the techniques required. Plan in 10-minute increments, taking into account that some

tasks can be dovetailed: you can assemble the salad while the rolls heat, or mash potatoes while the turkey stands waiting for carving time.

If you have kids or cooperative grownups near the kitchen, get them to help with a task or two. Dinner guests, too, usually mean it when they ask "How can I help?"

EMERGENCY SUBSTITUTIONS

It's always best to use the exact ingredients called for in a recipe. But if you don't have a particular ingredient on hand, look below for a substitute

that will give satisfactory results. We recommend that you avoid making more than one substitution in a single recipe, though.

Ingredient	Substitution
1 cup cake flour	1 cup all-purpose flour minus 2 tablespoons, or all-purpose flour sifted 3 times, then measured to make 1 cup
1 teaspoon baking powder	¼ teaspoon baking soda plus ½ teaspoon cream of tartar
1 envelope (1 tablespoon) active dry yeast	1 compressed yeast cake, crumbled
1 tablespoon cornstarch (used for thickening)	2 tablespoons all-purpose flour
1 cup buttermilk or sour milk	1 tablespoon white vinegar or lemon juice stirred into 1 cup milk and allowed to stand for 5 minutes
1 cup milk	½ cup evaporated milk plus ½ cup water, or ⅓ cup powdered whole milk stirred into 1 cup water
1 cup corn syrup	1 cup granulated sugar plus ¼ cup liquid*
1 cup honey	1¼ cups granulated sugar plus ¼ cup liquid*
2 egg yolks (used for thickening in custards)	1 whole egg
1 square (1 oz.) unsweetened chocolate	1 envelope (1 oz.) premelted chocolate, or 3 tablespoons unsweetened cocoa plus 1 tablespoon melted butter or margarine
Juice of 1 lemon	2 tablespoons bottled lemon juice
1 teaspoon grated fresh lemon peel or zest of 1 lemon	1 teaspoon dry lemon peel (purchased)
Juice of 1 medium orange	¼ cup reconstituted frozen orange juice
1 teaspoon grated fresh orange peel or zest of 1 orange	1 teaspoon dry orange peel (purchased)
1 cup regular-strength chicken or beef broth	1 chicken or beef bouillon cube plus 1 cup hot water
1 can (1 lb.) tomatoes	2½ cups chopped, peeled, fresh tomatoes, simmered for about 10 minutes
1 cup catsup or tomato-based chili sauce	1 can (8 oz.) tomato sauce plus ½ cup granulated sugar and 2 tablespoons white vinegar
1 teaspoon dry mustard	1 tablespoon prepared mustard
¼ cup minced fresh onion	1 tablespoon instant minced onion (let stand in liquid as directed)
1 medium-size onion	2 teaspoons onion powder
1 clove garlic	⅛ teaspoon garlic powder
2 tablespoons minced fresh parsley	1 tablespoon dehydrated parsley flakes
½ teaspoon grated fresh ginger	¼ teaspoon ground ginger

*Use a liquid called for in recipe. Equivalence is based on how product functions in recipe, not on sweetness.

SOUPS

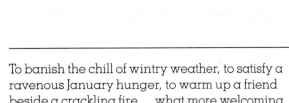

To banish the chill of wintry weather, to satisfy a ravenous January hunger, to warm up a friend beside a crackling fire... what more welcoming fare than a bowl or a mug of homemade soup?

Or suppose it's summertime, hot and humid, when appetites tend to languish in need of inspiration. Soup again, the perfect refreshment—this time iced, and singing with the pure flavors of seasonal vegetables.

Soup making was an endless process in the years when everyone had to start from scratch with meat or poultry bones, creating a stock that took hours to mellow to aromatic goodness. In this day of convenience foods, we can start with *canned* broths—beef or chicken—that are wonderfully flavorful. They simplify the making of soup while taking nothing away from its homemade quality. But if you wish to make your own chicken broth, turn to page 85.

Then you can move along to all manner of delicious additions. Practice with our recipes; enjoy the special hospitality they lend to your lunch or supper table.

Soup-making skills

Apart from handiwork with knife and cutting board, soups require few specialized cooking techniques. In soups you will later purée, vegetables are cut not so much for appearance, but simply to shorten their cooking time and to provide more surfaces from which the vegetables can release flavors. So when a recipe calls for slicing and dicing, consider it an opportunity to develop your chopping skills.

You can purée soup with a blender, food processor, or food mill. A blender produces the most velvety texture in the shortest time. With a food processor, you must spoon out solid ingredients from the soup first, then process them smooth before recombining them with the liquid. A food mill will also do the job for you, but it takes the most elbow power.

Even in smooth soups, you may prefer a little texture. On the other hand, if you want an ultra-smooth consistency, force the purée through a sieve to trap any remaining solids.

Taste before serving

Mysterious transformations take place in a soup kettle. Flavors blend and mellow, and sometimes—as in the case of salt—become absorbed by other ingredients and disappear. Because these changes occur, it's important to taste your soup before serving it, so you can adjust the seasonings to suit your own palate.

This is particularly true if you plan to serve cold soup. An herb that was pleasantly assertive when the soup was hot may fade to nothing after chilling and need an additional boost.

Chilling thickens soups, too, especially puréed soups. So be sure to stir a cold soup before serving it; then, if necessary, thin it with additional broth, water, milk, or cream.

First-course soups

Following is a mouth-watering selection of hot and cold soups, and a few that taste delicious either way. As a first course or as a hearty companion for a salad or sandwich, about 1 cup of soup makes a reasonable serving.

If more convenient, you can make these soups ahead. To reheat, cook the soup in an uncovered pan over medium-low heat, stirring occasionally, just until it's hot—but don't let it boil.

Creamy Tomato Soup

- 1 small onion, finely chopped
- 1 small carrot, finely chopped
- 2 tablespoons butter or margarine
- 1 large can (1 lb. 12 oz.) Italian-style tomatoes
- ½ teaspoon *each* thyme leaves and dry basil
  Salt and pepper
- ½ pint (1 cup) whipping cream
  Chopped parsley

In a 2-quart pan over medium heat, cook onion and carrot in butter until onion is soft. Add tomatoes and their liquid, thyme, and basil; sprinkle with salt and pepper to taste. Bring to a boil; cover, reduce heat, and simmer for 20 minutes.

In a blender or food processor, purée soup until smooth; return to pan. Whisk in whipping cream. Heat through; or cover, refrigerate, and serve cold. Garnish with parsley. Makes 4 cups.

Potato Bisque

- 1 medium-size onion, chopped
- ½ cup chopped celery (including some tops)
- 2 tablespoons butter or margarine
- 2 medium-size red or white thin-skinned potatoes, peeled and cut into ½-inch cubes
- 2 tablespoons chopped parsley
- 1 can (14½ oz.) regular-strength chicken broth or 1¾ cups homemade chicken broth (page 85)
- 2 cups milk
- 1½ tablespoons cornstarch mixed with 3 tablespoons water
  Salt and pepper
  Butter or margarine
  Chopped parsley

In a 3-quart pan over medium heat, cook onion and celery in the 2 tablespoons butter until onion is soft, then add potatoes, the 2 tablespoons parsley, and broth. Bring to a boil; cover, reduce heat, and simmer until potatoes are tender when pierced (about 20 minutes).

Stir in milk and cook, covered, until soup is thoroughly hot, but not boiling. Stir cornstarch mixture and add to soup. Cook, stirring, until soup bubbles and thickens slightly (about 5 minutes). Season to taste with salt and pepper. Serve hot. Garnish each serving with a small pat of butter and additional parsley. Makes about 6 cups.

MUSHROOM & POTATO BISQUE

Prepare **Potato Bisque,** but stir in ¼ pound sliced **mushrooms** when you add chicken broth.

SHRIMP BISQUE

Prepare **Potato Bisque,** but add ½ pound small cooked **shrimp** or 1 package (12 oz.) frozen, cooked shrimp, thawed, just before adding cornstarch mixture.

CRAB BISQUE

Prepare **Potato Bisque,** but add 1 small **bay leaf** when you add chicken broth. Just before adding cornstarch mixture, stir in ½ pound **crab meat.**

Mushroom Velvet Soup

- ½ pound mushrooms, sliced
- 1 medium-size onion, coarsely chopped
- ⅓ cup chopped parsley
- 4 tablespoons butter or margarine
- 1 tablespoon all-purpose flour
- 1 can (14½ oz.) regular-strength beef broth
- ½ pint (1 cup) sour cream

In a wide frying pan over medium-high heat, cook mushrooms, onion, and parsley in butter until mushrooms are soft and pan juices have evaporated (about 5 minutes). Stir in flour and cook for 1 minute to brown lightly. Slowly stir in broth; bring to a boil, stirring.

In a blender or food processor, purée soup with sour cream, a portion at a time, until smooth. Reheat without boiling. Makes about 4 cups.

...First-course soups

Carrot & Tarragon Soup

- 2 medium-size onions, chopped
- 2 cloves garlic, minced or pressed
- 2 tablespoons butter or margarine
- 1½ pounds carrots, peeled and thinly sliced
- 1 large can (49½ oz.) regular-strength chicken broth or 6 cups homemade chicken broth (page 85)
- ½ teaspoon dry tarragon
- ½ teaspoon salt
- ¼ teaspoon pepper
- ½ to ¾ cup orange juice
  Chopped parsley

In a 5-quart kettle over medium-high heat, cook onions and garlic in butter until onions are soft but not browned. Add carrot slices, broth, tarragon, salt, and pepper. Bring to a boil; cover, reduce heat, and simmer until carrots are very tender when pierced (about 35 minutes).

In a blender or food processor, purée soup, a portion at a time, until smooth. Stir in enough orange juice (up to ¾ cup) to give soup desired consistency. Heat through; or cover, refrigerate, and serve cold. Garnish with parsley. Makes about 7 cups.

Chilled Pea Soup

- 1 cup diced raw potatoes
- 1 cup fresh or frozen peas
- 2 green onions (including tops), sliced
- 1½ cups regular-strength chicken broth or homemade chicken broth (page 85)
- ⅛ teaspoon curry powder
- 1 cup whipping cream or half-and-half (light cream)
  Paprika
  Chopped chives

In a 3-quart pan, combine potatoes, peas, green onions, chicken broth, and curry powder. Bring to a boil; cover, reduce heat, and simmer until potatoes are just tender when pierced (about 20 minutes).

In a blender or food processor, purée soup, a portion at a time, until smooth. Stir in cream. Cover, refrigerate, and serve cold. Garnish with paprika and chives. Makes about 4 cups.

Icy Gazpacho

- 1 medium-size cucumber
- ½ green pepper, seeded and chopped
- 1 small onion, finely chopped
- 2 tomatoes, peeled, seeded, and diced
- 4 cups tomato juice
- 3 tablespoons olive oil or salad oil
- 2 tablespoons wine vinegar
- ½ teaspoon oregano leaves
- ½ avocado
  Salt
  Ice cubes (optional)

Peel cucumber and cut in half lengthwise. If seeds are large, scoop out with a spoon and discard. Chop cucumber, then place in a bowl with green pepper, onion, tomatoes, tomato juice, oil, wine vinegar, and oregano. Peel avocado, cut into ½-inch cubes, and stir into gazpacho. Add salt to taste. Cover and chill for at least 2 hours. To serve, ladle into bowls and add 1 or 2 ice cubes to each bowl, if desired. Makes about 6 cups.

Chilled Zucchini Soup

- 4 cups (about 1 lb.) sliced zucchini or crookneck squash
- 1 medium-size onion, thinly sliced
- 1 can (14½ oz.) regular-strength chicken broth or 1¾ cups homemade chicken broth (page 85)
- ½ cup sour cream or yogurt
- ¼ teaspoon dill weed
  Salt and pepper
  Shelled sunflower seeds

Combine squash, onion, and broth in a 2-quart pan. Bring to a boil; cover, reduce heat, and simmer until vegetables are very tender (about 30 minutes). In a blender or food processor, purée soup until smooth, a portion at a time. Whisk in sour cream (or yogurt, for tangier flavor), and dill weed. Season to taste with salt and pepper. Let cool, then cover and refrigerate for at least 4 hours for flavors to blend. Serve cold, garnished with sunflower seeds. Makes about 4 cups.

Full-meal soups

Though most of the preceding soups lend themselves to a light meal, the upcoming meal-in-a-bowl recipes are hearty enough to star in a dinner for family or friends. Crusty French bread or a hot quick bread from the chapter on breads (starting on page 144) would round out a comfortably informal country-style supper. You might start with a green salad, or follow the soup with fruit and cheese, or do both.

Meatball Minestrone

- 1 package (10 oz.) frozen chopped spinach, thawed
- 1½ pounds lean ground beef
- ⅓ cup fine dry bread crumbs
- 1 egg
- 1 teaspoon salt
- ¼ teaspoon pepper
- 2 tablespoons salad oil
- 1 large onion, coarsely chopped
- 4 cans (14½ oz. *each*) regular-strength beef broth
- 1 can (about 1 lb.) tomatoes
- 1 can (1 lb.) kidney beans
- ½ teaspoon *each* oregano leaves and dry basil
- 1 cup *each* sliced carrots and celery
- 1 cup rotelle (see page 116) or elbow macaroni
  Grated Parmesan cheese

With your hands, squeeze as much moisture as possible from spinach. In a large bowl, combine spinach, beef, bread crumbs, egg, salt, and pepper. Shape into 1-inch balls.

Heat oil in a Dutch oven over medium heat. When oil is hot, add a portion of meatballs and brown on all sides. Remove from pan with a slotted spoon, leaving drippings. Repeat until all meatballs are browned. Set meatballs aside. Add onion and cook, stirring occasionally, until soft. Stir in broth, tomatoes (break up with a spoon) and their liquid, beans and their liquid, oregano, and basil. Cover, reduce heat, and simmer for 10 minutes.

Add carrots and celery; cover and simmer for 10 more minutes. Stir in pasta; cover and simmer until pasta is *al dente* (about 10 minutes). Place meatballs in soup and heat through. Pass Parmesan at the table. Makes about 14 cups.

Aztec Soup

- ⅓ cup (about 1½ oz.) pine nuts
- ½ cup walnut halves
- 2 tablespoons butter or margarine
- 1 small onion, coarsely chopped
- 1 clove garlic, minced or pressed
- 1 large can (49½ oz.) regular-strength chicken broth or 6 cups homemade chicken broth (page 85)
- 2 cups diced, peeled butternut, acorn, or Hubbard squash
- 1 package (10 oz.) frozen corn
- 1 avocado
- ½ cup shelled pumpkin or sunflower seeds
- 2 cups (8 oz.) shredded jack cheese
- 2 to 3 cups tortilla chips

In a 4-quart pan over medium heat, stir pine nuts and walnuts in 1 tablespoon of the butter, cooking until golden (about 2 minutes). Remove from pan and reserve.

In same pan, melt remaining 1 tablespoon butter. Add onion and garlic and cook until onion is golden. Add broth and squash. Bring to a boil; cover, reduce heat, and simmer until squash is tender (10 to 15 minutes). Add corn and cook for 5 more minutes.

Just before serving, pit, peel, and dice avocado. Place avocado, reserved nut mixture, pumpkin seeds, cheese, and tortilla chips in individual small bowls. Pass condiments at the table to add to the soup. Makes about 10 cups.

GARNISHES FOR SOUPS

Though certainly not essential, garnishes do give soups a finishing flair that turns the ordinary into something special. Garnished soups look prettier than plain ones, and they usually taste a bit more interesting, too.

The list of possible garnishes is lengthy: a dollop of sour cream or yogurt, a pat of butter, chopped parsley or tiny whole parsley sprigs, sliced green onions or chives, croutons, crumbled cooked bacon, chopped fresh herbs (basil, dill, or mint), sunflower or pumpkin seeds, sliced almonds, lemon or orange slices, tiny cooked shrimp, and grated cheese.

...Full-meal soups

Vegetable Basil Soup

1 medium-size onion, chopped
1 large stalk celery, thinly sliced
1 large carrot, thinly sliced
3 tablespoons butter or margarine
1 large potato, peeled and cut into ½-inch cubes
2 large tomatoes, peeled, seeded, and diced
2 cans (14½ oz. *each*) regular-strength chicken broth or 3½ cups homemade chicken broth (page 85)
1 teaspoon dry basil
½ small head cauliflower, broken into flowerets
2 small zucchini, sliced ¼ inch thick
½ package (10 oz.) frozen peas
Salt and pepper
Grated Parmesan cheese

In a 5-quart pan over medium heat, cook onion, celery, and carrot in butter, stirring occasionally, until onion is soft but not browned. Add potato, tomatoes, broth, and basil. Bring to a boil; cover; reduce heat, and simmer for 15 minutes. Add cauliflower and zucchini; simmer for 10 minutes. Add peas and simmer until tender (about 5 minutes). Season to taste with salt and pepper. Pass Parmesan at the table. Makes about 10 cups.

Curried Split Pea Soup

1 medium-size onion, coarsely chopped
1 clove garlic, minced or pressed
4 strips bacon, cut into ½-inch pieces
1 cup dried yellow split peas
5 cups water
1 large carrot
2 stalks celery
1 can (about 1 lb.) tomatoes
1 teaspoon *each* salt and curry powder
¼ teaspoon pepper
2 tablespoons chopped parsley

In a 3-quart pan over medium heat, cook onion, garlic, and bacon until bacon is translucent. Add split peas and water. Bring mixture to a boil; cover, reduce heat, and simmer until peas are tender (about 1 hour). Meanwhile, split carrot lengthwise into 4 pieces. Thinly slice carrot and celery; set aside.

In a blender or food processor, purée pea mix-

ture, a portion at a time, until smooth; return to pan. Add carrot, celery, tomatoes (break up with a spoon) and their liquid, salt, curry powder, and pepper. Cover and simmer until carrots are tender when pierced (about 25 minutes). Stir in parsley. Makes about 10 cups.

French Onion Soup

(Pictured on facing page)

Dry-toasted French bread (directions follow)
2 tablespoons butter or margarine
1 tablespoon olive oil or salad oil
6 large yellow onions, thinly sliced
1 tablespoon all-purpose flour
3 cans (14½ oz. *each*) regular-strength beef broth
1 cup water
⅓ cup dry red wine
Salt and pepper
1 cup (4 oz.) shredded Swiss cheese
¼ cup grated Parmesan cheese

Prepare dry-toasted French bread. Then heat butter and oil in a 4-quart pan over medium-low heat, add onions, and cook, stirring occasionally, until soft and caramel-colored but not browned (30 to 40 minutes). Stir in flour and cook for 2 minutes to brown lightly. Pour in about 1 cup of the broth, stirring to blend flour and broth. Add remaining broth, water, and wine. Bring to a boil; cover, reduce heat, and simmer for 30 minutes. Season to taste with salt and pepper.

Ladle hot soup into six 1½ to 2-cup ovenproof soup bowls. Float a piece of dry-toasted French bread on top and sprinkle with Swiss and Parmesan cheeses. Place bowls in a 425° oven for 10 minutes; then broil about 4 inches from heat until cheese is lightly browned. Makes 6 servings.

Dry-toasted French bread. Trim six ½-inch-thick slices **French bread** to fit inside soup bowls. Place bread on an oven rack. Bake in a 325° oven for 20 to 25 minutes or until lightly toasted. Spread each slice with **butter** or margarine.

French Onion Soup (Recipe on facing page)

1 Cooking onions slowly in butter and oil develops their sweet flavor. Stir occasionally, scraping pan bottom as juices caramelize.

2 Float dry-toasted French bread in hot soup, sprinkle with cheeses, then bake. Use baking pan as tray to slide bowls in and out of oven.

3 Golden brown and bubbly, French Onion Soup makes a simple meal with flavors to remember.

SALADS & DRESSINGS

One of the simplest and zestiest creations of the culinary arts is a crisp salad—it's just leafy green freshness (sometimes crunchy vegetables get tossed in, too) enhanced and brought to splendor by a flavorful dressing.

Besides our classic salads and savory vinaigrettes, you can whip up a perfectly luscious mayonnaise to top your garden (or grocery store) produce. We've left fruit ideas to the desserts chapter, but we do include a mild chutney mayonnaise that enhances fresh fruit salads.

Choosing & handling salad greens

The versatile green salad—just greens and dressing—fits more menus than any other type. Keep freshness in mind as you select greens—look for tender and crisp heads with untarnished leaves. Any yellow, wilted, or dry and curled outer leaves are signs the greens are over the hill.

Contrast is fun in salads. For varying flavors and textures, try a combination of two or more greens. Combine mild leaves with spicy-flavored ones, crisp with tender, and green with pale or red-tinged leaves. Choose from juicy, mild-flavored romaine (also called cos); delicate and velvety butter lettuce (butterhead, Bibb, Boston); crisp, mild-flavored iceberg; tender crinkled leaf lettuce; wiry and bitter curly endive (chicory); spicy watercress; slightly bitter escarole (broad-leaf endive); robust head cabbage (purple or green); or crunchy, spirited spinach.

Scan the selections below for a glimpse of some of the greens to be found for your salad making.

Always handle greens tenderly because they bruise easily. Try to wash them a day ahead of preparing your salad so they can chill and crisp.

Before washing iceberg lettuce, core it, then hold the head under cold running water, gently separating the leaves. Wash romaine, butter lettuce, leaf lettuce, endive, and spinach piece by piece. Bathe watercress by the bunch in several changes of water.

Shake off as much water as possible; then drain on paper towels or a clean dish towel, or whirl in a lettuce drying basket. When drained and barely damp, wrap leaves loosely in a clean dish towel or paper towel and store them in a plastic bag in your refrigerator for several days. Before serving, pat off any excess moisture and break greens into bite-size pieces; dress and serve.

Before washing cabbage, slice the head in half; then wash it in cold running water, and drain and store as directed for lettuce.

Caesar Salad from the Kitchen

Caesar salad is usually tossed at the table where everyone can watch. This hassle-free version is assembled in the kitchen, with no last-minute fuss.

> 1 clove garlic, cut in half
> 6 to 8 anchovy fillets, halved
> ¼ cup olive oil or salad oil
> 2 tablespoons *each* lemon juice and grated Parmesan cheese
> 1 egg yolk
> 1½ teaspoons Worcestershire
> ⅛ teaspoon freshly ground pepper
> 1 large head romaine, torn into bite-size pieces
> 1 cup garlic-flavored croutons

In a blender or food processor, whirl garlic, anchovy halves, oil, lemon juice, cheese, egg yolk, Worcestershire, and pepper until anchovies are finely chopped. If made ahead, cover and refrigerate; bring to room temperature before using.

To serve, place romaine in a salad bowl. Stir dressing, pour over romaine, and toss until every leaf is glossy. Add croutons and mix gently. Serve immediately. Makes 4 to 6 servings.

Wilted Spinach Salad

> ¾ to 1 pound fresh spinach
> 5 green onions (including tops), thinly sliced
> 2 hard-cooked eggs, chopped
> 1 egg
> 2 tablespoons *each* sugar, white wine vinegar, and red wine vinegar
> ½ to 1 pound sliced bacon, cut into ½-inch pieces

Remove and discard tough spinach stems; tear leaves into bite-size pieces and place in a salad bowl. Add onions and chopped eggs to spinach. If made ahead, cover and refrigerate.

In a small dish, lightly beat raw egg with sugar, white vinegar, and red vinegar; set aside.

In a large frying pan over medium heat, cook bacon until crisp, stirring occasionally to separate. Remove bacon pieces with a slotted spoon and drain on paper towels; set aside. Discard all but 3 tablespoons drippings from pan. Stirring constantly with a wire whisk, slowly pour egg-vinegar mixture into warm bacon drippings; cook until mixture has slightly thickened (about 1 minute). Immediately pour hot dressing over spinach, add cooked bacon, and toss to coat each leaf. Serve at once. Makes 4 to 6 servings.

Vinaigrette Vegetable Salads

Whatever the time of year, a vegetable salad refreshes a menu. Here, we marinate seasonal vegetables in the various vinaigrette dressings that appear on page 25. Each vegetable is then presented on a small lettuce-lined plate, or in individual mounds on one larger plate—either way, the colorful salads can be arranged to create a kaleidoscopic effect. Serve as a first course at dinner, or with crusty bread and wine for lunch.

For maximum effect, we recommend that you choose, from the suggestions below, three to five vegetables of varying colors and textures.

In ½ cup **Basic Vinaigrette** (page 25), marinate 2 thinly sliced **tomatoes;** or 2 cups diced green or red **bell peppers;** or ½ pound **green beans,** cooked crisp-tender, rinsed under cold water, and drained; or 2 cups shredded purple or green **cabbage.**

In ½ cup **Mustard Vinaigrette** (page 25), marinate 2 cups **cauliflowerets,** cooked crisp-tender, rinsed under cold water, and drained; or 4 red or white thin-skinned **potatoes,** cooked, peeled, and sliced, or 2 cups diced **celery;** or 2 cups shredded **celery root.**

In ¼ cup **Lemon Vinaigrette** (page 25), marinate 2 cups shredded **carrots.**

Using a separate bowl for each vegetable, marinate your choices for at least 2 hours. If refrigerated, bring to room temperature before serving.

Cobb Salad (Recipe on facing page)

1 To chop egg, first quarter it. Then hold knife in one hand and rest fingers of other hand on top ridge of knife. Move knife up and down, chopping through egg on board.

2 Cut avocado in half lengthwise around pit. Cup avocado in both hands and twist in half. Holding half with pit in one hand, thrust knife into pit and twist out.

3 For lunch or a light supper, this beautifully arranged Cobb Salad has a delicious blend of flavors and textures. Wine and bread round out the meal.

Cobb Salad

(Pictured on facing page)

Traditionally this famous Hollywood salad stars chicken, but turkey, shrimp, and crabmeat make excellent stand-ins. You can prepare the tomatoes, chicken, bacon, and eggs in advance, but assemble the salad just before serving. Present it at the table, then toss and serve at once.

   1 **medium-size head iceberg lettuce, shredded**
   6 **tablespoons white wine vinegar**
  ½ **teaspoon salt**
  ⅛ **teaspoon** *each* **garlic powder and freshly ground pepper**
   3 **tablespoons chopped chives**
  ½ **cup salad oil**
   1 **large tomato, seeded and chopped**
1½ **cups diced cooked chicken**
   1 **large avocado, peeled, pitted, diced, and tossed with 1 tablespoon lemon juice**
   1 **pound sliced bacon, crisply cooked, drained, and crumbled**
   2 **hard-cooked eggs, chopped**
   3 **ounces blue-veined cheese, finely crumbled**
      Watercress (optional)

Place lettuce in a large, wide salad bowl. In a jar, combine vinegar, salt, garlic powder, pepper, chives, and oil; blend well. Pour dressing over lettuce and toss well; then spread lettuce in an even layer in bowl. On top of lettuce make a second layer—tomato, chicken, avocado, bacon, and eggs, arranged in separate, wedge-shaped sections. Place crumbled cheese in center. Garnish with watercress, if desired. Toss at the table. Makes 4 servings.

Coleslaw

(Pictured on page 62)

   1 **medium-size head cabbage (about 1¼ lbs.)**
   1 **cup** *each* **chopped parsley and chopped green onions (including tops)**
  ½ **cup white wine vinegar**
   1 **tablespoon sugar**
   1 **teaspoon salt**
  ⅓ **cup salad oil**

Shred cabbage; you should have about 8 cups. In a salad bowl, combine cabbage, parsley, and onions. Cover and refrigerate if made ahead. In a jar, combine vinegar, sugar, salt, and oil; blend well. Pour dressing over salad and toss to coat cabbage. Makes 6 to 8 servings.

Carrot-Raisin Slaw

   5 **large carrots, shredded**
   1 **cup thinly sliced celery**
  ½ **cup thinly sliced green onions (including tops)**
  ¾ **cup raisins**
   4 **tablespoons sour cream**
   4 **tablespoons mayonnaise, purchased or homemade (page 26)**
   1 **tablespoon lemon juice**
  ½ **teaspoon salt**
      Dash of pepper

In a salad bowl, combine carrots, celery, onions, and raisins. In a small bowl, combine sour cream, mayonnaise, lemon juice, salt, and pepper; blend well. Pour over vegetables and toss to coat. Cover and refrigerate for at least an hour or until next day. Makes 4 to 6 servings.

Cucumbers in Sour Cream

   3 **large cucumbers, peeled and cut into ⅛-inch-thick slices**
   1 **teaspoon salt**
  ½ **pint (1 cup) sour cream**
  ⅓ **cup mayonnaise, purchased or homemade (page 26)**
   1 **tablespoon tarragon vinegar**
   2 **green onions (including tops), thinly sliced**
   1 **tablespoon finely minced parsley**
   1 **small clove garlic, minced or pressed**
   1 **teaspoon Worcestershire**

In a bowl, mix cucumbers and salt and let stand for about 15 minutes; drain well on paper towels. In a small bowl, combine sour cream, mayonnaise, and vinegar; blend well. Stir in onions, parsley, garlic, and Worcestershire. Pour dressing over cucumbers and stir to coat. Cover and refrigerate for at least 2 hours. Serve chilled. Makes 6 to 8 servings.

Classic Crab Louis

- 1 **cup mayonnaise, purchased or homemade (page 26)**
- ¼ **cup** *each* **tomato-based chili sauce, finely chopped green pepper, and sliced green onions (including tops)**
- ¼ **cup whipping cream, whipped**
  Salt
  Lemon juice
- 2 **small heads iceberg lettuce**
- 1 **pound crabmeat**
- 4 **large tomatoes, cut into wedges**
- 4 **hard-cooked eggs, cut into wedges**
  Parsley sprigs
  Lemon wedges

In a small bowl, thoroughly combine mayonnaise, chili sauce, green pepper, and onions; fold into whipped cream. Season with salt and lemon juice to taste.

Arrange outer leaves of lettuce on 4 large plates; shred remaining lettuce and divide evenly among the plates. Place crabmeat on top of shredded lettuce, and arrange tomatoes and eggs around crab. Spoon dressing over crab; garnish with parsley and lemon wedges. Makes 4 servings.

Potato Salad

Thin-skinned potatoes keep their shape better than baking varieties when tossed in a salad.

- 6 **medium-size red or white thin-skinned potatoes (about 2½ lbs.** *total***)**
- 3 **tablespoons white vinegar**
- 2 **large stalks celery, chopped**
- 6 **green onions (including tops), thinly sliced**
- 3 **hard-cooked eggs, chopped**
- 1 **to 1½ cups mayonnaise, purchased or homemade (page 26)**
- ¾ **teaspoon salt**
  Dash of pepper
- 1 **tablespoon prepared mustard**

In a pan with 1 inch of boiling water, place potatoes; cover and cook until tender when pierced (20 to 25 minutes). Drain, cool slightly, peel, and cut into cubes. Place in a large salad bowl; sprinkle with vinegar. Add celery, onions, and eggs.

In a bowl, combine mayonnaise, salt, pepper, and mustard; mix thoroughly. Spoon dressing over potato mixture and stir gently to coat potatoes evenly. Cover and chill for 4 to 6 hours or until next day. Makes about 8 servings.

POTATO SALAD VARIATIONS

To lend variety to your potato salad, add ¼ to ½ cup of one or more of the following: shredded **carrots,** shredded **Cheddar cheese,** sliced **radishes,** crisp cooked **bacon,** diced **dill pickle** or **sweet pickle,** sliced **pimentos,** sliced **olives,** or chopped **green pepper.**

Roasted Pepper & Tomato Salad

- 6 **large green or red bell peppers or a combination of both, roasted (directions follow)**
- 5 **large tomatoes (about 2½ lbs.** *total***), peeled, seeded, and cut into bite-size pieces**
- 20 **pitted ripe olives**
- ¼ **cup olive oil**
- ½ **teaspoon salt**
- ¼ **teaspoon pepper**
- 1 **teaspoon ground cumin**
- 4 **cloves garlic, minced or pressed**
- 1 **tablespoon chopped parsley**
  Lettuce leaves

Cut roasted peppers into strips ½ to 1 inch wide and place in a bowl. Stir in tomatoes and olives.

In a cup, combine oil, salt, pepper, cumin, garlic, and parsley; blend well, then stir into pepper mixture. Cover and let stand at room temperature for about 4 hours, or refrigerate for as long as 2 days, but bring to room temperature before serving. To serve, line individual plates with lettuce leaves and mound pepper mixture on leaves. Makes 6 servings.

Roasted peppers. Set whole peppers in a shallow pan and place under broiler so that peppers are about 1 inch from heat source. Broil, turning frequently with tongs, until peppers are well blistered and charred on all sides (see page 131). Then place in a plastic bag, close bag tightly, and let peppers sweat for 15 to 20 minutes to loosen skins. Peel and discard skins.

Vinaigrette dressings

Vinaigrette dressings (sometimes called French dressings) are a mixture of oil, an acid such as vinegar or lemon juice, salt, pepper, and sometimes spices. Most commonly used is olive oil or a mild vegetable oil. Salt and pepper are the only essential seasonings; after that you're on your own. You can add paprika or mustard; fresh or dried herbs such as basil, oregano, or tarragon; seeds like coriander, fennel, or mustard.

Perfect flavor balance emerges from the marriage of salad ingredients with just the right vinaigrette dressing. But go lightly on the amount of dressing—it should just add a sparkle to each leaf, not leave a puddle in the bottom of the bowl. The desired taste is light, refreshing, and crisp. Too much acid in the vinaigrette—or just too much vinaigrette—can overpower the delicate greens. On the other hand, if the dressing is too bland, the salad will lack spirit.

The proportion of oil to vinegar depends on your taste, so experiment to determine your preference. A dressing of three to four parts oil to one part vinegar will produce a slightly tart vinaigrette. Since individual vinegars and oils vary greatly, be sure to taste the dressing before adding it to your greens. If the vinegar tastes too strong, dilute the dressing with wine. If the taste of olive oil is too strong, dilute the dressing with a bland vegetable oil, such as corn or peanut oil.

Below are brief descriptions of the different vinegars and oils available in most supermarkets.

Oils

Nut oils. Pressed from walnuts, almonds, or hazelnuts (filberts). To dress green or fruit salads, use 2 to 3 parts walnut or almond oil to 1 part lemon juice or wine vinegar; hazelnut oil is more potent—use only 1 to 2 parts oil to 1 part lemon juice. Store bottled oils in a dark, cool place (don't refrigerate); will keep for many months.

Olive oil. Offered in many grades. The highest quality olive oil comes from the first light pressing of the olives and is graded "extra virgin" or "virgin." Subsequent pressings release stronger flavored oils. Purchase in quantities small enough to use up within 2 months. Don't refrigerate—temperature changes oxidize the oil and it will become rancid more rapidly than if left at room temperature. Pair with wine vinegar.

Vegetable oils (salad oil). Pressed from the seeds of plants (corn, cottonseed, peanut, safflower), these all-purpose oils are very bland and mild in flavor. They go well with most vinegars.

Vinegars

Cider vinegar. Golden in color, this vinegar is made from hard apple cider. Its strong flavor could overpower delicate greens. Use in potato salad or for marinated vegetables.

Distilled white vinegar. This colorless vinegar is made from grain alcohol. It is also strong, so use as you would cider vinegar.

Fruit vinegars. With their pronounced fruit flavors and colors, these pair well with mild vegetable oils on mixed green or fresh fruit salads.

Wine vinegars. Produced from both red and white wines. Their flavors are delicate compared with those of cider or malt vinegar, so they're the preferred choice for most salad dressings. They complement olive oil or vegetable oil.

Basic Vinaigrette

> ½ cup wine vinegar
> 1 teaspoon salt
>   Dash of pepper
> 1½ cups salad oil or olive oil, or a combination of both

In a jar, combine vinegar, salt, pepper, and oil; mix thoroughly. If made ahead, cover and refrigerate, but bring to room temperature and mix again before adding to a salad. Makes 2 cups.

MUSTARD VINAIGRETTE

Prepare **Basic Vinaigrette** and add 2 tablespoons **Dijon or prepared mustard.**

LEMON VINAIGRETTE

Prepare **Basic Vinaigrette,** but substitute ½ cup freshly squeezed **lemon juice** for vinegar, and decrease oil to ½ cup. Add salt to taste.

Mayonnaise & mayonnaise-based dressings

Mayonnaise has an intimidating reputation, but there's a secret to success, and nothing is better than this all-purpose sauce, fresh from your kitchen. Wonderful on its own, it also serves as a base for other dressings—here we offer recipes for five of them.

The secret to making mayonnaise is to add the oil to the egg-vinegar base in a slow, steady stream. If you use olive oil, choose a brand and grade that is light and delicate in flavor.

You can use one whole egg, or one whole egg plus one yolk, or simply three egg yolks to achieve the flavor and spreading consistency you prefer. Whole egg mayonnaise is softer than mayonnaise made with egg yolks alone. One egg plus a yolk gives you a medium-thick, pale-yellow dressing. Using only egg yolks produces a thicker, stiffer dressing with a noticeably richer flavor. As you practice the method, try more than one approach to find your own preference.

Mayonnaise

- 1 **large egg, or 1 large egg plus 1 egg yolk, or 3 egg yolks**
- 1 **teaspoon Dijon or other prepared mustard**
- 1 **tablespoon wine vinegar or lemon juice**
- 1 **cup salad oil (or use part olive oil)**
  Salt and pepper

Using a blender, food processor, or electric mixer, beat egg, mustard, and vinegar at high speed until well blended. Beating constantly, add oil—a few drops at a time at first, then increasing to a slow, steady stream about $\frac{1}{16}$ inch wide as mixture begins to thicken and form an emulsion.

This emulsion can separate if overbeaten—it will appear curdled. But take heart—you can repair the damage. Start over with a new egg yolk, vinegar, and mustard; then gradually add the separated mayonnaise to the egg-vinegar mixture in place of additional oil.

Stir in salt and pepper to taste, and a few more drops of vinegar, if desired. If made ahead, cover and refrigerate. Makes 1 to 1½ cups.

GREEN HERBED MAYONNAISE
(Pictured on facing page)

In a blender or food processor, place ¼ cup lightly packed chopped **parsley;** ⅓ cup chopped **chives;** 1 **green onion** (including top), chopped; ¼ to ½ teaspoon **dill weed;** and 2 teaspoons **lemon juice.** Whirl until finely chopped. Stir into ½ cup **mayonnaise.** If made ahead, cover and refrigerate. Makes about 1 cup.

THOUSAND ISLAND DRESSING

In a bowl, stir together 1 cup **mayonnaise;** ¼ cup **tomato-based chili sauce;** 2 hard-cooked **eggs,** finely chopped; 1 tablespoon chopped **green pepper;** 1 **green onion** (including top), chopped; 2 tablespoons **sweet pickle relish;** and a dash of **paprika.** Stir well to blend. If made ahead, cover and refrigerate. Makes about 1½ cups.

GREEN GODDESS DRESSING

In a blender or food processor, place 1 clove **garlic,** minced or pressed; ¼ cup *each* coarsely chopped **parsley, green onions** (including tops), and **watercress;** ½ teaspoon **salt;** 1 teaspoon **dry tarragon;** 1 teaspoon **anchovy paste** or finely chopped anchovy fillets; and 2 teaspoons **lemon juice.** Whirl until finely chopped. Stir into 1 cup **mayonnaise.** If made ahead, cover and refrigerate. Makes about 1½ cups.

CHUTNEY DRESSING

In a bowl, stir together ½ cup *each* **mayonnaise** and **sour cream,** and 2 to 4 tablespoons finely chopped **chutney.** If made ahead, cover and refrigerate. Serve on fresh fruit. Makes 1 to 1¼ cups.

HERBED BUTTERMILK DRESSING

In a bowl, combine 1 cup **buttermilk;** 2 tablespoons *each* **parsley** and **minced onion;** ¼ teaspoon *each* **dry basil, oregano leaves, dry rosemary,** and **savory leaves;** and one clove **garlic,** minced or pressed. Let stand for 5 minutes. Stir in 1 cup **mayonnaise** until mixture is smooth, and season to taste with **salt** and **pepper.** If made ahead, cover and refrigerate. Before serving, gently stir in 6 ounces crumbled **blue-veined cheese,** if desired. Makes about 2 cups.

How to make Mayonnaise (Recipe on facing page)

1 The secret of successful mayonnaise, whether you use a food processor, blender, or electric mixer, is to add oil to egg/vinegar base in a slow, steady 1/16-inch stream.

2 One egg plus an extra yolk gives you mayonnaise that is fluffy, velvety smooth, and of spreading consistency—all characteristics of a well-emulsified mayonnaise.

3 The finished product can be this Green Herbed Mayonnaise (recipe on facing page) surrounded by such tasty and colorful dippers as raw and cooked vegetables and rolled ham slices.

EGGS & CHEESE

EGGS

No one has ever determined whether the little red hen came before the egg she laid—but without a doubt, it's the virtuoso egg that wins first place for sheer versatility. Commonplace in cuisines of the world from Paris to Bangkok, the egg slips its special sunshine into every imaginable dish—from hors d'oeuvres to frothy, light desserts.

As you shop for this masterpiece of naturally packaged nourishment, be selective. Choose only the freshest refrigerated eggs, and open their cartons to check that none are cracked. Grade AA eggs are freshest and most widely available. Eggs are also graded by size—jumbo, extra large, large, medium, and small. **All recipes in this book are based on large eggs.**

Generally speaking, eggs maintain good quality for as long as a month if stored in the refrigerator. The sign of a fresh egg is a plump yolk that sits up a bit higher than the surrounding white, which—in a very fresh egg—is thick and dense. Freshness matters most when you're frying or poaching—or separating the egg for a more elaborate concoction. Save the slightly less fresh, though perfectly nutritious eggs for hard cooking or for well-mixed creations like omelets, scrambled eggs, or egg-based sauces.

If you crack an egg and see a fleck of blood, don't be alarmed. Just remove it with a spoon. It won't affect the egg's flavor or quality.

Eggs are delicate; even slight shifts of temperature can affect them appreciably in cooking. When a recipe calls for eggs at room tempera-ture, take the advice seriously; don't expect chilly subjects to perform as energetically as the recipe promises. You can bring refrigerated eggs to room temperature quickly by covering them for a minute or two with hot tap water.

When you cook eggs, always keep the dial in the moderate range. High heat and overcooking produce disappointingly rubbery results.

Soft or hard-cooked eggs

Though the expression "hard-boiled eggs" is familiar to us all, in fact you should *never* boil eggs. If you do, you'll court such mishaps as cracked, leaking shells and waterlogged, rubbery whites. Eggs are delicate and need only a gentle simmer.

To cook eggs in their shells, place the eggs in a single layer in a pan and cover with cold tap water. Set pan, uncovered, over high heat and bring water to simmering (bubbles will just begin to rise to the surface). **For soft-cooked eggs,** reduce heat and continue to simmer for 3 to 5 minutes, depending on your taste; serve immediately.

For hard-cooked eggs (to stuff or use in salads), simmer for 15 to 18 minutes; drain immediately and cover with cold water to stop them from cooking any further and to make shells easier to remove. If you don't plan to use them right away, store cooled, unshelled eggs in the refrigerator.

To shell a hard-cooked egg, tap gently all over on a flat surface or with the back of a spoon. Under cold running water, roll the egg between the palms of your hands to loosen the shell.

DEVILED EGGS

Shell 6 cool hard-cooked **eggs** and slice in half, lengthwise. Remove yolks and mash with ¼ cup **mayonnaise** until creamy. Season to taste with **salt** and **pepper.** Fill hollow of each egg white with yolk mixture. Garnish with chopped **chives,** minced **parsley,** or **paprika.**

ALMOND DEVILED EGGS

Follow directions for **Deviled Eggs,** but mash yolks with 2 tablespoons *each* **mayonnaise** and **sour cream,** 1 teaspoon **prepared mustard,** and **salt** to taste. Fill hollow of each egg white with yolk mixture. Garnish with chopped or slivered **almonds.**

Scrambled eggs

For tender, velvety-textured scrambled eggs you need to mix a little liquid into the eggs before cooking.

Break **eggs** into a bowl. Add 1 teaspoon to 1 tablespoon **milk,** cream, or water for each egg, plus a dash of **salt.** Beat with a fork until thoroughly blended but not frothy. Heat **fat** (1 teaspoon butter, margarine, salad oil, or bacon fat per egg) in a wide frying pan over medium heat. Use an 8-inch pan for 2 to 4 eggs, a 10 or 12-inch pan for a larger quantity (but no more than 1 dozen).

When pan is hot, pour in egg mixture. Cook eggs slowly and gently *(Illustration 1).* Lift cooked portion to allow uncooked egg to flow underneath *(Illustration 2).* Never rush eggs—they should

Illustration 1

Illustration 2

cook slowly and gently. Remove pan from heat when eggs are still creamy; they will finish cooking in their own heat.

CREAMY SCRAMBLED EGGS

Unlike most scrambled eggs, which taste best when served immediately after cooking, these eggs stay creamy and warm for as long as an hour on an electric warming tray.

In a small pan over medium heat, melt 2 tablespoons **butter** or margarine. Stir in 2 tablespoons **all-purpose flour** and cook until bubbly. Remove from heat and stir in 1 cup **sour cream.** Return to heat and cook until bubbly and smooth; set aside.

In a large bowl, beat together 2 dozen **eggs,** ¾ teaspoon **salt,** and ⅛ teaspoon **pepper.** In a wide frying pan over medium-low heat, melt 2 tablespoons **butter** or margarine; pour in eggs and cook, gently lifting cooked portion to allow uncooked egg to flow underneath, until eggs are softly set. Remove from heat and gently stir in sour cream mixture.

Turn eggs into a serving dish and garnish with **parsley.** Serve plain or with the following condiments set in individual bowls: crisp **bacon** bits, shredded Cheddar or blue-veined **cheese,** sliced **ripe olives,** sliced **green onions,** small cooked **shrimp, caviar,** and **sour cream.** Makes about 12 servings.

Fried eggs

You can fry eggs without any fat if you use a nonstick pan as the manufacturer directs. But most people prefer the added flavor of a little fat— butter, margarine, bacon fat, or salad oil.

For tender, evenly cooked fried eggs, always start with a preheated pan over medium heat. The eggs should not be crowded in the pan or they will be hard to turn. Melt fat (1 to 2 teaspoons per egg) in a wide frying pan over medium heat. When pan is hot, break eggs directly into pan. Eggs should begin to set almost immediately.

For over-easy style, fry just until whites are set on one side, then with a spatula turn over and fry briefly on the other side. For opaquely covered yolks, sprinkle 1 to 2 teaspoons water over each egg in pan; cover and cook for about 2 minutes.

Four stages of beaten egg whites

Separating an egg

1 Frothy. Lightly beaten egg whites look bubbly and fluid. This is stage at which you would add cream of tartar to stabilize whites—such as in soufflé on page 34.

2 Soft peaks. Whites have moist, shiny, small bubbles. When beaters are lifted, peaks form, but tips fold over. This is correct stage to fold in beaten egg yolks for a soufflé.

1 Gently crack egg against rim of bowl and break into two halves. With yolk in one shell, let most of white drain into bowl.

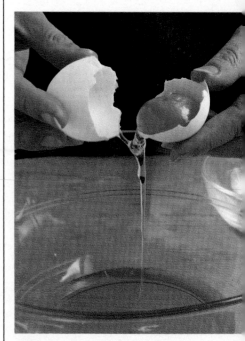

3 Stiff peaks. Whites have lost their sheen. When beaters are lifted, tips stand upright in short, distinct peaks. It's not advisable to beat whites beyond this point.

4 Overbeaten. Whites appear dull, dry, and curdled. This unstable dry foam begins to collapse immediately and will be lumpy if added to other ingredients. You can't correct it and must start over.

2 Using other shell, transfer yolk back and forth until all white is in bowl. Place yolk in a separate bowl.

Baked eggs

To cook eggs by this simple method, you'll need individual custard cups or ramekins. Because each egg bakes in its own dish, you can time each one according to individual preferences.

For each serving, thickly butter a 10-ounce custard cup or 1-cup ramekin; sprinkle lightly with **thyme leaves** or fines herbes. Carefully break 1 **egg** into cup; top with 1 teaspoon **half-and-half** (light cream) and sprinkle with **salt** and **pepper.** Arrange 2 **precooked link sausages** around egg and sprinkle with **paprika.** Bake in a 400° oven for about 10 minutes or until egg is just set to your liking; it will continue to cook slightly after removal from oven. Makes 1 serving.

Baked Eggs with Asparagus & Chicken

- 2 **tablespoons butter or margarine**
- 2 **tablespoons all-purpose flour**
- ¼ **teaspoon salt**
- ⅛ **teaspoon** *each* **white pepper and ground nutmeg**
- 1 **teaspoon dry mustard**
- 2 **cups milk**
- 1¼ **cups (5 oz.) shredded Cheddar cheese**
- 1 **pound fresh asparagus, cooked according to chart on page 127, or 1 package (about 9 oz.) frozen asparagus pieces, cooked and drained**
- 2 **cups diced cooked chicken**
- 4 **eggs**
- 4 **teaspoons butter or margarine, melted and cooled**

In a pan over medium heat, melt the 2 tablespoons butter. Stir in flour, salt, pepper, nutmeg, and mustard; cook until bubbly. Remove from heat. Stirring constantly, gradually pour in milk. Return to heat; continue cooking and stirring until sauce boils and thickens. Stir in cheese until melted. Stir in asparagus pieces and chicken; remove from heat.

Thickly butter four 1½ to 2-cup ramekins. Pour equal amounts of sauce into each and make a hollow in center; carefully break an egg into each hollow. Pour 1 teaspoon melted butter over each egg. Bake, uncovered, in a 375° oven for 15 to 20 minutes or until eggs are set to your liking. Makes 4 servings.

Puffy omelet

To achieve the puffy quality of this popular type of omelet, you beat the egg whites and yolks separately, then fold them together. This produces an airy, delicate texture. You can do some of the preparation ahead of time, but once you beat the egg whites, you must proceed with the recipe before the whites lose their fluffiness.

Sour Cream & Ham Omelet

- 5 **eggs, separated**
- ½ **cup sour cream**
- 3 **tablespoons** *each* **chopped parsley and green onions**
- 1 **cup finely diced cooked ham**
- 1½ **tablespoons butter or margarine**
  Sour cream

In a bowl, beat egg yolks until very thick and lemon colored. Whisk sour cream into yolks, then stir in parsley, onions, and ham. In a large bowl, using clean beaters, beat egg whites until stiff, moist peaks form (see photos on facing page). Pour yolk mixture over beaten whites and gently fold together (see page 35).

In a 10-inch frying pan with sloping sides and ovenproof handle, melt butter over medium heat. Tilt pan so butter coats bottom and sides of pan. Pour omelet mixture into pan; gently smooth surface of mixture with a spoon to ensure even cooking. Reduce heat to low and cook until edges are lightly browned (about 7 to 10 minutes); lift edge of omelet with a spatula to test.

Place pan in a 325° oven and bake for 12 to 15 minutes or until a knife inserted in center comes out clean.

Run a spatula around edge of omelet, then slide spatula under omelet to loosen from pan. Slide omelet onto a warm serving plate. Separate into wedges with two forks or gently cut with a knife. Serve with additional sour cream. Makes about 4 servings.

Plain omelet

An omelet, sometimes called a French omelet, is one of the easiest, speediest, yet most elegant creations in cooking. Even with a filling added, the transition from eggshell to table happens almost like magic—in less than 5 minutes. When perfectly made, an omelet is smooth and creamy inside, golden and tender outside.

A large omelet may use as many as 6 eggs, but for practice, start with an easier-to-manage 2 to 3-egg omelet, a generous size for an individual serving. For more than one person, cook individual omelets in succession.

The traditional omelet pan has sides that curve outward from the bottom, making it easier to slide or roll an omelet out neatly. But we go a step further and strongly recommend that all but the most experienced omelet makers use a pan with a nonstick finish. A 7 to 8-inch size comfortably accommodates a 2 to 3-egg omelet. It's a good idea to reserve this pan just for omelets.

Individual Omelet

If you plan to use a filling, be sure to have it ready and nearby before you begin cooking.

> 2 or 3 eggs
> ¼ teaspoon salt
> Dash of pepper
> 1 tablespoon water
> 1 tablespoon butter or margarine

For each omelet, break eggs into a small bowl and add salt, pepper, and water. Beat with a fork just enough to mix yolks and whites.

In a 7 to 8-inch omelet pan (with a nonstick finish) over medium-high heat, melt 1½ teaspoons of the butter and heat until foam begins to subside. Pour in egg mixture all at once. As edges begin to set (almost at once), lift with a spatula and shake

or tilt pan to let uncooked egg flow underneath (Illustration 1). When egg no longer flows freely, run a spatula around edge, fold omelet in half, (Illustration 2) and slide onto a warm serving plate. Spread remaining 1½ teaspoons butter over top of omelet. Makes 1 serving.

FILLED OMELET

Follow directions for **Individual Omelet,** but when egg no longer flows freely, spoon one or a combination of the following down center of omelet: shredded **cheese** (jack, Cheddar, or Parmesan); diced **avocado; alfalfa sprouts;** sliced **mushrooms** (raw or sautéed in butter); cooked crumbled **bacon;** thinly sliced **ham; salami** slivers; small cooked **shrimp** (or flaked crab or tuna); **salted sunflower seeds;** diced **tomatoes.**

Herb Omelets with Tomato Sauce

> Tomato sauce (recipe follows)
> 2 tablespoons chopped chives or green onion (including top)
> 1 small clove garlic, minced or pressed
> ¼ teaspoon *each* dry basil and thyme leaves
> ⅛ teaspoon dry tarragon
> 2 tablespoons grated Parmesan cheese
> 6 eggs
> 2 tablespoons water
> ¼ teaspoon salt
> 1 tablespoon butter or margarine

Prepare tomato sauce and keep warm. In a small bowl, combine chives, garlic, basil, thyme, tarragon, and Parmesan cheese. In another bowl, beat eggs, water, and salt just until blended.

In a 7 to 8-inch omelet pan (with a nonstick finish) over medium-high heat, melt 1½ teaspoons of the butter and heat until foam begins to subside. Pour in half the egg mixture. As edges begin to set (almost at once), lift with a spatula and shake or tilt pan to let uncooked egg flow underneath. When egg no longer flows freely, spoon half the chive mixture down center of omelet. Run a spatula around edge, fold omelet in half, and slide onto a warm serving plate.

Repeat for second omelet. Spoon hot tomato sauce over omelets before serving. Makes 2 servings.

Illustration 1

Illustration 2

Tomato sauce. Cut 1 small **onion** into chunks. In a blender or food processor, whirl onion and 1½ tablespoons melted **butter** or margarine until smooth; pour into a small pan. Stir in 1 can (8 oz.) **tomato sauce** and cook, stirring, over medium heat until slightly thickened; keep warm.

Country Omelet

Serve this open-faced omelet right from the pan, cut into wedges like a pie.

- 4 **strips bacon**
  About 8 walnut halves
- 1 **small red or white thin-skinned potato, cut in ⅛-inch dice**
- ¼ **cup diced onion**
- 2 **tablespoons butter or margarine**
- 3 **to 4 eggs, lightly beaten**
- ⅓ **cup shredded Swiss cheese**
- 1 **tablespoon minced parsley**
  About ¼ cup sour cream
  Salt

In a wide frying pan, cook bacon over medium heat until crisp. Remove bacon from pan, crumble, and set aside. Add walnuts to drippings and cook, stirring, over medium heat for 1 to 2 minutes or until nuts are lightly browned; set nuts aside. Discard all but 2 tablespoons drippings. Add potato and onion and cook, stirring, over medium-low heat until potato is fork-tender but only slightly browned (about 10 minutes); remove from pan, set aside, and keep warm.

In a 7 to 8-inch omelet pan over medium-high heat, melt butter and heat until foam begins to subside. Pour in eggs. As edges begin to set, lift with a spatula and shake or tilt pan to let uncooked egg flow underneath. When egg no longer flows freely and top of omelet is still moist, sprinkle eggs with potato, cheese, bacon, and parsley. Remove from heat. Mound sour cream in center of omelet. Garnish with toasted walnuts. Cut into wedges to serve, and salt to taste. Makes 2 servings.

Zucchini Frittata

A frittata is an omelet that is cooked on both sides, with vegetables mixed right in with the eggs. Not folded, it is cut into individual wedges and served hot or cool.

- 4 **tablespoons olive oil**
- 2 **cloves garlic, minced or pressed**
- 1 **pound zucchini, sliced into ⅛-inch rounds**
- 8 **eggs**
- 3 **tablespoons whipping cream or water**
- ½ **teaspoon each oregano leaves and salt**
  Dash of pepper
- 3 **tablespoons grated Parmesan cheese**
- ½ **cup sliced green onions (including tops)**
- 1 **can (2¼ oz.) sliced ripe olives, drained**

In a 10 or 11-inch frying pan with ovenproof handle, heat 3 tablespoons of the olive oil over medium-high heat. When oil is hot, add garlic and zucchini; cook, stirring occasionally, until zucchini is crisp-tender (about 5 minutes). Remove from heat.

In a bowl, lightly beat eggs and cream. Stir in oregano, salt, pepper, cheese, onions, olives, and zucchini mixture.

Add the remaining 1 tablespoon olive oil to pan; place over medium heat. When oil is hot, pour in egg mixture and cook without stirring. As egg mixture begins to set, lift edges with a metal spatula and tilt pan to allow uncooked egg to flow underneath. Continue cooking until eggs are softly set and the top still looks moist and creamy.

Remove from heat. Place in preheated broiler about 6 inches from heat, just until tops of eggs are set (about 2 to 3 minutes). Cut into wedges to serve. Makes 4 to 6 servings.

Soufflés

An aura of mystery has always surrounded soufflés yet they're surprisingly simple to make once you've mastered a few techniques. For a main-dish soufflé, the ingredients are simply a thick white sauce, eggs, and your choice of vegetables, fish, poultry, meat, or cheese. Make the sauce first and let it cool while you prepare the egg whites.

To achieve the greatest volume, start with eggs that are at room temperature and separate them carefully (see photos on page 30). If a bit of yolk falls into the whites, remove it before beating. If you can't remove all trace of yolk, save the eggs for another purpose, because the slightest amount of yolk—or, for that matter, an oily bowl or beaters—will decrease the volume of beaten whites.

Beaten whites should hold soft, moist peaks (see page 30). If whites are overbeaten and become dry, they'll be difficult to fold into the sauce-yolk mixture.

You can help the beaten whites maintain their volume by adding cream of tartar to them early in the beating. You lighten the heavy sauce by first folding a portion of the beaten egg white into the sauce, then gently folding the lightened sauce into the egg whites.

A traditional soufflé dish is ideal but not essential. Any straight-sided, deep, ovenproof baking dish will do, as long as its volume is equal to what the recipe specifies. Whatever dish you use, it must be well greased.

Once your soufflé is assembled and in the baking dish, put it directly into a *preheated* oven —it must be preheated because a soufflé bakes from the bottom up and needs quick, high bottom heat to achieve height.

The soufflé is done when the top is golden or feels firm to the touch, and jiggles only slightly when gently shaken. The French prefer their soufflés, like their eggs, moist and creamy. Americans, on the other hand, often prefer theirs more firm.

Once baked, your soufflé should ideally be served immediately, but it can remain in the turned-off oven for about 10 minutes before it begins to collapse. It will continue to cook slightly, though, and become more firm.

Once you've mastered this soufflé and wish to experiment, you can substitute ½ cup chopped cooked meat, fish, poultry, or vegetable for the cheese and add it to your white sauce. Season sauce mixture with ½ teaspoon herb or spice (see inside back cover for suggestions).

Cheese Soufflé
(Pictured on facing page)

- 3 tablespoons *each* butter and all-purpose flour
- ¼ teaspoon salt
- ⅛ teaspoon ground nutmeg
  Dash of freshly ground pepper
- 1 cup milk
- 4 eggs, separated
- ¾ to 1 cup shredded sharp Cheddar, Swiss, or Gruyère cheese
- ¼ teaspoon cream of tartar

Preheat oven to 450°. In a 1-quart pan over medium heat, melt butter. To make *roux* (cooked butter-flour base for sauces), stir in flour, salt, nutmeg, and pepper and cook until mixture bubbles continuously for 1 minute. Remove from heat. Stirring constantly with a wire whisk, gradually add milk. Return to heat and cook, continuing to stir constantly, until sauce boils and thickens to the consistency of a thick paste. Turn off heat.

With a spoon, lightly beat egg yolks. Spoon about 2 tablespoons of the sauce into the yolks and stir until all the sauce has been incorporated. Stir egg yolk mixture back into sauce. Stir in cheese until it melts; set aside.

Beat egg whites until frothy. Add cream of tartar and beat until soft, moist, stiff peaks form. Fold about ⅓ of the beaten whites into the sauce mixture (see photo 3 on facing page). Then add sauce to egg whites by carefully pouring sauce into space left when first ⅓ of the egg whites was removed. Gently fold sauce and whites together.

Pour into a well-buttered 1½-quart soufflé dish. For flat-top soufflé (pictured on facing page), gently smooth top with spatula. For a "top-hat," draw a circle on surface of soufflé, an inch or so in from rim, with tip of knife or spoon. Bake for 10 minutes at 450°, then reduce oven temperature to 250° and bake for 10 to 15 more minutes, or until top is golden and center jiggles only slightly when gently shaken. When you do this test for doneness, make it quick and close oven door promptly—if temperature drops excessively, soufflé may sink. Spoon onto plates. Makes 4 servings.

Making a perfect soufflé (Recipe on facing page)

1 Spoon about 2 tablespoons of the thick, hot, *roux*-based sauce into slightly beaten egg yolks; stir to blend well.

2 Slowly pour egg yolk mixture back into hot sauce, whisking constantly until completely incorporated.

3 Spoon ⅓ of the beaten egg whites into sauce mixture. Fold together by cutting straight down center of pan with spatula, lifting mixture up and over; repeat until incorporated.

4 To prevent egg whites from collapsing as you fold in sauce, slowly pour lightened yolk sauce into space left in egg white bowl.

5 To fold, cut down center and turn flat side of spatula toward you as you lift sauce up against side of bowl; fold sauce atop whites. Repeat, turning bowl, until sauce is almost incorporated.

6 Behold the billowy soufflé. It deflates within minutes, so have everyone seated and ready to eat when you take it from the oven. Spoon it out to serve.

Oven pancakes

For sheer showmanship, a giant oven pancake runs close competition to a soufflé. The elasticity of eggs produces spectacular height in both, but with quite different results. A soufflé puffs and bursts into a rounded crown; an oven pancake billows on all sides, leaving a hollow in the center. Like a soufflé, an oven pancake holds its puffiness for only a very short time, so it should be served promptly. It's great for breakfast, lunch, or supper.

Giant Oven Pancake

If you wish, you can make the batter an hour or two ahead and refrigerate it until needed. Though we like to dust the pancake with powdered sugar and squeeze a little lemon juice over it, you can choose your own toppings. Warm honey, maple or fruit syrup, strawberries, sliced peaches, blueberries, sautéed apples and sour cream are some of the possibilities.

⅓ **cup butter or margarine**
4 **eggs**
1 **cup** *each* **milk and all-purpose flour**
  Powdered sugar
  Lemon wedges

Place butter in a 3 to 4-quart round or oval shallow baking dish or casserole and set in a 425° oven. Meanwhile, in a blender or food processor, whirl eggs at high speed for 1 minute. With motor running, gradually pour in milk, then slowly add flour; continue to whirl for 30 more seconds. Or, in a bowl, beat eggs until blended; gradually beat in milk, then flour.

When butter is melted, remove pan from oven and quickly pour in batter. Return pan to oven and bake for 20 to 25 minutes or until pancake is puffy and well browned. Cut into wedges and serve immediately. Offer powdered sugar and lemon wedges at the table. Makes 4 servings.

Quiche

Its versatility—along with its elegance—has made quiche very popular. You can serve it warm or at room temperature. Besides offering it as a stylish brunch entrée, you can pair it with salad for a light dinner, or pass small servings as an hors d'oeuvre, or transport it to a picnic or potluck.

The basic filling—eggs, milk, and cheese—is a snap to assemble. The pastry shell takes more time. We like Butter Pastry (page 167) for its tender texture and ease of handling. If you have trouble rolling it out on a board, you can press it by hand into your pie pan or quiche dish—handling won't make it tough. We recommend that you prebake the crust so it won't become soggy when it bakes with the filling; bake it the day before, if you like.

Quiche Lorraine

  Butter Pastry (page 167)
10 **strips bacon, crisply cooked, drained, and crumbled**
1 **cup (4 oz.) shredded Swiss or Gruyère cheese**
3 **eggs**
1½ **cups half-and-half (light cream)**
⅛ **teaspoon ground nutmeg**

Preheat oven to 450°. On a lightly floured board, roll out pastry to about ⅛-inch thickness. Fit into a 1½-inch-deep, 9-inch pie pan; flute edges. Or press into a quiche dish (see page 110). Place a piece of foil inside pastry shell and partially fill

---

WHITES & YOLKS—HOW TO STORE & MEASURE THEM

When a recipe calls for egg whites only, you can store the remaining yolks in the refrigerator for several days. Place yolks in a small bowl, cover them with a slight amount of cold water, then cover the bowl airtight with plastic wrap. Measuring out 1 tablespoon yolk for each large egg yolk needed, you can use yolks to enrich sauces or scrambled eggs.

In the opposite situation, when your recipe uses only egg yolks, store remaining whites in a jar with a screw-on lid. Measure out 2 tablespoons egg white for each large egg white needed.

If you halve a recipe and find you need only half an egg, beat a whole egg, then pour off half of it (about 1½ tablespoons). Cover the remaining egg and store in the refrigerator for other uses.

with uncooked beans or rice (see page 110). Bake in the preheated 450° oven for 10 minutes. Lift off foil and beans; return pastry to oven for 5 more minutes or until lightly browned. Let cool. Reduce oven temperature to 350°.

Scatter bacon in pastry shell; sprinkle evenly with cheese. In a bowl, beat eggs with half-and-half, then pour onto cheese. Sprinkle nutmeg over filling. Bake for 35 to 40 minutes or until a knife inserted in center comes out clean. Let stand for 10 minutes before cutting. Makes 6 servings.

CHEESE & CHILE QUICHE

Follow directions for **Quiche Lorraine,** but omit bacon, and substitute 1½ cups (6 oz.) shredded mild **Cheddar cheese** for Swiss cheese. Sprinkle 1 can (4 oz.) **diced green chiles** over cheese before pouring in egg-cream mixture. Sprinkle with ⅛ teaspoon **ground cumin** instead of nutmeg.

Spinach & Feta Quiche

If you're in a hurry, or trimming calories, bake this without crust.

> 9-inch baked pastry shell as for Quiche Lorraine (optional)
1 package (10 oz.) frozen chopped spinach, thawed
6 ounces (1½ cups) feta cheese, crumbled
½ cup cottage cheese
6 green onions (including tops), sliced
1 tablespoon olive oil
1 teaspoon dry basil
½ teaspoon pepper
¼ teaspoon garlic salt
4 eggs
½ cup milk

Prepare and bake pastry shell, if desired.

With your hands, squeeze as much moisture from spinach as possible; set spinach aside. In a blender or food processor, whirl feta cheese, cottage cheese, green onions, oil, basil, pepper, and garlic salt until smooth. Add eggs and milk; blend well. Pour into a bowl and stir in spinach.

Pour into baked pastry shell or a greased 9-inch pie pan. Bake in a 325° oven for 35 to 40 minutes or until a knife inserted in center comes out clean. Let stand for 10 minutes before cutting. Makes 6 servings.

Mushroom Crust Quiche

> 5 tablespoons butter or margarine
½ pound mushrooms, coarsely chopped
½ cup finely crushed saltine crackers
¾ cup chopped green onions
2 cups (8 oz.) shredded jack or Swiss cheese
1 cup cottage cheese
3 eggs
¼ teaspoon *each* ground red pepper (cayenne) and paprika

In a frying pan over medium heat, melt 3 tablespoons of the butter. Add mushrooms and cook until soft; stir in crushed crackers. Turn mixture into a well-greased 9-inch pie pan and press evenly into pan bottom and up the sides.

In same frying pan over medium heat, melt remaining 2 tablespoons butter. Add onions and cook until soft. Spread onions over mushroom crust; sprinkle evenly with shredded cheese. In a blender, whirl cottage cheese, eggs, and cayenne until smooth. Pour into crust and sprinkle with paprika. Bake in a 350° oven for 20 to 25 minutes or until a knife inserted in center comes out clean. Let stand for 10 minutes. Makes 6 servings.

Tuna Quiche

> 9 eggs
1½ cups half-and-half (light cream) or milk
1 teaspoon prepared horseradish
1 tablespoon lemon juice
½ teaspoon *each* salt and dry basil
2 large cans (12½ oz. *each*) chunk-style tuna, well drained
1 package (10 oz.) frozen peas, thawed
1 can (about 8 oz.) water chestnuts, chopped
⅓ cup sliced green onions
1½ cups *each* shredded jack cheese and Cheddar cheese

In a large bowl, blend eggs and half-and-half; stir in horseradish, lemon juice, salt, and basil. Then stir in tuna, peas, water chestnuts, onions, jack cheese, and 1 cup of the Cheddar cheese.

Pour mixture into a greased 10 by 15-inch jelly-roll pan. Top with remaining Cheddar. Bake in a 375° oven for 25 to 30 minutes or until a knife inserted in center comes out clean. Let stand for 10 minutes. Makes 12 servings or 60 appetizers.

Poaching eggs for Eggs Benedict (Recipe on facing page)

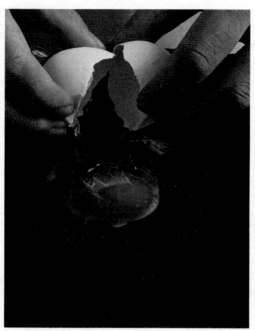

1 Into a wide, greased frying pan, pour water to a depth of 1½ inches. Heat until tiny bubbles form on pan bottom. Add 1 table-spoon vinegar to help set egg whites.

2 Break eggs directly into water; do not overcrowd. Adjust heat, if necessary, to keep water simmering, and cook eggs, uncovered, for 3 to 5 minutes.

3 Test for doneness with light finger pressure. White should be firm; yolk should be opaquely covered and cooked to the firmness you like.

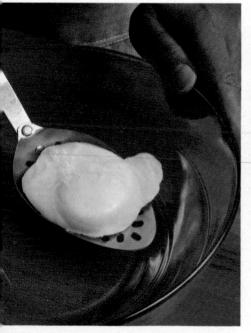

4 To stop the cooking, transfer to bowl of cold water. Cover and chill for up to 24 hours. To reheat, place eggs in bowl of very hot tap water for 5 to 10 minutes.

5 A simple poached egg becomes an elegant brunch entrée when served on toasted muffin half and Canadian bacon. Creamy hollandaise sauce forms the golden mantle.

Poached eggs

A beautifully poached egg has a well-centered yolk snugly surrounded by the white, the whole of it cooked just to the firmness you like.

To achieve such perfection, pour water into a wide, greased frying pan to a depth of 1½ inches. Heat until bubbles form on the pan bottom. Add 1 tablespoon white or cider vinegar. Break each egg into the water, keeping them separate. (Cook no more than 6 at a time in a 10-inch pan.) Cook, with water barely simmering, until eggs are done to your liking (touch yolk gently to check firmness). For soft yolks and firm whites, allow 3 to 5 minutes.

With a slotted spoon, lift eggs from hot water. To use eggs at once, drain well on paper towels.

To make poaching easier for entertaining, and to eliminate a lot of last-minute work, we suggest prepoaching your eggs a day ahead and then reheating them at serving time. To do this, immerse poached eggs in cold water as soon as you lift them from the hot water. Cover and chill for as long as 24 hours. To reheat, transfer cooked eggs to a bowl of very hot tap water for 5 to 10 minutes or until eggs are hot to touch.

Huevos Rancheros

　　　Hot sauce (recipe follows)
　6　corn or flour tortillas
　6　hot poached or fried eggs
　　　Garnishes: sliced avocado, sliced radishes, shredded jack or mild Cheddar cheese

Prepare sauce and keep warm.

In an ungreased heavy frying pan over medium-high heat, place tortillas, one at a time, and heat until soft and hot (about 30 seconds on each side). Put immediately into a covered ovenproof container or foil packet; keep in a 200° oven until all tortillas are heated.

For each serving, place 1 tortilla on a plate; top with a well-drained poached or fried egg and about ½ cup sauce. Sprinkle with garnish of your choice. Makes 6 servings.

Hot sauce. In a wide frying pan over medium-high heat, cook 2 medium-size **onions,** chopped, and 1 **green pepper,** seeded and chopped, in 3 tablespoons **salad oil** until vegetables are soft. Add 1 can (14 oz.) **Italian-style tomatoes** (break up with a spoon) and their liquid, 1 can (14½ oz.) regular-strength **chicken or beef broth,** 2 to 4 tablespoons canned **diced green chiles,** and ½ tea-

spoon each **oregano leaves** and **ground cumin.** Boil rapidly, stirring to prevent sticking, until sauce is reduced to about 2½ cups.

Eggs Poached in Tomatoes

　3　or 4 large tomatoes
　1　pound mushrooms, thinly sliced
　2　tablespoons butter or olive oil
　6　to 8 eggs
　　　Salt and pepper
　¾　cup (3 oz.) shredded jack cheese
　　　Chopped parsley

Cut tomatoes into cubes and drain in a colander for several minutes. Meanwhile, in a 10 to 11-inch frying pan over medium-high heat, cook mushrooms in butter, stirring, until mushrooms are soft and juices have evaporated. Add tomatoes and stir to heat through. Reduce heat to low. With a spoon make 6 or 8 depressions in mushroom-to-mato mixture; break an egg into each depression. Sprinkle with salt and pepper and cover evenly with cheese. Cover pan and cook over low heat until eggs are set as you like and cheese is melted. Garnish with parsley. Makes 3 or 4 servings.

Eggs Benedict

(Pictured on facing page)

Eggs can be poached and the hollandaise prepared ahead of time for this easy brunch entrée.

　6　eggs
　½　pound Canadian bacon or boneless cooked ham, sliced ⅛ to ¼ inch thick
　3　English muffins, halved
　　　Hollandaise sauce (page 132)

Poach eggs. Or, if poached the day before, reheat in a bowl of very hot tap water for 5 to 10 minutes. In a wide frying pan over medium heat, cook bacon until lightly browned on both sides and heated through. Toast muffin halves and reheat hollandaise sauce as directed on page 132.

To serve, place 1 or 2 muffin halves on each plate. Cover each half with bacon. Lift eggs from hot water, drain well, and place 1 egg on each bacon-topped muffin. Spoon about 2 tablespoons hollandaise over each egg. Makes 3 to 6 servings.

CHEESE

A connoisseur once observed that cheese was milk's leap into immortality. One of our oldest and most satisfying foods, cheese comes in a glorious and bountiful array.

Today's market displays reflect the influence of Europe, where this simple milk product has long been an everyday food in many forms and flavors. You can find both European and domestic versions of many cheeses; others are unique to a single region.

Natural cheeses (those without additives) derive directly from milk—most often cows' milk, occasionally milk from sheep or goats. These cheeses differ considerably in flavor and texture, depending on how they're made and how long they've been "ripened" (aged) to develop a characteristic flavor.

Cheeses fall into several basic families, according to the way they're made; sharpness and texture may vary within a family, but flavors are similar. Also classified by consistency, cheeses come in soft or firm unripened, and in several ripened varieties—soft, semisoft, firm, very hard, and blue-vein mold.

In general, the harder the natural cheese, the longer it will keep in the refrigerator. Soft ricotta or cottage cheese should be used within a few days after purchase, but hard cheeses keep for several weeks. After opening, any cheese should be enclosed tightly in plastic wrap (don't use foil—the acid in cheese may react with it) and stored in the coldest part of the refrigerator. If a little mold appears, just cut or scrape it away; the remaining cheese is perfectly safe. Wrap strong-smelling cheeses and store them separately.

When cooking with cheese, use low temperatures—325° to 350°—and short cooking times. Excessive heat and overcooking cause cheese to become tough and stringy, and fat may separate. If possible, add cheese at the last minute; it melts quickly and blends in easily if it is first shredded or grated. In general, 4 ounces yields a cup of shredded cheese, but with hard grating types like Parmesan or Romano, 3 ounces of cheese equals a cup.

Serve ripened cheeses at room temperature to enjoy their fullest aroma, flavor, and texture. Unripened cheeses taste best when they're chilled. Light and fruity wines enhance the milder ripened cheeses; a full-bodied red wine complements stronger, tangier cheese varieties.

You can freeze most kinds of cheese (except ricotta and cottage cheese), but changes in texture are likely, and it's by far the best idea to enjoy cheese while it's fresh. To use cheese from the freezer, thaw it, unopened, in the refrigerator and use as soon as possible.

Often you can substitute one cheese for another with similar texture and flavor. Use the chart below as your guide to experimentation and discovery.

A CHEESE SAMPLER

(Pictured on page 43)

Cheese and country of origin	Personality profile	Serving suggestions
Blue France	Semisoft ripened cheese; pasty, sometimes crumbly texture; white interior marbled with blue green veins. Pungent, tangy flavor.	Use in appetizers or dips, crumbled into salads or salad dressings, in cooking, with pears or apples for dessert.
Brie France	Soft cheese with edible thin white crust; creamy yellow interior becomes satiny and spreadable when fully ripened. Mild to pungent flavor.	Present with crackers or French bread as an appetizer with raw vegetables, or for dessert with grapes, pears, or other fresh fruit.
Camembert France	Soft cheese with edible thin white crust; smooth creamy yellow interior when fully ripened. Mild to pungent flavor grows stronger with age.	Serve small wheels or wedges as an appetizer paired with crackers or French bread, or as dessert with grapes, melon, or pears.
Cheddar England	Firm ripened cheese with smooth body; ivory to medium yellow orange in color. Mild to very sharp flavor grows stronger with age. Domestic forms include Colby, Coon, Longhorn, Tillamook.	Enjoy as an appetizer, in sandwiches, with fresh fruit for dessert. Shred to use in omelets, cheese sauce, or other cooking, or as casserole topping.
Cottage cheese Unknown	Soft unripened white cheese; lumpy large or small curds. Mild, slightly acid flavor. Less moist than ricotta.	Eat as a snack or use in appetizers and dips, in salads with fruit, in cooking and baking, in cheesecake.
Cream cheese U.S.A.	Soft unripened white cheese with smooth, buttery texture. Mild flavor, slightly acid.	Use in appetizers, dips and spreads, sandwiches, salads, cheesecake, frostings.

Cheese and country of origin	Personality profile	Serving suggestions
Edam Netherlands	Firm ripened cheese; creamy yellow interior has small holes. Sold in cannonball shape with red wax coating. Mild, nutlike flavor.	Good table cheese served with crackers or fresh fruit; also use in sandwiches or salads.
Emmentaler Switzerland	Firm ripened cheese; light yellow wheels have large holes, natural rind. Sweet, nutlike flavor, slightly salty tang. The original Swiss cheese, it has been widely copied.	Perfect for sandwiches, as a snack, in salads, with fruit for dessert. A good cooking cheese, it shreds well and melts readily.
Feta Greece	Soft ripened white cheese, made from sheep's or goats' milk and "pickled" in brine; flaky texture. Sharp, tangy flavor, usually very salty.	Serve with Greek olives as an appetizer; use in salads and cooking.
Fontina Italy	Semisoft to firm ripened cheese; yellow interior; may have wax coating. Bland to nutty flavor. European kinds more full flavored than domestic.	Use in appetizers and sandwiches, in cooking, for dessert with crusty bread.
Gorgonzola Italy	Semisoft ripened cheese; pasty, sometimes crumbly texture; creamy white interior marbled with blue green veins; light tan surface. Piquant, tangy flavor; most pungent of the blues.	Classic dessert cheese served with pears and crackers or dark breads; also use in salads and salad dressings, and in cooking.
Gouda Netherlands	Semisoft to firm ripened cheese; compact texture with a few holes. Flattened balls of yellow cheese may have wax coating. Mild to mellow flavor.	Favorite for snacks or appetizers, in sandwiches and salads, in cooking, for dessert served with crackers and fresh fruit.
Gruyère Switzerland	Firm ripened cheese; light yellow with texture similar to Emmentaler but with smaller and fewer holes. Buttery, slightly nutty flavor.	Classic cooking cheese used in fondue, quiche, and other dishes; also enjoy as an appetizer or with fruit for dessert.
Jack (Monterey) U.S.A.	Semisoft ripened cheese produced in creamy white wheels; smooth open texture. Mild flavor.	All-purpose cheese, good for snacks, in sandwiches, in cooking.
Jarlsberg Norway	Firm ripened, buttery cheese similar to Swiss in appearance but less nutty in flavor.	Serve for snacks, in sandwiches and salads, on cheese board. Good melting cheese.
Limburger Belgium	Soft cheese, smooth when fully ripened; creamy white interior usually contains small, irregular holes; yellow orange rind. Robust flavor and aroma. Made extensively in Germany.	Use in sandwiches, as a snack with crackers or dark breads. Keep separate from other cheeses, since Limburger's strong aroma can affect their flavor.
Mozzarella Italy	Slightly firm unripened cheese; creamy white; supple texture. Mild, delicate flavor. Italian imports are more tender, less rubbery than domestic types.	Use as appetizer, in sandwiches and salads, and in cooking—especially Italian dishes. Serve mellow Italian mozzarella (bufalo) as a dessert cheese.
Münster France	Semisoft ripened cheese has creamy white interior with many small holes; yellow tan surface. Mild to pungent flavor.	Serve in sandwiches, on cheese boards, with fruit for dessert.
Neufchâtel U.S.A.	Soft unripened white cheese; smooth and creamy texture. Mild flavor. Similar to cream cheese.	Use for snacks, in dips and spreads, salads, cheesecake, for dessert with fruit.
Parmesan Italy	Very hard ripened grating cheese; granular brittle texture; creamy white or light yellow with brown or black coating. Sharp, piquant flavor. Pregrated version much less flavorful.	Grate or shred for cooking; use in Italian dishes, especially pasta; for garnishing soups or casseroles; on toasted bread or croutons. Serve wedges for dessert with fresh fruit.
Provolone Italy	Firm ripened cheese; compact, flaky texture; creamy interior with light golden brown surface; firm, smooth shapes bound with cord. Mild to sharp flavor, depending on age; smoky, salty.	Use for snacks and appetizers, in sandwiches and salads, with fruit for dessert. Good for cooking, especially in Italian dishes. Suitable for grating when fully cured and dried.
Ricotta Italy	Soft unripened white whey cheese; moist and grainy texture. Bland but semisweet flavor.	Use in cooking, especially Italian dishes; also for appetizers, in salads, for dessert.
Romano Italy	Very hard ripened grating cheese; hard granular texture; yellow white interior with greenish black surface. Sharp, piquant flavor.	Grate or shred for seasoning or garnishing soups, salads, or cooked dishes, especially pasta, or for use in sauces.
Roquefort France	Semisoft cheese made from sheep's milk and ripened in limestone caves; pasty and sometimes crumbly texture; creamy white interior marbled with blue green veins. Sharp, pungent flavor.	Enjoy with crackers or crusty bread as an appetizer, or with pears or apples for dessert. Crumble in salads or salad dressings, or use in cooking.
Swiss U.S.A.	Firm ripened, light yellow cheese resembles Emmentaler; smooth texture with large round holes. Sweet, nutlike flavor.	Serve in sandwiches, as a snack, in salads. Shred to use in cooking sauces, fondue; grate to sprinkle atop soup.

The Cheese Board

Simple yet sophisticated, a cheese board fills the bill for many purposes, from appetizer to dessert as well as for between-meal entertaining almost any time. For variety, choose three to five cheeses ranging from mild to pronounced flavor and soft to firm texture. (The cheese chart on pages 40–41 offers many suggestions.) Arrange your selection on a bread board or in a shallow basket.

As accompaniments, we recommend crackers (preferably one of the many unsalted varieties), small pieces of crusty bread, and vegetables. Zucchini sticks, cucumber rounds, cherry tomatoes, and green pepper slices go well with cheeses and grace them with color, too.

A dessert cheese board is light and appealing. You can build an arrangement around a Baked Brie (see recipe this page), adding, perhaps, wedges of fontina and crisp quartered red apples or a creamy Camembert with juicy green-gold pears.

Freezer Cheese Balls

    2 cups (8 oz.) shredded sharp Cheddar cheese
    1 large package (8 oz.) cream cheese or
       Neufchâtel, cut into pieces
    4 ounces blue cheese, cut into pieces
    4 tablespoons butter or margarine
    1 clove garlic, minced or pressed
    ⅔ cup coarsely chopped walnuts or pecans

Allow cheeses and butter to stand at room temperature until soft. Place Cheddar, cream cheese, blue cheese, and butter in a large bowl; with an electric mixer, beat until blended. Add garlic and beat until creamy.

Cover and chill mixture until firm enough to shape into balls, but not hard (about 2 hours). Divide in half and shape each half into a smooth ball. Sprinkle nuts on a piece of wax paper and roll each ball in about half of the nuts, pressing in lightly. Place balls in separate plastic bags and seal; refrigerate or freeze until needed.

Before serving, allow cheese balls to stand at room temperature, unwrapped, for 30 minutes if refrigerated, or for 3 to 4 hours if frozen. Serve with assorted crackers or wafers. Makes 2 balls, each about 3 inches in diameter.

Zesty Tomato Fondue

Bubbling fondue makes a fun do-it-yourself party appetizer. For dippers, you can offer cubes of crusty French bread, cooked artichoke leaves, lightly steamed whole baby carrots, green beans, broccoli and cauliflower florets, or pieces of cooked Italian sausage.

    1 medium-size onion, finely chopped
    1 clove garlic, minced or pressed
    2 tablespoons butter or margarine
    1 small can (about 8 oz.) stewed tomatoes
    ½ teaspoon dry basil
    ¼ teaspoon oregano leaves
    ⅛ teaspoon pepper
    2 cups (8 oz.) shredded mild Cheddar cheese
    ¼ cup grated Parmesan cheese
    1 tablespoon cornstarch

In a 2-quart pan over medium heat, cook onion and garlic in butter until golden. Add tomatoes (break up with a spoon) and their liquid, basil, oregano, and pepper; heat to simmering. Meanwhile, combine Cheddar and Parmesan cheeses with cornstarch.

Reduce heat to low and add cheese mixture, a handful at a time, stirring until cheeses are melted and blended. Transfer to fondue pot or chafing dish, and keep warm over heat source. Makes about 2 cups (8 appetizer servings).

Baked Brie

Let guests spread the hot Brie on slices of French bread, and serve with grapes and sliced pears or apples.

    2 tablespoons butter, softened
    7 to 8-ounce whole ripe Brie or Camembert
       cheese with rind
    2 tablespoons sliced almonds

Preheat oven to 350°. Spread butter over top and sides of cheese. Place cheese on an ovenproof rimmed serving plate and sprinkle almonds over top. Bake for 12 to 15 minutes or until cheese just begins to melt. (Very ripe cheese may melt completely.) Makes 4 to 6 appetizer or dessert servings.

A cheese sampler (See chart on pages 40–41)

Provolone

Parmesan

Gruyère

Romano

Emmentaler

Domestic Swiss

Jarlsberg

Provolone

Monterey jack

Natural cream cheese

Cream cheese

Cottage cheese

Neufchâtel

Ricotta

Roquefort

Gorgonzola

Münster

Italian fontina

Feta

Blue

Mozzarella

Cheddar

Camembert

Brie

Gouda

Edam

Limburger

Brie

In this collection of cheeses, textures range from creamy to crumbly, flavors from mild to pungent. Table cheese tastes best at room temperature. To serve, cut wheels or ball shapes into wedges, and cut flat, square, or rectangular cheeses into slices, bars, or cubes. Descriptions of these cheeses appear on pages 40–41.

MEATS
Beef · Pork · Lamb · Veal

BEEF

Some days confusion seems to reign at the meat counter. The only clear label is the price tag, and it's not always easy to know what you're actually buying. Names and cuts vary from region to region and even from store to store.

Simply put, meats fall into two categories—naturally tender cuts and those that are fibrous and tougher. The least exercised parts of any animal (those in the middle of the back, called the loin) are the most tender. The parts adjacent to the loin get more exercise, so they are less tender. In fact, meat becomes increasingly less tender as its distance from the loin increases. Really hard-working muscles, such as the shoulder (or chuck) and neck, produce tough meat.

Obviously, it helps to become familiar with basic animal anatomy. Our drawing of a steer (page 48) showing the wholesale (or primal) cuts applies as a general guide for all meats. The loin portion of a steer that yields tender porterhouse and T-bone steaks is the same portion of the lamb, pig, or calf that produces lamb chops, pork chops, and veal loin chops.

Cooking methods

The anatomical origin of a cut of meat determines its tenderness, and the tenderness determines the cooking method. Tender cuts (from the loin or rib) should be cooked with dry heat—roasting, broiling, grilling, pan-broiling, or frying. Tougher cuts (from the shoulder or shank) require moist heat—stewing or braising—in which the long, slow cooking in liquid breaks down the connective tissue that causes the meat's toughness. The results can be appetizingly tender.

Another option with less tender cuts of meat is to tenderize them before cooking—this will allow you to use one of the dry-heat methods. One method of tenderizing (often done in the market) involves mechanically breaking down the meat's muscle fibers by pounding with a cleated mallet or a tenderizing machine.

You also can tenderize raw meat in a marinade of wine, vinegar, or citrus juice. Or you can buy packaged chemical tenderizers (usually papaya derivatives) to apply to the meat. When using these tenderizers, be sure to follow the manufacturer's directions—if the tenderizer is applied too liberally or left to stand on the meat too long before cooking, the meat may go beyond tenderness to mush.

How much meat to buy

Appetites vary, but usually it's enough to allow ¼ to ⅓ pound per serving of lean, boneless meat with little or no fat—such as ground meat, filets, or boned, rolled roasts. For meat with a medium amount of bone and some edge fat—loin, rib, and shoulder roasts; steaks and chops; and bone-in ham—allow about ½ pound per serving. For very bony cuts—shank, spareribs, short ribs, and breast of veal or lamb—allow 1 full pound per serving.

MEAT ROASTING TIME & TEMPERATURE CHART

The suggested cooking times are merely a guide—the only *accurate* measure for doneness is a meat thermometer. First, estimate total cooking time by multiplying minutes-per-pound (for doneness you prefer) by weight of roast. Then insert a meat thermometer in meat's thickest portion (without touching bone); roast until thermometer registers degree specified for preferred doneness. Remove roast from oven and let stand for 10 to 20 minutes before carving; internal temperature will rise 5 to 10 degrees.

All testing was done with meat taken directly from the refrigerator and roasted on a rack in a shallow pan, in a conventional electric or gas oven; unless otherwise indicated, oven temperature is 325°.

Cut	Approximate weight (lbs.)	Approximate cooking time (minutes per lb.)	Meat thermometer reading (°F)
BEEF (Illustrated on page 48)			
Standing rib	4–6	26–32	135° (R)
		34–38	155° (M)
		40–42	170° (W)
Standing rib	6–8	23–25	135° (R)
		27–30	155° (M)
		32–35	170° (W)
Rib eye (Delmonico) (use 350° oven)	4–6	18–20	135° (R)
		20–22	155° (M)
		22–24	170° (W)
Tenderloin (use 425° oven)	4–6	45–60 (total cooking time)	135° (R)
Boneless rolled rump	4–6	25–30	150°–170°
Sirloin tip	3½–4	32–40	135°–155°
VEAL			
Leg	5–8	22–32	170°
Loin	4–6	22–28	170°
Shoulder, boneless	4–6	35–45	170°
FRESH PORK (Illustrated on page 60)			
Loin roasts			
Center, bone-in	3–5	30–35	170°
Half, bone-in	5–7	35–40	170°
Half, boneless, rolled	3–5	35–40	170°
End, bone-in	3–4	35–40	170°
Top, boneless	2–4	30–35	170°
Crown	4–6	35–40	170°
Picnic shoulder			
Bone-in	5–8	30–35	170°
Boneless	3–5	35–40	170°
Boston shoulder (butt)	4–6	40–45	170°
Leg (fresh ham)			
Whole, bone-in	12–16	22–26	170°
Whole, boneless	10–14	24–28	170°
Half, bone-in	5–8	35–40	170°
Tenderloin	½–1	45–60 (total cooking time)	—

Cut	Approximate weight (lbs.)	Approximate cooking time (minutes per lb.)	Meat thermometer reading (°F)
SMOKED PORK (Illustrated on page 60)			
Ham (cook-before-eating)			
Whole	10–14	18–20	160°
Half	5–7	22–25	160°
Shank portion	3–4	35–40	160°
Butt portion	3–4	35–40	160°
Ham (fully cooked)			
Half	5–7	18–22	140°
Loin	3–5	25–30	160°
Picnic shoulder (cook-before-eating)	5–8	30–35	170°
Picnic shoulder (fully cooked)	5–8	25–30	140°
Shoulder roll (butt)	2–4	35–40	170°
LAMB (Illustrated on page 69)			
Leg, bone-in			
Whole	5–9	20–25	140° (R)
		25–30	160° (M)
		30–35	170°–180° (W)
Shank half	3–4	25–30	140° (R)
		30–35	160° (M)
		35–40	170°–180° (W)
Sirloin half	3–4	20–25	140° (R)
		25–30	160° (M)
		30–35	170°–180° (W)
Leg, boneless	4–7	25–30	140° (R)
		30–35	160° (M)
		35–40	170°–180° (W)
Crown	2½–4	30–35	140° (R)
		35–40	160° (M)
		40–45	170°–180° (W)
Shoulder			
Square cut	4–6	25–30	160° (M)
		30–35	170°–180° (W)
Boneless	3½–5	30–35	140° (R)
		35–40	160° (M)
		40–45	170°–180° (W)
Cushion	3½–5	30–35	170°–180° (W)
Rib (use 375° oven)	2–3	25–30	140° (R)
		30–35	160° (M)
		35–40	170°–180° (W)

(R) Rare   (M) Medium   (W) Well done

Standing Rib Roast (Recipe on facing page)

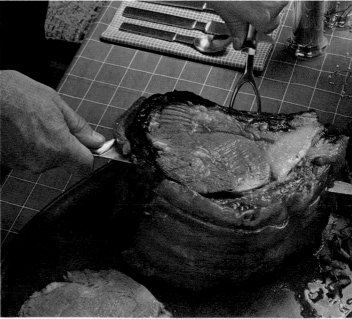

1 Place roast, fat side up, on a rack in a shallow baking pan. Insert a meat thermometer into thickest portion of meat without touching bone; roast according to the chart on page 45.

2 To carve, place roast on board or platter, large end down and ribs to your left. Insert fork between ribs. Cut across grain into ¼ to ½-inch-thick slices.

3 With tip of knife, free slice from rib by cutting down along edge of rib. Transfer slice to board or serving platter before starting to cut the next slice.

4 After slicing below first rib, cut bone off and set aside. Continue slicing meat and removing rib bones.

Beef: dry roasting

When it comes to beef roasts, the standing rib is king. The same cut, boned and tied, is sold as a rib eye or Delmonico roast. Equally impressive, and even more tender, is the tenderloin—4 to 6 pounds of pure meat, with no bones or fat. All three of these roasts are naturally tender cuts you cook with dry heat, using the same basic method of oven roasting. (See chart, page 45, for oven temperatures and approximate cooking times.)

You can use dry heat to roast other less expensive (and less tender) cuts, too, such as sirloin tip and certain boneless cuts from the chuck (cross rib, mock tender, Jewish filet). Generally these are at their best when dry roasted rare to medium—still pink and juicy. When cooked well done, they become dry and stringy.

Standing Rib Roast

(Pictured on facing page)

You can make Yorkshire pudding from the pan drippings—it's simply popover batter (see page 151) that bakes in the flavorful meat juices.

> 4 **to 6-pound standing rib beef roast**
> ⅔ **cup regular-strength beef broth, dry red wine, or water**
> **Salt and pepper**

Place roast, fat side up, on a rack in a shallow baking pan. Insert a meat thermometer into thickest portion of meat without touching bone. Roast, uncovered, in a 325° oven until meat thermometer registers degree of doneness preferred (see chart, page 45).

Remove from oven and transfer roast to a carving board or platter. Cover roast with a tent of foil and let stand for 10 to 20 minutes before carving.

Meanwhile, skim and discard fat from pan drippings; pour broth into pan and place over medium-high heat. Cook, stirring and scraping browned particles free from pan, until sauce is reduced to ½ to ⅓ cup. Season to taste with salt and pepper and pour into a small serving dish.

Slice meat and spoon a small amount of sauce over each slice. Makes 8 to 12 servings.

Herb-crusted Beef Roast

> 2 **cloves garlic, minced or pressed**
> 2 **tablespoons salad oil**
> 2 **teaspoons dry basil**
> ⅛ **teaspoon pepper**
> 4 **pound sirloin tip or cross rib beef roast**
> 2 **to 3 slices firm white bread**
> ½ **cup finely chopped parsley**
> 2 **green onions (including tops), finely chopped**
> 4 **tablespoons butter or margarine, melted**

Stir together garlic, oil, basil, and pepper; brush evenly over meat. Place roast, fat side up, on a rack in a shallow baking pan. Insert a meat thermometer into thickest portion of meat. Roast, uncovered, in a 325° oven for 1 hour.

Meanwhile, with your fingers crumble enough bread to make 1 cup crumbs; combine with parsley, onions, and butter. Remove roast from oven; quickly pat crumb mixture over meat. Return to oven and roast until meat thermometer registers 135° (for rare) to 155° (for medium). Let stand for 10 to 20 minutes before carving.

To serve, cut meat crosswise into thin slices. Makes about 8 servings.

One Rib for Two

A single rib, frozen solid and then cooked at a high temperature, is the secret to a juicy, succulent roast for two.

> 1 **tablespoon salad oil or olive oil**
> 1 **small clove garlic, minced or pressed**
> 1 **rib (about 2½ lbs.) standing rib beef roast, frozen solid**
> 2 **large russet potatoes**

Combine oil and garlic; rub evenly over cut surfaces of frozen meat. Stand rib, bone side down, in a shallow baking pan between potatoes placed like book ends.

Roast, uncovered, in a 400° oven for 1 hour. Insert a meat thermometer through fat layer into center of roast without touching bone; continue to cook until meat thermometer registers degree of doneness preferred (see chart, page 45). Let stand for 5 minutes before carving. Makes 2 servings.

Beef primal cuts

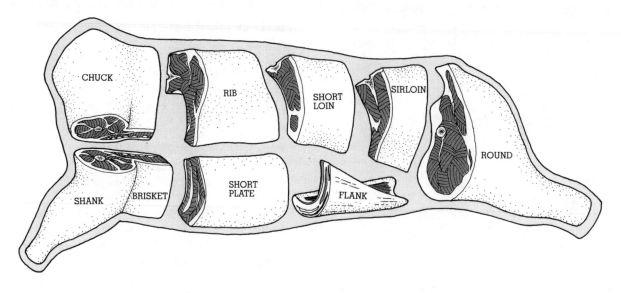

RETAIL CUTS—AND HOW TO COOK THEM

7-bone Chuck Steak
(From the Chuck)
Braise • Cook in
  liquid

Blade Steak
(From the Chuck)
Braise • Cook in
  liquid

Arm Roast • Steak
(From the Chuck)
Braise • Cook in
  liquid

Rib Roast
(From the Rib)
Roast

Rolled Rump Roast
(From the Round)
Braise • Cook in
  liquid

Bottom Round
Roast
(From the Round)
Braise • Cook in
  liquid

Porterhouse Steak
(From the Short Loin)
Broil • Pan-broil •
  Grill

T-bone Steak
(From the Short Loin)
Broil • Pan-broil •
  Grill

Club, Top Loin
Steak
(From the Short Loin)
Broil • Pan-broil •
  Grill

Full Cut Round
Steak
(From the Round)
Braise • Cook in
  liquid

Shank Cross Cuts
(From the Shank)
Braise • Cook in
  liquid

Short Ribs
(From the Short Plate)
Braise • Cook in
  liquid

Corned Brisket
(From the Brisket)
Braise • Cook in
  liquid

Flank Steak
(From the Flank)
Broil • Braise • Grill

Tip Roast
(From the Round)
Braise • Cook in
  liquid

Beef: Broiling

Best broiler candidates are tender steaks such as porterhouse, T-bone, club, rib, and top sirloin (see "Retail cuts" on facing page). When cooked rare to medium-rare by this speedy dry-heat method, the meat remains tender and juicy.

Less tender steaks, such as flank and top round, also broil well if you marinate them first, then cook to rare or medium-rare.

Chili Orange Steak

  1 teaspoon *each* grated orange peel and salad oil
  ½ teaspoon chili powder
  1 porterhouse steak (1½ to 2 lbs.), cut 1½ inches thick
  1 medium-size orange, cut in half
     Salt

In a small bowl, stir together orange peel, oil, and chili powder; rub all over steak. Place steak on a rack in a broiler pan (see "How to Broil Meat," at right). Broil about 3 inches below heat for about 5 minutes on each side for rare or until done to your liking when slashed.

Transfer steak to a carving board with a well to collect meat juices. Squeeze orange over steak; sprinkle with salt. Cut meat from bone; then slice, dipping each slice in accumulated juices before serving. Makes 3 or 4 servings.

Lemon Steak

  2 tablespoons *each* olive oil and lemon juice
  2 large New York steaks, cut 1½ inches thick (¾ to 1 lb. *each*) or 2 pounds top sirloin, cut 1½ inches thick
  1 lemon, cut in half
     Salt and pepper

In a small bowl, stir together oil and lemon juice. Place steaks, side by side, in a close-fitting pan and pour oil mixture over steaks. Let stand at room temperature for about 1 hour. Place steaks on a rack in a broiler pan (see "How to Broil Meat," at right). Broil about 3 inches below heat for about 5 minutes on each side for rare or until done to your liking when slashed.

Transfer steaks to a carving board and cut into thin slices. Squeeze lemon over slices and season to taste with salt and pepper. Makes 4 servings.

Broiled Flank Steak

  ½ cup soy sauce
  1 large clove garlic, minced or pressed
  1 teaspoon ground ginger
  2 tablespoons *each* brown sugar, lemon juice, salad oil, and minced onion
  ¼ teaspoon pepper
  1 flank steak (about 1½ lbs.)

In a small bowl, combine soy, garlic, ginger, sugar, lemon juice, oil, onion, and pepper. Place steak in a close-fitting baking dish; pour soy mixture over steak. Cover and refrigerate for 6 hours or until next day, turning steak occasionally.

Remove steak from marinade and drain briefly, reserving marinade. Place steak on a rack in a broiler pan (see "How to Broil Meat," below). Broil about 3 inches below heat for 3 to 4 minutes on each side for rare or until done to your liking when slashed.

Meanwhile, heat reserved marinade in a small pan over medium heat until bubbly; pour into a small serving bowl. Transfer meat to a carving board and cut across the grain into thin slanting slices. Pass marinade at the table. Makes 4 servings.

HOW TO BROIL MEAT

To broil, choose a large, shallow pan with a rack, and place the meat on the rack. Position the pan below the heat source in your broiler, adjusting the pan (or the oven rack on which the pan is resting) until the top of the meat is the recommended distance below the heat source.

Remove the meat from the broiler, leaving the pan and rack inside. Preheat the broiler for 5 to 7 minutes. Meanwhile, if the meat has a border of fat, slash through the fat to the lean meat at 1-inch intervals to prevent curling. Remove the pan from the broiler and lightly grease the hot rack.

Place the meat on the rack and broil, turning as needed, for the time specified in the recipe or until it's done to your liking when slashed in the thickest portion.

Beef: Pan-broiling & pan-frying

For hearty dinners in a hurry, you can cook these beef entrées on top of the range in just minutes. Whether you pan-broil or pan-fry, the technique is the same—the only difference is the amount of fat you use. Pan-broiling takes little or no fat—at the most a thin film to prevent sticking. Pan-frying, on the other hand, requires several tablespoons, depending on the recipe. With either method, pat the surface of the meat dry before cooking.

If you wish, you can enhance the quickly cooked meat with a well-seasoned sauce, as in our Beef Stroganoff.

Flank Steak with Mustard-Caper Sauce
(Pictured on facing page)

> 4 tablespoons butter or margarine
> 1 tablespoon salad oil
> 1 flank steak (about 1½ lbs.)
> 3 tablespoons dry vermouth or dry white wine
> 1 tablespoon Dijon mustard
> ¼ teaspoon Worcestershire
> 1½ tablespoons capers, drained well
> Watercress (optional)

Melt 1 tablespoon of the butter with the oil in a wide frying pan over medium-high heat. Place meat in pan and cook, uncovered, until meat is browned on both sides but still pink in center when slashed (5 to 6 minutes *total*).

Transfer meat to a carving board and cover loosely to keep warm. Over low heat, melt the remaining 3 tablespoons butter in pan drippings. Mix in vermouth, mustard, Worcestershire, and capers; stir briskly to blend. Cut meat across the grain into thin slanting slices. Spoon sauce over meat. Garnish with watercress, if desired. Makes 4 servings.

Pan-fried Liver & Onions

> 12 strips bacon
> 4 large onions, cut into ¼-inch-thick slices
> Salt and pepper
> 1½ pounds baby beef liver, cut into ½-inch-thick slices
> ¼ cup all-purpose flour

In a wide frying pan over medium heat, cook bacon until crisp. Remove bacon from pan, drain,

and keep warm. Pour off and reserve all but 2 tablespoons drippings. Add onions to drippings in pan and cook over medium-low heat, stirring often and adding more drippings as needed, until onions are golden (about 25 minutes). Season to taste with salt and pepper. Remove onions from pan and keep warm.

Remove membrane from liver. Dredge each slice in flour; shake off excess. Add 3 to 4 tablespoons of the reserved drippings to pan over medium-high heat. Add liver and cook until browned on both sides but still pink in center when slashed (about 2 minutes on each side). Spoon onions onto 4 dinner plates; top with liver slices and bacon strips. Makes 4 servings.

Beef Stroganoff

> ¾ pound lean boneless beef (flank steak, chuck, or top round)
> Pepper
> 3 tablespoons butter or margarine
> 1 tablespoon salad oil
> 1 small onion, finely chopped
> ¼ pound mushrooms, sliced
> 1½ tablespoons all-purpose flour
> ½ cup regular-strength beef broth
> ½ tablespoon Dijon mustard
> ⅛ teaspoon ground nutmeg
> ¼ cup whipping cream
> Salt
> Hot, cooked, buttered noodles
> Chopped parsley

Cut beef across the grain into ⅛ to ¼-inch-thick slanting slices about 3 inches long. Sprinkle generously with pepper.

Melt 1 tablespoon of the butter with oil in a wide frying pan over high heat. Add beef and cook until just browned on all sides (about 1½ minutes total). Remove beef and set aside. Reduce heat to medium.

Melt the remaining 2 tablespoons butter in pan. Stir in onion and mushrooms and cook until soft; then stir in flour and cook until bubbly. Stir in broth and mustard and cook, stirring, until thickened. Return meat to pan. Add nutmeg and cream, season to taste with salt, and heat through. Serve over noodles and garnish with parsley. Makes 2 or 3 servings.

Pan-frying flank steak (Recipe on facing page)

1 Use a heavy frying pan for very even browning. If meat is damp, pat dry with paper towels. Heat butter and oil, then cook meat in hot pan.

2 To make sauce, melt remaining butter in pan drippings. Pour in vermouth, then add mustard, Worcestershire, and capers; stir briskly to blend.

3 Cut meat across grain in thin slanting slices. This slicing technique, and cooking only to rare stage, keep flank steak juicy and tender.

4 Brown on the outside, rare on the inside, and topped with a zesty sauce, this company entrée is ready in minutes.

Reduction sauces made from pan drippings

Many a chef has built a reputation on deftly seasoned sauces that lend sophistication to simply cooked food. Perhaps the sauce that restaurateurs rely on most to embellish roasted, pan-broiled, and fried meats is a reduction sauce—and for good reason. It has a smooth texture, distinctive sheen, and rich flavor; yet it's surprisingly simple and quick to prepare.

The essential flavor comes from the liquid —generally broth or wine—used to deglaze the pan drippings from the meat or roast. Seasonings such as herbs, mustard, or shallots further enhance the flavor. (Salt is never added until the sauce is completed; always taste it first.) The liquid, along with drippings and seasonings, is reduced (boiled down) to about half the original volume to concentrate the flavor. You can then serve this simple reduction sauce (see Standing Rib Roast, page 47), or, to make a more elaborate version, continue with the steps that follow.

The texture of the more elaborate reduction sauces depends on whether you thicken them with whipping cream, or whipping cream and butter (or margarine), or just butter (or margarine). Cream alone makes a thick, satiny sauce; you just boil it down to reach the desired thickness. For an even thicker, silky-smooth sauce, add butter to the liquid-cream mixture, stirring constantly to force the liquid droplets apart and hold them in suspension. For a lighter, more sheer sauce, use only butter or margarine to thicken the reduced liquid.

Making reduction sauces

Lift pan-cooked or roasted meat from pan; set aside and keep warm. Spoon off and discard most of the fat from pan drippings, if necessary. Pour pan drippings into a glass measure, add enough liquid (suggestions follow) to make 1 cup. Return liquid to pan. Add seasonings (suggestions follow), if desired. Boil, uncovered, over high heat, scraping browned particles free from pan, until reduced to ½ cup. At this point you may serve sauce or, if desired, you can add cream, or cream and butter, or just butter.

To add cream, pour in ⅓ to ½ cup whipping cream and boil again until big shiny bubbles form all over the surface, and sauce is again reduced to ½ cup. You may serve sauce immediately, or keep warm, or add butter.

To add butter to the reduced liquid or to the liquid-cream mixture, reduce heat to low or re-move pan from heat to prevent liquid from evaporating too quickly. Add 2 to 6 tablespoons butter or margarine all at once (amount depends on consistency desired), stirring constantly to incorporate butter as it melts. Butter will thicken sauce. Serve immediately or keep warm. Makes 4 to 6 servings.

Liquids. Use regular-strength beef broth or chicken broth; or use dry red or white wine, dry vermouth, dry sherry, Madeira, or port; or use half broth and half wine.

Seasonings. Use about ½ teaspoon dry tarragon, dry basil, or thyme leaves; or 1 or 2 teaspoons Dijon mustard; or 1 to 2 tablespoons minced shallots.

Keeping a reduction sauce warm

Since a reduction sauce goes together so quickly, there's little need to prepare it ahead. But if it's more convenient to hold the sauce for a time, set the serving container, uncovered, in hot-to-touch water. Stir occasionally, and if the water becomes cool, replace it with more hot-to-touch water. (Reduction sauces tend to break down if reheated.)

Restoring a broken sauce

If you boil away too much of the liquid base before adding the cream or butter, the sauce will break down or separate, just as it will if you reheat the sauce over direct heat. To form the sauce again, heat 2 to 4 tablespoons whipping cream or wine in a pan over low heat. Beating constantly, whisk in broken sauce, a few drops at a time, until all the broken sauce is incorporated.

KEEPING COOKED FOODS WARM

When you remove cooked foods from heat to prevent overcooking, but need to keep them warm until serving, use a tent of foil. Simply tear off a piece of foil large enough to loosely cover the platter of food. Make a tent by placing foil, shiny side down (to reflect heat downward), over the food. (Don't tuck foil edges under the platter; this would cause condensation of steam that could drip into the food and make it watery.)

Reduction sauce variations

With the directions just given, you can make any number of reduction sauces to enhance not only meats, but poultry and fish as well. Practice with the specific recipes that follow. They'll get you started. Then, as you master the technique, you can apply it to an endless number of dishes.

Beef with Madeira-Mushroom Sauce

> About 1½ pounds lean ground beef,
> or 4 small beef filets cut 1 to 1½ inches thick
>
> 1 tablespoon butter or margarine
> 1 tablespoon salad oil
> 4 slices French bread, cut ¾ inch thick
> Butter or margarine
> ½ pound mushrooms, thinly sliced
> ⅔ cup Madeira (or regular-strength beef broth blended with 1½ teaspoons lemon juice)
> ½ cup whipping cream
> 1 ripe avocado, pitted, peeled, and sliced
> Watercress (optional)

If using ground beef, shape into 4 oval patties, each about 1 inch thick. In a wide frying pan over medium-high heat, melt the 1 tablespoon butter with oil. Add patties or steaks and cook until well browned on both sides and cooked to desired doneness when slashed (3 to 5 minutes on each side for rare).

Toast French bread. Spread with butter and put a slice on each plate; top with patties or steaks and keep warm.

Add mushrooms to pan and cook, stirring, over high heat until lightly browned. Add Madeira and bring to a boil, scraping browned particles free from pan. Stir in cream and boil until liquid is reduced to about ½ cup. Spoon sauce over meat and garnish with avocado slices and watercress, if used. Makes 4 servings.

LAMB PATTIES IN MUSHROOM SAUCE

Prepare **Beef with Madeira-Mushroom Sauce,** but substitute **lean ground lamb** for the ground beef; discard all but 2 tablespoons drippings. When adding mushrooms to pan, also add ¼ teaspoon **dry rosemary** and ⅓ cup sliced **green onions** (including tops) and cook as directed. Instead of Madeira, use the beef broth with lemon juice. Makes 4 servings.

Pork Chops with Caper Sauce

> 2 pounds shoulder pork chops, cut about ½ inch thick (cut large chops in half)
> ¾ cup *each* dry white wine and regular-strength beef broth
> 2 tablespoons capers, drained well
> ½ cup whipping cream
> 4 tablespoons butter or margarine

Put pork chops in a wide frying pan over medium-high heat. Cover and cook for 5 minutes to draw out some of the juices, then uncover and cook over medium heat until juices evaporate and chops are well browned on all sides. Set chops aside.

Add wine and broth to pan and scrape bottom to loosen browned particles. Stir in capers, then return chops to pan. Bring to a boil; cover, reduce heat, and simmer until meat near bone is no longer pink when slashed (15 to 20 minutes). Arrange chops on a rimmed platter; keep warm.

Boil juices in pan over high heat until reduced to ½ cup; stir in cream and boil until mixture is reduced to ½ cup. Reduce heat to low or remove pan from heat; with a wire whisk, stir in butter, blending constantly to incorporate butter as it melts. Spoon over chops. Makes 6 servings.

Veal Chops with Sage

> 4 to 6 loin veal chops, cut 1 inch thick
> Pepper
> 7 tablespoons butter or margarine
> 1 teaspoon rubbed sage leaves
> ¾ cup dry vermouth

Sprinkle chops with pepper. Melt 3 tablespoons of the butter in a wide frying pan over medium-high heat; add chops, reduce heat to medium, and cook on one side until browned (8 to 10 minutes). Turn chops, sprinkle sage into butter, and cook until chops are browned and meat near bone is no longer pink when slashed (about 10 minutes). Arrange chops on a platter; keep warm.

Add vermouth to pan and boil over high heat, scraping browned particles free from pan, until reduced to ½ cup. Reduce heat to low or remove pan from heat; with a wire whisk, stir in the remaining 4 tablespoons butter, blending constantly to incorporate butter as it melts. Spoon over chops. Makes 4 to 6 servings.

How to make Beef Pot Roast (Recipe on facing page)

1 Place flour-rubbed roast in foamy butter mixture. Use two spoons to turn roast so it browns on all sides. Browning seals in juices and flavors drippings for gravy.

2 When meat is done and transferred to a platter, skim fat from pan drippings and reserve drippings for gravy.

3 Rich meat drippings have been whisked into a smooth and flavorful brown gravy that pours like thick cream.

4 Hearty dinner fare for a wintry evening—succulent, tender beef pot roast surrounded by carrots, onions, and turnips. Serve with boiled red thin-skinned potatoes and gravy on the side.

Beef: Braising & stewing

Less tender cuts of beef, such as rump, shank, brisket, and short ribs (see "Retail cuts," page 48), require moist heat to transform them from sinewy to succulent. The technique, called "braising" or "stewing," is basically long slow cooking in a liquid in a tightly covered kettle or baking pan—either on top of the range or in the oven.

To enhance the flavor and color of the meat, you usually brown it first in a small amount of fat before adding the liquid (broth, stock, wine, fruit juice, or water). But the browning step can be eliminated, as in our Spiced Short Ribs and Oven-simmered Beef Brisket (page 56). Sometimes aromatic vegetables join the simmering meat for an energy-saving, hearty, one-dish meal.

Beef Pot Roast

(Pictured on facing page)

>   All-purpose flour
> 4   to 5-pound boneless beef rump roast
>   or chuck roast
> 2   tablespoons salad oil
> 5   tablespoons butter or margarine
> 1   bay leaf
> 1   teaspoon pepper
> 1½ teaspoons thyme leaves
> 1   can (14½ oz.) regular-strength beef broth and
>   1 can water
> 12 small white boiling onions, peeled
> 3   medium-size turnips, peeled and quartered
> 8   medium-size carrots, cut into 3-inch lengths
> 3   tablespoons all-purpose flour

Rub flour into roast; brush off excess. Heat oil and 2 tablespoons of the butter in a 5-quart kettle over medium-high heat. Add meat and brown well on all sides. Add bay leaf, pepper, thyme, beef broth, and water; bring to a boil. Cover and place in a 350° oven for 1½ hours.

Add onions, turnips, and carrots; continue to cook, covered, until meat and vegetables are tender when pierced (about 1 hour).

Transfer meat and vegetables to a rimmed platter and keep warm. Skim fat from drippings. Pour drippings into a 2-cup glass measure and add water, if necessary, to make 2 cups total.

Melt the remaining 3 tablespoons butter in kettle over medium heat. Add the 3 tablespoons flour and cook, stirring, until bubbly; remove from heat. With a wire whisk, gradually stir in re-

served drippings. Return pan to heat and cook, stirring, until thickened. Pour into a gravy boat; pass at the table. Makes about 6 to 8 servings.

POT ROAST FOR TWO

Following directions for **Beef Pot Roast,** prepare and brown 2 **beef shank slices** (about 1 lb. *each*), but use only 1 tablespoon **oil** and 1 tablespoon **butter** or margarine for browning. Add 1 **bay leaf,** ½ teaspoon **pepper,** ¾ teaspoon **thyme leaves,** and 1 can (14½ oz.) **regular-strength beef broth.** Omit water. Cook as for roast, adding 4 **onions,** 1 **turnip,** and 2 or 3 **carrots.** Use 1 cup **drippings** (add water to make 1 cup, if needed); thicken with 1½ tablespoons **butter** or margarine and 1½ tablespoons **all-purpose flour.** Makes 2 servings.

Hungarian Beef Stew

> 2   tablespoons salad oil
>   About 1½ pounds lean boneless beef chuck,
>   cut into 1-inch cubes
> 1   can (14½ oz.) regular-strength beef broth
> 1   clove garlic, minced or pressed
> 1   tablespoon paprika
> 3   to 4 medium-size leeks
> 1   large red or green bell pepper
> ½   pound small mushrooms
> ¼   cup whipping cream
> 1   tablespoon cornstarch mixed with 2
>   tablespoons dry sherry or apple juice
>   Salt and pepper
>   Hot cooked rice (optional)

Heat oil in a 5-quart kettle over medium-high heat; add meat, a few pieces at a time, and cook until browned on all sides. Stir in broth, garlic, and paprika. Bring to a boil; cover, reduce heat, and simmer until meat is tender when pierced (about 1 hour).

Meanwhile, trim and discard tops from leeks, leaving about 1½ inches of green leaves. Split leeks lengthwise, rinse well, then cut into 1-inch lengths. Seed pepper and cut into 1-inch squares. Add leeks, pepper, and mushrooms to meat; cover and simmer until vegetables are tender when pierced (15 to 20 minutes). Stir in cream and cornstarch mixture; cook, stirring, over high heat until thickened. Season to taste with salt and pepper. Serve with rice, if desired. Makes 4 servings.

...Beef: Braising & stewing

Spiced Short Ribs

About 4 pounds lean beef short ribs
Pepper and all-purpose flour
4   medium-size onions, thinly sliced
1   clove garlic, minced or pressed
1   bay leaf
3   whole cloves
½   teaspoon dry rosemary
1   can (14½ oz.) regular-strength beef broth
1½ tablespoons red wine vinegar
1   teaspoon Dijon mustard
Salt
Chopped parsley

Sprinkle short ribs lightly with pepper. Then dredge in flour on all sides; shake off excess. Place about half the onions in a 4 or 5-quart kettle; arrange ribs on top of onions, then cover with remaining onions. Add garlic, bay leaf, cloves, and rosemary. Pour broth over all.

Cover and bake in a 350° oven for 3 to 3½ hours or until meat is very tender when pierced. Remove meat to a rimmed platter; keep warm. Skim fat from cooking liquid, then stir in vinegar and mustard. Bring to a boil and continue to boil, stirring, until sauce is slightly reduced. Season to taste with salt. Pour sauce over ribs, and sprinkle with parsley. Makes about 4 servings.

Barbecue-style Swiss Steak

2   pounds bottom round beef steak, cut about ¾ inch thick
Pepper
2   tablespoons all-purpose flour
About 2 tablespoons salad oil
2   large onions, sliced
2   beef bouillon cubes, crushed
½   cup tomato-based chili sauce or catsup
½   cup water
2   tablespoons lemon juice
1   teaspoon *each* Worcestershire and Dijon mustard

Trim and discard fat from meat; cut meat into 4 to 6 serving-size pieces. Lay pieces on wax paper; sprinkle with pepper and 1 tablespoon of the flour. With a mallet or edge of a saucer, pound flour into meat. Turn pieces over; sprinkle with pepper and remaining 1 tablespoon flour, then pound again.

Heat 2 tablespoons of the oil in a 4-quart kettle over medium-high heat. Add meat, a few pieces at a time, and brown well on all sides; remove meat as it browns and set aside. Add more oil to pan, if needed; then add onions and cook over medium heat, stirring often, until soft. Return meat to pan.

In a small bowl, stir together bouillon cubes, chili sauce, water, lemon juice, Worcestershire, and mustard; pour over meat. Cover and bake in a 325° oven for 1½ hours or until meat is tender when pierced. Transfer meat to a rimmed platter. Skim fat from sauce, then spoon onions and sauce over meat. Makes 4 to 6 servings.

Oven-simmered Beef Brisket

You marinate the brisket overnight, then oven-simmer it until tender. Serve hot for dinner, or chill and thinly slice for a buffet.

1   fresh beef brisket (about 4 lbs.)
2½ cups apple juice
½   cup soy sauce
¼   cup salad oil
2   bay leaves
1   clove garlic, minced or pressed
1   large onion, chopped
½   teaspoon ground ginger
¼   teaspoon pepper
¼   cup *each* cornstarch and water
Bread, butter, and mustard (optional)

Trim and discard fat from meat; place brisket in a roasting pan. In a bowl, stir together apple juice, soy sauce, oil, bay leaves, garlic, onion, ginger, and pepper; pour over meat. Cover and refrigerate until next day.

Leaving meat and marinade in roasting pan, bake, covered, in a 350° oven for 3 hours or until tender when pierced.

To serve hot, transfer meat to a platter. Skim fat from pan juices and discard bay leaves. Mix cornstarch and water; stir into juices. Place over medium heat and cook, stirring, until thickened. Serve in a small bowl at the table.

To serve cold, omit cornstarch and water. Cool meat in cooking liquid; cover and refrigerate for up to 2 days. Remove meat from liquid and slice thinly. If desired, serve with bread, butter, and mustard. Makes 8 to 10 servings.

Ground beef

Popular, versatile, and economical, today's ground beef offers the consumer a range of choices, all determined by fat content. Federal regulations specify that meat labeled *regular ground beef*, *hamburger*, or simply *ground beef* can contain up to 30 percent fat. *Lean ground beef* has no more than 20 percent fat; *extra lean ground beef* has 15 percent or less.

Ground beef can also be labeled by cut, though. Beef labeled *ground chuck* has about the same fat content as lean ground beef; beef labeled *ground round* is generally equivalent in fat content to extra lean ground beef.

If you compare these "grades" in the market, you can see the difference at a glance. As fat content increases, the meat becomes paler and the price goes down. But remember that fat is waste—it cooks out of the meat, only to be discarded. It follows, then, that you can expect more shrinkage in hamburgers made from ground beef than in those made from lean ground beef.

Basic Hamburgers

> 1 **pound lean ground beef**
> 1 **egg**
> ¼ **cup fine dry bread crumbs**
> 1 **small onion, chopped**
> ⅛ **teaspoon pepper**
> 1 **teaspoon Worcestershire**
>   **Salt**
> 4 **hamburger buns, split and toasted**

Crumble ground beef into a bowl. Add egg, bread crumbs, onion, pepper, and Worcestershire; mix well. Divide mixture into 4 equal portions; lightly shape each portion into a patty ¾ to 1 inch thick.

Sprinkle salt in a wide frying pan over medium to medium-high heat. Add patties and cook until browned on both sides and done to your liking when slashed (about 4 minutes on each side for medium-rare). Serve patties in buns. Makes 4 servings.

BASIC MEATLOAF

Prepare mixture for **Basic Hamburgers,** but add 1 can (8 oz.) **tomato sauce** and ½ teaspoon **garlic salt;** mix well. Pat evenly into a 4 by 8-inch loaf pan. Bake, uncovered, in a 350° oven for 45 to 50 minutes or until meat in center is no longer pink when slashed. Makes about 4 servings.

CHEESE STUFFED HAMBURGERS

Prepare mixture for **Basic Hamburgers.** Divide mixture into 8 equal portions; shape each portion into a patty ¼ to ½ inch thick.

In a small bowl, stir together 1 cup (4 oz.) shredded **sharp Cheddar cheese,** 2 tablespoons **butter** or margarine (softened), 1½ teaspoons **catsup,** ½ teaspoon **prepared mustard,** and 1 tablespoon finely chopped **green onion** (including top). Spread equal amounts of filling over 4 of the patties to within ¼ inch of edges. Dampen edge of each patty with water. Top with remaining patties and pinch edges of meat together to completely enclose cheese filling (see *Illustrations 1* and *2*).

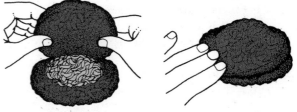

Illustration 1   *Illustration 2*

Cook as for Basic Hamburgers. Meanwhile, split and toast 4 **hamburger buns** or English muffins. Serve patties in buns. Makes 4 servings.

BURGUNDY-GLAZED BEEF PATTIES

Prepare and shape **Basic Hamburgers.** Place on a rack in a broiler pan (see "How to Broil Meat," page 49). Broil 3 inches below heat for 3 to 4 minutes on each side for medium-rare.

Meanwhile, heat 1 teaspoon **salad oil** in a small frying pan over medium heat. Add 2 tablespoons chopped **green onion** (including top) and 1 clove **garlic** (minced or pressed); cook, stirring, for 2 to 3 minutes. In a small bowl, combine 1 **beef bouillon cube** (crushed), ½ teaspoon **Dijon mustard,** and ¾ cup **dry red wine.** Pour into pan; boil rapidly, uncovered, until reduced by half. Add 3 tablespoons **butter** or margarine and heat, stirring, until melted.

Split and toast 2 **English muffins.** Top each muffin half with a beef patty; spoon sauce over each patty. Makes 4 servings.

...Ground beef

BASIC MEATBALLS

Prepare mixture for **Basic Hamburgers** (page 57). Shape into 1¼-inch balls and place in baking pans. Bake, uncovered, in a 450° oven for 15 minutes or until meatballs are well browned and slightly pink in center when slashed.

Serve plain or top with Curry, Mornay, or Mushroom Sauce (page 133). Makes 4 servings.

Joe's Special

- ¼ teaspoon salt
- 1 pound lean ground beef
- 1 large onion, finely chopped
- 1 clove garlic, minced or pressed
- ¼ teaspoon *each* pepper, ground nutmeg, and oregano leaves
- 1 package (10 oz.) frozen chopped spinach
- 4 eggs, lightly beaten
  Grated Parmesan cheese

Sprinkle salt in a wide frying pan over medium-high heat; crumble beef into pan and cook until browned. Reduce heat to medium; add onion and garlic. Cook, stirring often, until onion is soft. Stir in pepper, nutmeg, and oregano; add frozen spinach. Cover and cook, breaking up spinach as it thaws, until hot and well combined with meat. Pour in eggs and cook, stirring, until eggs are set. Pass cheese at the table. Makes 4 servings.

Beef Tacos

- ¼ teaspoon garlic salt
- 1 pound lean ground beef
- 1 medium-size onion, finely chopped
- 1½ teaspoons chili powder
- ½ teaspoon *each* oregano leaves and paprika
- ¼ teaspoon *each* ground cumin and pepper
- 3 tablespoons prepared taco sauce
- 2 teaspoons Worcestershire
  Salad oil
- 10 to 12 corn tortillas
  Toppings (suggestions follow)

Sprinkle garlic salt in a wide frying pan over medium-high heat; crumble beef into pan and cook until browned. Add onion and cook, stirring, until soft. Stir in chili powder, oregano, paprika, cumin, pepper, taco sauce, and Worcestershire; heat through.

Heat ¼ inch salad oil in a wide frying pan over high heat. Fry each tortilla for about 15 seconds, then fold in half (fried side in) and fry for 15 seconds on each side until slightly crisp. Drain on paper towels; keep warm until all are cooked.

Fill each taco shell with 2 to 3 tablespoons beef mixture. Pass toppings at the table to garnish individual tacos. Makes 5 or 6 servings.

Toppings. In separate bowls, offer shredded **iceberg lettuce, tomato wedges,** chopped **green onions** (including tops), shredded **sharp Cheddar cheese,** and **prepared taco sauce.**

Greek Meatballs

(Pictured on facing page)

- Yogurt sauce (recipe follows)
- 1 pound lean ground beef
- ½ pound lean ground lamb
- 1½ tablespoons finely chopped fresh mint or 2 teaspoons dry mint
- ½ cup soft bread crumbs
- 2 eggs
- 1 medium-size onion, finely chopped
- 1 teaspoon salt
- ⅛ teaspoon pepper
  All-purpose flour
- 2 tablespoons salad oil
- ½ teaspoon dry basil
- 1 can (about 1 lb.) tomatoes

Prepare yogurt sauce; cover and refrigerate until needed. In a bowl, combine beef, lamb, mint, bread crumbs, eggs, onion, salt, and pepper; mix well. Shape mixture into walnut-size meatballs; roll in flour, and shake off excess.

Heat oil in a wide frying pan over medium-high heat. Add meatballs, a few at a time, and brown on all sides; remove from pan when browned. Discard drippings. Return meatballs to pan; add basil along with tomatoes (break up with a spoon) and their liquid. Bring to a boil; cover, reduce heat, and simmer until meatballs are tender (about 15 minutes). Pass yogurt sauce at the table. Makes 4 or 5 servings.

Yogurt sauce. In a small bowl, combine 1 cup **unflavored yogurt,** 1 clove **garlic** (minced or pressed), and ¼ cup chopped **parsley;** mix well.

Making Greek Meatballs the easy way (Recipe on facing page)

1 Pinch off equal portions (about 1½ tablespoons each) of meat mixture and drop in mounds on counter. Roll mounds into balls and drop into flour in baking pan.

2 Shake pan back and forth until each ball is coated with flour. Shake off excess flour as you place meatballs in hot oil in frying pan.

3 Sauté meatballs, without crowding, until browned on all sides. Shake frying pan occasionally to prevent meat from sticking and to keep meatballs round.

4 Browned meatballs, simmered to tenderness in basil-flavored tomato sauce, are served with yogurt sauce and buttered noodles.

PORK

Today's methods of breeding and feeding produce fresh pork that's much younger and leaner than a generation ago—a boon to those who relish this rich-tasting, vitamin-packed meat but are concerned about calories or cholesterol.

To stay tender, lean pork must not overcook—if it does, it will become dry and stringy. For best results when roasting pork, insert a meat thermometer into the thickest part of the meat, without touching bone. An internal temperature of 140°

will kill any trichinae possibly present in pork; but stretching the point a bit for safety's sake, the current recommended internal temperature for cooked fresh pork is 170°. Fried or braised pork is done when there is no longer any trace of pink when meat is slashed.

Complement pork with the mellow sweetness of fruit (apples are a classic partner) or with such robustly flavored vegetables as sauerkraut, cauliflower, broccoli, or cabbage.

PORK PRIMAL CUTS

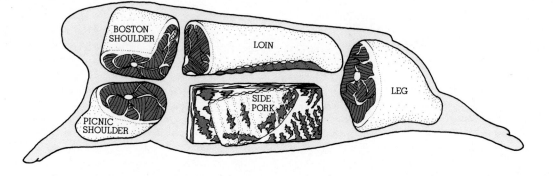

RETAIL CUTS—AND HOW TO COOK THEM

Blade Steak
(From the Boston
Shoulder)
Pan-fry • Braise

Center Loin Roast
(From the Loin)
Roast

Rib Chop
(From the Loin)
*Pan-broil •
Pan-fry • Braise*

Smoked Arm Picnic
(From the Picnic
Shoulder)
*Roast • Cook in
liquid*

Fresh Hock
(From the Picnic
Shoulder)
*Braise • Cook in
liquid*

Spareribs
(From the Side Pork)
*Bake • Braise •
Cook in liquid*

Slab Bacon
(From the Side Pork)
Broil • Pan-broil

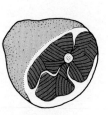

Rump Butt Portion
(From the Leg)
*Roast • Cook in
liquid*

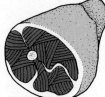

Shank Portion
(From the Leg)
*Roast • Cook in
liquid*

Center Ham Slice
(From the Leg)
Broil • Pan-broil

Pork: Dry roasting

It's hard to resist the aroma of pork roasting in the oven with its promise of a feast close at hand. Because fresh pork cuts vary little in tenderness, you can dry roast most of them (see page 45). Marinate beforehand; or simply roast unadorned or basted with a sauce.

Roast Leg of Pork

    About 7-pound bone-in shank end leg of pork
½ large unpeeled orange, cut into pieces
½ large unpeeled lime, cut into pieces
1 clove garlic, quartered
3 tablespoons salad oil
2 tablespoons vinegar
¼ teaspoon *each* rubbed sage and thyme leaves

With a sharp knife, cut off and discard leathery skin from pork. Score fat by making diagonal cuts at ½ to ¾-inch intervals through fat just to, but not into, flesh. Place meat in a deep, close-fitting container.

In a blender or food processor, combine orange, lime, garlic, oil, vinegar, sage, and thyme; whirl until well blended. Spread orange mixture over meat; cover and refrigerate until next day.

Place pork on a rack in a shallow roasting pan. Insert a meat thermometer into thickest part of meat, without touching bone. Roast, uncovered, in a 325° oven for about 4 hours or until thermometer registers 170°. Makes about 10 servings.

Spiced Pork Roast with Pears

4 to 4½-pound bone-in pork loin roast
1 clove garlic, halved
½ teaspoon salt
¼ teaspoon pepper
¾ teaspoon *each* ground ginger and ground cinnamon
¼ cup firmly packed brown sugar
2 tablespoons lemon juice
½ cup dry sherry or apple juice
3 or 4 ripe Anjou pears
1 tablespoon cornstarch mixed with 2 tablespoons water

Place roast, fat side up, on a rack in a shallow roasting pan. Rub meat with cut garlic, then drop garlic into pan. Insert a meat thermometer into thickest part of meat, without touching bone. Roast, uncovered, in a 325° oven for about 1½ hours or until thermometer registers 140°.

Meanwhile, in a small bowl, stir together salt, pepper, ginger, cinnamon, sugar, lemon juice, and sherry. Just before thermometer reaches 140°, peel, quarter, and core pears. Remove roast and rack from pan. Place meat directly in pan, add pears, and pour sherry mixture evenly over roast and pears. Turn pears to coat all sides.

Return pan to oven and continue roasting for about 45 more minutes or until thermometer registers 170°; baste roast and pears often with pan drippings. Lift out pork and pears; arrange on a platter and keep warm.

Discard garlic; skim and discard fat from drippings. Pour drippings into a pan, scraping browned particles free from roasting pan. Stir cornstarch mixture into drippings and cook over medium heat, stirring, until sauce boils and thickens. Pass sauce at the table. Makes 6 to 8 servings.

Pork Tenderloin with Onion-Apple Cream

¾ to 1-pound pork tenderloin
6 tablespoons whipping cream
2 tablespoons cream sherry
1 teaspoon Dijon mustard
½ teaspoon prepared horseradish
2 tablespoons butter or margarine
1 large onion, thinly sliced
1 small golden Delicious apple, thinly sliced
    Salt and pepper

Place pork on a rack in a shallow roasting pan. In a small bowl, stir together whipping cream, sherry, mustard, and horseradish; brush half of mixture over pork. Roast, uncovered, in a 325° oven, brushing often with cream mixture, for 45 to 60 minutes or until pork meat in center is no longer pink when slashed.

Melt butter in a wide frying pan over medium heat; add onion and apple and cook, stirring often, until onion is soft (about 20 minutes).

Transfer pork to a platter and keep warm. Pour pan drippings and any remaining cream mixture into onion mixture. Bring to a boil over high heat; season to taste with salt and pepper. Pass sauce at the table. Makes 2 servings.

How to make Oven-barbecued Spareribs (Recipe on facing page)

1 Choices of pork ribs, clockwise from top left; spareribs, Chinese-style ribs (cut in narrow strip and in pieces), back ribs, and country-style ribs.

2 Place ribs in pan and top with lemon and onion. Add water. Cover pan tightly with foil. During initial oven cooking, meat releases excess fat.

3 Cut ribs into serving-size pieces; discard pan juices. Brush ribs with barbecue sauce and return to oven. Bake until fork-tender, basting often.

4 Mahogany-hued spareribs make good eating any time of year. For a summertime feast, serve with corn on the cob and Coleslaw (page 23).

Pork: Spareribs

Though spareribs have a high ratio of bone to meat, it's never detracted from their popularity. Part of their appeal, in fact, is the satisfaction of chewing on the bones to reach every last morsel of meat. You can cook ribs in a variety of ways, depending on the kind of ribs you buy.

Neapolitan Country-style Spareribs

- 2 tablespoons salad oil
- 3 to 4 pounds country-style spareribs, cut into serving-size pieces
- 1 can (16 oz.) tomato purée
- 1 clove garlic, minced or pressed
- ¼ cup chopped parsley
- ¼ pound mushrooms, sliced
- 2 teaspoons dry basil
- 1 teaspoon *each* salt and oregano leaves
- ¼ teaspoon *each* pepper and sugar
- ¾ cup water
  Hot cooked spaghetti

Heat oil in a 5 to 6-quart kettle over medium-high heat. Add ribs and cook until browned on all sides. Add tomato purée, garlic, parsley, mushrooms, basil, salt, oregano, pepper, sugar, and water. Bring to a boil; cover, reduce heat, and simmer until meat is fork-tender (1 to 1½ hours).

Arrange meat on a platter; skim and discard fat from sauce. Pass sauce at the table to spoon over spaghetti. Makes 6 servings.

Oven-barbecued Spareribs

(Pictured on facing page)

- 1 side pork spareribs (3 to 4 lbs.), uncut
- 1 lemon, thinly sliced
- 1 small onion, thinly sliced
- 1 cup *each* water and catsup
- ¼ cup *each* firmly packed brown sugar and vinegar
- 1 teaspoon *each* dry mustard and chili powder
- ½ teaspoon *each* salt and paprika
- 2 tablespoons Worcestershire

Trim and discard excess fat from ribs. Arrange ribs in a single layer in a shallow roasting or broiler pan. Distribute lemon and onion evenly over meat. Pour in ½ cup of the water. Cover with foil and bake in a 350° oven for 1 hour.

Meanwhile, in a small pan over medium heat, combine catsup, brown sugar, vinegar, mustard, chili powder, salt, paprika, Worcestershire, and remaining ½ cup water. Cook, uncovered, until sauce thickens slightly (about 10 minutes).

Remove ribs from the oven; lift off and discard lemon and onion. Lift out ribs and cut into serving-size pieces. Discard pan drippings. Return meat to pan and brush with about a third of the barbecue sauce. Return ribs to oven and continue baking, uncovered, brushing often with sauce for 45 more minutes or until meat is fork-tender. Makes 4 servings.

Szechwan Spareribs

- About 1½ pounds pork spareribs, cut Chinese-style into 1½-inch lengths
- 3 tablespoons salad oil
- ⅓ cup water
- 1 tablespoon soy sauce
  Cooking sauce (recipe follows)
- 2 cloves garlic, minced or pressed
- 1 teaspoon minced fresh ginger
- ¼ to ½ teaspoon crushed red pepper
- 1 green pepper, seeded and cut into 1-inch squares

Trim and discard excess fat from ribs; cut between bones into individual pieces. Heat 2 tablespoons of the oil in a wide frying pan over high heat. Add ribs and cook, stirring often, until browned (about 4 minutes). Remove pan from heat and let cool briefly. Add water and soy and return pan to low heat; cover and simmer until ribs are fork-tender (about 30 minutes). Meanwhile, prepare cooking sauce and set aside.

Remove ribs from pan and discard drippings. Rinse pan and wipe dry. Heat the remaining 1 tablespoon oil in pan over medium-high heat. Add garlic, ginger, red pepper, and green pepper and stir-fry for 1 minute. Add meat and stir-fry for 2 minutes. Stir cooking sauce, pour into pan, and cook, stirring, until sauce thickens slightly. Makes 2 or 3 servings.

Cooking sauce. In a small bowl, combine 1 tablespoon *each* **Worcestershire** and **dry sherry**, 2 tablespoons **catsup**, ¼ cup **water**, 2 teaspoons **sugar**, ¼ teaspoon **salt**, and 1½ teaspoons **cornstarch**.

Pork: Braising

You can braise various cuts of pork the same way you braise beef—just cook in liquid in a tightly covered container either on top of the range or in the oven. But because many pork cuts—rib or loin chops and cubes of pork butt, for example—are more tender than the beef cuts you braise, the cooking time for pork is often considerably shorter.

Fruit-stuffed Pork Chops

> 1 package (12 oz.) mixed dried fruits, chopped
> ⅔ cup water
> ¼ cup *each* chopped onion and celery
> ½ teaspoon *each* dry rosemary and salt
> Dash of pepper
> 6 large rib or loin pork chops, cut 1 inch thick
> 2 tablespoons butter or margarine
> About 1 cup apple juice
> 2 tablespoons cornstarch

In a 1-quart pan over medium heat, combine fruits, water, onion, celery, and rosemary; cook, stirring, until liquid is absorbed. Stir in salt and pepper; set aside.

With a sharp knife, slash through edge fat of each chop almost to bone to form a pocket (see *Illustration 1*). Stuff each pocket with about 3 tablespoons of the fruit mixture. Set aside any remaining filling. Bring meat together, closing pocket, and secure with a metal or bamboo skewer (see *Illustration 2*).

Illustration 1   Illustration 2

Melt butter in a wide frying pan over medium heat. Add chops, a few at a time, and cook until well browned on both sides. Pour in ¾ cup of the apple juice and bring to a boil. Cover, reduce heat, and simmer until meat near bone is no longer pink when slashed (35 to 40 minutes). Turn chops over after 20 minutes.

Lift out chops; arrange on a platter and keep warm. Pour drippings into a 2-cup glass measure; skim and discard fat. Stir cornstarch into ¼ cup of the apple juice and stir into drippings; add more apple juice, if needed, to make 2 cups total. Pour liquid into pan and add any remaining filling; cook, stirring, over medium heat until sauce boils and thickens slightly. Pour some of the sauce over chops; pass remaining sauce at the table. Makes 6 servings.

Piquant Oven Pork Stew

> 3 pounds lean boneless pork (butt)
> 2 tablespoons salad oil
> 1 medium-size onion, thinly sliced
> 3 tablespoons soy sauce
> ¼ cup cider vinegar
> 1 clove garlic, minced or pressed
> 2 bay leaves
> 1 cup water
> 2 teaspoons cornstarch mixed with 1 tablespoon water
> Sliced green onions (including tops)
> Hot cooked rice

Trim and discard excess fat from pork; cut meat into 1-inch cubes. Pour oil into a 9 by 13-inch baking pan; place pan in oven while it preheats to 500°. When oil is hot, add meat and onion to pan and bake, uncovered, stirring occasionally, for 15 minutes or until meat is browned. Meanwhile, in a small bowl, stir together soy, vinegar, garlic, bay leaves, and water.

Reduce heat to 350°. Pour soy mixture over meat, cover, and continue baking for 30 more minutes or until meat is tender when pierced.

With a slotted spoon, transfer meat to a shallow serving dish; keep warm. Pour drippings into a 1-quart pan; skim and discard fat. Discard bay leaves. Boil over high heat until reduced to 1 cup. Add cornstarch mixture and cook, stirring, until sauce boils and thickens slightly. Pour over meat and sprinkle with green onions. Serve over rice. Makes 6 servings.

Pork: Pan-frying

Bone-in or boneless, pan-fried pork is a boon to the busy cook, thanks to its simple and speedy preparation. Choose chops or steaks cut from the shoulder, leg, or loin. Or surprise your family with lean ground pork. "Burgers" take on a lively new dimension when you substitute ground pork for the usual ground beef.

Browned Pork Chops

>   4   to 6 shoulder pork chops or steaks,
>   cut ½ inch thick
>   Salt and pepper
>   2   tablespoons salad oil
>   ⅔   cup dry white wine
>   About ¼ cup thinly sliced dill pickle
>   (optional)
>   Dijon mustard

Sprinkle pork chops lightly with salt and pepper. Heat oil in a wide frying pan over medium-high heat; cook chops, 2 or 3 at a time, turning as needed, until they're browned on both sides and meat near bone is no longer pink when slashed (5 to 7 minutes on each side). Lift out chops; arrange on a platter and keep warm.

Skim and discard fat; add wine and cook, scraping browned particles free from pan, until reduced to about ⅓ cup. Pour over chops and sprinkle with pickle, if desired. Serve with mustard. Makes 4 to 6 servings.

Pork Chops with Olives

>   6   loin pork chops, cut ¾ inch thick
>   ¾   cup each dry white wine and whipping
>   cream
>   1   teaspoon grated lime peel
>   2   tablespoons sliced pimento-stuffed olives
>   Salt and pepper
>   Chopped parsley

In a wide frying pan over medium-high heat, set chops on their fat edge close together so they stay upright; cook until fat is browned. Swirl drippings across pan, then lay chops flat. Cover and cook, turn after 5 minutes, until meat near bone is no longer pink when slashed (8 to 12 minutes).

Lift out chops; arrange on a rimmed platter and keep warm. Add wine, cream, lime peel,

and olives to pan. Boil over high heat until liquid is reduced to about half. Add any juices that have drained from pork, and season to taste with salt and pepper. Pour sauce over chops and sprinkle with parsley. Makes 6 servings.

PORK CHOPS WITH GREEN PEPPERCORNS

Follow directions for **Pork Chops with Olives,** but substitute 3 tablespoons **green peppercorns,** rinsed and drained well, for olives.

Pineapple Pork Patties

>   1½ pounds lean ground pork
>   1   egg
>   2   cloves garlic, minced or pressed
>   1   medium-size onion, finely chopped
>   1   medium-size green pepper, seeded
>   and finely chopped
>   ½   teaspoon each salt, pepper, and
>   oregano leaves
>   ¾   teaspoon ground cumin
>   4   English muffins, split and toasted
>   8   slices canned pineapple, drained well

In a bowl, combine pork, egg, garlic, onion, green pepper, salt, pepper, oregano, and cumin. Divide into 8 equal portions; shape each into a 4-inch patty.

Heat a wide frying pan over medium heat; add patties and cook, turning once, until meat is well browned on both sides and no longer pink when slashed (6 to 7 minutes on each side). Place patties on muffin halves and keep warm. Add pineapple to pan and cook, turning, until lightly browned on both sides. Place on top of patties. Makes 4 to 8 servings.

SWEET & SOUR PORK PATTIES

Prepare **Pineapple Pork Patties,** but substitute **ground ginger** for oregano leaves. Omit ground cumin. Substitute **hot cooked rice** for muffins. Prepare **sweet-sour sauce** (page 66). Arrange pineapple-topped patties on rice. Stir sweet-sour sauce, add to pan, and cook, stirring, over high heat until sauce boils and thickens slightly. Spoon over patties. Makes 4 to 8 servings.

Pork: Stir-frying

Stir-frying has only one prerequisite for success: everything must be ready before you start to cook. Because the food cooks so quickly, there's literally not a minute to stop and chop the next ingredient or prepare a sauce.

Sweet & Sour Pork

(Pictured on facing page)

> ½ to 1-pound lean boneless pork butt, cut into 1-inch cubes
> 1 cup water
> 1 slice fresh ginger
> 1 tablespoon soy sauce
> Sweet-sour sauce (recipe follows)
> 1 egg
> ½ cup cornstarch
> About 4 tablespoons salad oil
> 1 medium-size onion, cut into wedges, with layers separated
> 1 green pepper, seeded and cut into 1-inch squares
> 1 clove garlic, minced or pressed
> 2 small tomatoes, cut into wedges
> ½ cup canned pineapple chunks, drained

Place pork, water, ginger, and soy in a pan; bring to a boil over high heat. Cover, reduce heat, and simmer for 5 minutes. Drain and let cool. Prepare sweet-sour sauce and set aside.

Beat egg in a small bowl. Place cornstarch in a bag. Dip pork cubes in egg, then shake in cornstarch until lightly coated; shake off excess. Heat about 2 tablespoons of the oil in a wok or wide frying pan over medium-high heat. When oil is hot, add meat (cook half at a time if using more than ½ lb.) and stir-fry until browned (2 to 3 minutes). Remove meat and set aside; discard pan drippings.

Increase heat to high and add remaining 2 tablespoons oil. When oil is hot, add onion, green pepper, and garlic and stir-fry for 1 minute, adding a few drops of water if pan appears dry. Stir sweet-sour sauce, add to pan, and cook, stirring, until sauce boils and thickens slightly.

Stir in tomatoes, pineapple, and meat and cook just until heated through (about 30 seconds). Makes 2 to 4 servings.

Sweet-sour sauce. In a bowl, combine ¾ cup **water;** 1 tablespoon *each* **cornstarch, catsup,** and **soy sauce;** ¼ cup *each* **sugar** and **wine vinegar,** and a few drops of **liquid hot pepper seasoning.**

SWEET & SOUR SPARERIBS

Follow directions for **Sweet & Sour Pork,** substituting about 1½ pounds **pork spareribs,** cut into pieces Chinese-style (see photo on page 62) for pork butt. Increase water to 2 cups, ginger to 2 slices, and soy sauce to 2 tablespoons. Simmer ribs in seasoned water until fork-tender (about 30 minutes); then proceed with recipe.

SWEET & SOUR CHICKEN

Follow directions for **Sweet & Sour Pork,** substituting 1 whole **chicken breast** (1 lb.—boned, skinned, and cut into 1-inch cubes) for pork butt. Do not simmer chicken in seasoned water. Dredge in egg and cornstarch and stir-fry over high heat until golden brown (about 3 minutes); then proceed with recipe.

Curried Sausage Sauté

> About 1½ pounds fully cooked sausages (kielbasa, knackwurst, bratwurst, or garlic frankfurters)
> 4 tablespoons butter or margarine
> 4 teaspoons curry powder
> 1 medium-size mild white onion, cut into 1-inch squares
> 1 large green pepper, seeded and cut into 1-inch squares
> 2 medium-size tomatoes, cut into wedges
> 1 can (1 lb.) applesauce (optional)

Cut sausages into ½-inch-thick slanting slices; set aside. Melt butter in a wide frying pan over medium heat; stir in curry powder and mix well. Add onion and green pepper and cook, stirring, until tender-crisp (about 2 minutes). Stir in sausages and cook until meat is lightly browned (about 4 minutes). Add tomatoes and cook, stirring gently, until they give up some juice (1 to 2 minutes). Turn into a dish. Pass applesauce at the table to accompany sausage, if desired. Makes 4 to 6 servings.

How to stir-fry Sweet & Sour Pork (Recipe on facing page)

1 Place simmered and coated pork cubes in hot pan. Stir-fry until coating is crunchy and browned. Remove from pan.

2 After stir-frying firm vegetables until crisp-tender, pour sweet-sour sauce into pan around pan edge so sauce heats and cooks quickly.

3 Stir continuously—cornstarch-thickened sauces cook quickly. Sauce is done when it boils, thickens slightly, and turns from opaque to clear.

4 Add tomatoes, pineapple, and pork, stirring just until heated through and coated with sweet-sour sauce. Serve piping hot.

Smoked pork

Curing and smoking certain cuts of fresh pork produce versatile meats with wide appeal—ham from leg of pork, Canadian bacon from pork tenderloin, smoked loin from center-cut pork loin, picnic ham from picnic shoulder, bacon from side pork, and smoked sausage from seasoned ground pork.

Until recently, these smoked cuts, like their fresh counterparts, needed to be cooked; but today, most of them carry the label "fully cooked" or "ready to eat."

Country hams such as Smithfield, Tennessee, Kentucky, and Virginia—more heavily cured and smoked than other hams—require soaking and precooking (follow the package directions).

Sausage & Sauerkraut

- 1 to 1½ pounds fully cooked sausages (kielbasa, bratwurst, or frankfurters)
- 2 strips bacon, diced
- 1 medium-size onion, finely chopped
- 1 can (1 lb. 11 oz.) sauerkraut, drained well
- 1 medium-size golden Delicious apple, cored and diced
- 1 tablespoon *each* brown sugar and dry sherry
- ½ teaspoon caraway seeds
- ½ cup regular-strength beef broth
  Chopped parsley

At about 1-inch intervals, cut ¼-inch deep slashes in each sausage; set aside. In a wide frying pan over medium heat, cook bacon and onion, stirring, until onion is soft. Stir in sauerkraut, apple, sugar, sherry, caraway seeds, and broth. Cook, stirring, for about 2 minutes. Arrange sausages on top; cover, reduce heat, and simmer until sausages are heated through and apple is fork-tender (20 to 25 minutes). Garnish with parsley. Makes 4 to 6 servings.

Baked Ham with Madeira Sauce

- 6 to 7-pound fully cooked half ham (bone-in shank or butt)
- 2 tablespoons Dijon mustard
- ½ cup *each* firmly packed brown sugar and Madeira

With a sharp knife cut off and discard leathery skin from ham. Place ham, fat side up, on a rack in a shallow pan; insert meat thermometer into thickest part of meat without touching bone. Roast, uncovered, in a 325° oven for 1 hour. Remove from oven; score fat by making diagonal cuts at ½ to ¾-inch intervals through fat but not into meat.

In a small bowl, stir together mustard, sugar, and Madeira until blended; brush half the sauce evenly over ham. Return to oven and continue roasting, uncovered, for 45 to 60 more minutes or until thermometer registers 140° and glaze is browned; baste often with remaining sauce. Makes about 10 servings.

JAM-GLAZED BAKED HAM

Prepare **Baked Ham with Madeira Sauce**, substituting 1 **egg yolk** and ¾ cup **apricot-pineapple jam** for mustard, brown sugar, and Madeira. Spread all the jam mixture over ham after scoring fat; press about ¼ cup **pecan halves** on ham and continue baking as directed.

Smoked Pork Chops with Sweet Potatoes

- 4 medium-size sweet potatoes (about 2 lbs. *total*)
- 4 tablespoons butter or margarine, melted
- ¾ cup firmly packed brown sugar
- ¼ teaspoon ground cinnamon
- 4 smoked pork chops, cut ¾ inch thick
- 1 can (about 8 oz.) sliced pineapple, packed in its own juice
  Parsley sprigs

Prepare and boil sweet potatoes (see page 130). Drain, peel, and cut in half lengthwise. Pour 2 tablespoons of the butter into a 9-inch square baking dish and stir in ¼ cup of the sugar. Arrange potatoes in dish in an even layer and sprinkle with cinnamon and remaining ½ cup sugar.

Arrange chops over potatoes. Drain pineapple, reserving liquid. Cut pineapple slices in half and place over chops. Pour reserved liquid and remaining 2 tablespoons butter over all.

Cover and bake in a 350° oven for 10 minutes. Uncover, baste with pan juices, and continue baking for 20 to 30 more minutes or until fruit and chops are lightly browned; baste several times. Garnish with parsley. Makes 4 servings.

LAMB

The most tender part of a lamb is the loin section down the center of its back. The average lamb lives only 5 to 10 months, though, so most of the other sections are relatively tender, too. That's why nearly all cuts of lamb can be cooked with dry heat—roasted, broiled, pan-broiled, or pan-fried. The few tougher cuts of lamb, such as those near the shoulder or shank, are easily coaxed to juicy tenderness when braised.

Lamb's delicate and distinctive flavor mingles well with a myriad of diverse seasonings, from garlic, mustard, and marjoram to sweet spices, nuts, and fruits.

Most epicures agree that lamb tastes its best when cooked medium-rare to medium—still pink and juicy inside. Even so, many people prefer well-done lamb, so in the roasting chart on page 45 we include two or three thermometer readings.

LAMB PRIMAL CUTS

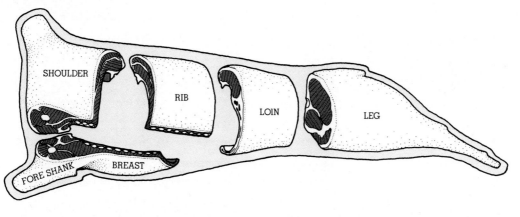

RETAIL CUTS—AND HOW TO COOK THEM

Square Shoulder
(From the Shoulder)
Roast

Blade Chop
(From the Shoulder)
Broil • Pan-broil •
Pan-fry

Arm Chop
(From the Shoulder)
Broil • Pan-broil •
Pan-fry

Crown Roast
(From the Rib)
Roast

8-Rib Rack
(From the Rib)
Roast

Loin Chops
(From the Loin)
Broil • Pan-broil •
Pan-fry

Leg (Sirloin Half)
(From the Leg)
Roast

Leg (Shank Half)
(From the Leg)
Roast

Lamb Shank
(From the Fore
Shank)
Braise

Breast
(From the Breast)
Roast • Braise

Preparing Mustard-coated Roast Leg of Lamb (Recipe on facing page)

1 Cut a small gash in lamb surface and insert a garlic sliver. Make more gashes, about 1½ inches apart, inserting a garlic sliver in each gash as you go.

2 Brush about half the thick mustard mixture over surface of lamb on one side; turn and completely coat other side with remaining mixture.

3 Insert meat thermometer into thickest portion of meat without touching bone.

4 Meat will be golden brown and done to perfection when internal temperature reaches 140°. Red arrow indicates desired temperature for rare. Upon standing, temperature will climb about 10° to 150°.

5 To carve lamb, grasp narrow end of leg (protect hand) and slice meat parallel to leg bone. Those who like well done meat get outside slices; inner meat is pinkest for those who like rare.

Lamb: Dry roasting

When a lamb roast has star billing on your dinner menu, you can choose the supporting cast from a variety of side dishes. One established favorite is a pilaf of rice or cracked wheat (page 121). Also complementary are lightly cooked green vegetables, such as asparagus, broccoli, or green beans. And our curry sauce (page 73) dresses any leftover meat to make a tasty encore.

Rolled Lamb Shoulder Roast

    2   cloves garlic, minced or pressed
    ½   teaspoon *each* salt and oregano leaves
    ¼   teaspoon pepper
    4   to 4½-pound boneless lamb shoulder, rolled
        and tied
    ½   cup water
    1½ teaspoons *each* cornstarch and water

In a small bowl, combine garlic, salt, oregano, and pepper; rub mixture all over meat. Place meat on a rack in a shallow roasting pan. Insert a meat thermometer into thickest portion of meat.

Roast, uncovered, in a 325° oven for 2 to 2½ hours or until meat thermometer registers 145° for medium-rare or degree of doneness preferred (see chart, page 45). Baste occasionally with pan drippings. Place meat on carving board; keep warm.

Skim fat from pan drippings; add ½ cup water to pan and scrape browned particles free from pan. Combine cornstarch and water; stir into drippings. Place over medium-high heat and cook, stirring, until bubbly. Pour into a serving container.

Cut roast across the grain into thick slices. Pass sauce at the table. Makes 8 servings.

Mustard-coated Roast Leg of Lamb

(Pictured on facing page)

    3   cloves garlic
    ½   cup Dijon mustard
    1   tablespoon soy sauce
    ½   teaspoon ground ginger
    1   teaspoon dry rosemary
    ¼   cup salad oil
    5   to 6-pound leg of lamb

Mince or press 1 clove of the garlic. In a small bowl, stir together minced garlic, mustard, soy, ginger, rosemary, and oil; set aside.

Place meat on a rack in a shallow roasting pan. Cut remaining 2 cloves garlic into slivers. Cut small gashes in surface of lamb and insert garlic slivers (see photo 1 on facing page). With a brush, completely coat roast with mustard mixture. Insert a meat thermometer into thickest portion of meat without touching bone; let stand at room temperature for 1 hour.

Roast, uncovered, in a 325° oven until meat thermometer registers degree of doneness preferred (see chart, page 45). Remove lamb to a platter; let stand for 10 to 15 minutes. Skim fat from pan drippings; reheat drippings and pour into a small container.

To carve, grasp narrow end of leg (protect hand with a potholder or cloth) and slice meat, cutting parallel to leg bone. Serve with juices. Makes 6 to 8 servings.

Luau Racks of Lamb

    2   racks of lamb, 2 to 2½ pounds *each*
    1   pineapple (2½ to 3 lbs.) or 1 can (1 lb. 4 oz.)
        sliced pineapple, packed in its own juice
    ¼   cup firmly packed brown sugar
    1   teaspoon *each* dry mustard, ground ginger,
        and soy sauce

Place lamb, fat side up, in a shallow roasting pan. Insert a meat thermometer into thickest portion of meat without touching bone. Roast, uncovered, in a 375° oven for about 45 minutes or until meat thermometer registers 125°.

Meanwhile, peel and core pineapple; cut crosswise into ½-inch-thick slices. In a blender or food processor, purée 2 of the slices, then strain mixture to obtain ⅓ cup juice. (Or drain canned pineapple, reserving ⅓ cup liquid.) In a 1-quart pan, stir together juice (or reserved liquid), sugar, mustard, ginger, and soy. Bring glaze to a boil; set aside.

When lamb has reached an internal temperature of 125°, arrange fruit around meat; brush meat and fruit with glaze. Continue to roast, basting often with remaining glaze, until meat thermometer registers 145° for medium-rare or degree of doneness preferred (see chart, page 45).

To serve, cut down between rib bones into chops. Offer fruit and pan juices on the side. Makes 6 servings.

Lamb: Broiling & pan-broiling

Which lamb cuts should you buy to broil or pan-broil? Let dinner plans and your budget provide the answer. For guests, choose lamb steaks cut from the leg; one steak makes a generous serving. Or buy small loin or rib chops, allowing two chops per person. These cuts are the most tender, but they carry a higher price tag than, say, shoulder chops.

For everyday fare, round bone or blade shoulder chops provide a delicious and more economical meal. One large chop apiece is ample. To make kebabs, use boneless lamb from the leg or shoulder.

Broiled Lamb Nuggets

1 can (8 oz.) pineapple chunks, packed in their own juice
1 beef bouillon cube
⅓ cup hottest tap water
2 tablespoons lemon juice
2 teaspoons curry powder
1 teaspoon *each* ground ginger, garlic powder, and marjoram leaves
1½ pounds lean boneless lamb, cut into 1½-inch cubes
2 teaspoons cornstarch

Drain pineapple, reserving ⅓ cup of the liquid; set pineapple aside. Dissolve bouillon cube in hot water, then stir in reserved pineapple liquid, lemon juice, curry powder, ginger, garlic powder, and marjoram; set aside.

Divide meat and pineapple into 4 equal portions; alternating fruit and meat, thread onto 4 metal skewers. Place in a shallow baking dish; pour bouillon mixture over kebabs. Cover and refrigerate for 4 hours or until next day, turning skewers several times.

Lift skewers from marinade and drain briefly, reserving marinade. Place skewers on a rack in a broiler pan (see "How to Broil Meat," page 49). Broil 2½ to 3 inches below heat, turning as needed, until meat is lightly browned on all sides but still pink in center when slashed (10 to 15 minutes *total*).

Transfer skewers to individual plates. Remove broiler rack and set aside. Stir cornstarch into reserved marinade; pour into broiler pan and cook, stirring, over medium-high heat until thickened. Pour into a small container to serve with meat. Makes 4 servings.

Lamb Pocket Burgers

1 pound lean ground lamb
1 small onion, finely chopped
¼ cup fine dry bread crumbs
⅓ cup finely chopped moist-pack dried apricots
1 egg
2 teaspoons curry powder
3 pocket breads, halved
Condiments (suggestions follow)

In a bowl, combine lamb, onion, crumbs, apricots, egg, and curry powder. Divide mixture into 6 equal portions; shape each portion into a 3 to 4-inch oval patty.

Heat a wide frying pan over medium-high heat; add patties and cook until well browned on both sides and still slightly pink in center when slashed (8 to 10 minutes total).

To serve, place each patty in a pocket bread half; pass condiments to top individual servings. Makes 6 servings.

Condiments. Offer each in a separate bowl: Major Grey's **chutney** (chopped), **unflavored yogurt,** and thinly sliced **cucumbers.**

Lamb Chops with Pine Nut Stuffing

4 rib or loin lamb chops, cut 1 inch thick
2 teaspoons butter or margarine
¼ cup pine nuts
1 clove garlic, minced or pressed
½ teaspoon grated lemon peel
1½ tablespoons *each* finely minced green onion and parsley
1½ tablespoons lemon juice
⅛ teaspoon *each* oregano leaves, salt, and pepper

With a sharp knife, slash through edge fat of each chop almost to bone to form a pocket (see *Illustration 1*, page 64).

Melt 1 teaspoon of the butter in a small frying pan over medium heat; add nuts and garlic and cook, stirring, until nuts are golden. Remove from heat and stir in lemon peel, onion, and parsley. Stuff each pocket with about 1 tablespoon of the nut mixture. Close each pocket and secure with a small metal or bamboo skewer (see *Illustration 2*, page 64).

Melt the remaining 1 teaspoon butter in pan over medium heat; stir in lemon juice, oregano, salt, and pepper. Lightly brush chops with some of the lemon juice mixture. Place chops on a rack in a broiler pan (see "How to Broil Meat," page 49). Broil about 3 inches below heat, basting with remaining lemon juice mixture, for 4 to 5 minutes on each side or until browned and meat near bone is still pink when slashed. Makes 2 servings.

CURRY SAUCES TRANSFORM LEFTOVERS

Yesterday's cooked meat, chicken, or turkey sheds its leftover status and becomes instant party food when treated to our curry sauce.

Curry sauce. Melt 3 tablespoons **butter** or margarine in a wide frying pan over medium heat; add 1 large **onion,** chopped, and 2 cloves **garlic,** minced or pressed, and cook until onion is soft. Stir in 1 tablespoon **curry powder** and 3 tablespoons **all-purpose flour** and cook until bubbly. Remove pan from heat. Gradually stir in 1 can (14½ oz.) regular-strength **beef or chicken broth.** Return to heat and cook, stirring, until thickened. Add 1 **red-skinned apple,** cored and diced, and 2 to 3 cups **cooked meat,** chicken, or turkey. Cover, reduce heat, and simmer for 15 to 20 minutes or until apple is fork-tender.

Serve over **hot cooked rice** and offer 3 or 4 condiments such as **unflavored yogurt,** Major Grey's **chutney, peanuts,** chopped **hard-cooked egg,** toasted shredded **coconut,** and crisply fried and crumbled **bacon.** Makes 4 servings.

Curry tomato sauce. Prepare **Curry sauce,** but omit flour and broth. Instead, add 1 can (14½ oz.) **pear-shaped tomatoes** (break up with spoon) and their liquid. Uncover for the last 5 minutes of cooking, or until sauce is slightly thickened.

Broiled Lamb Chops with Mustard-Honey Glaze

¼ cup *each* Dijon mustard and honey
1 teaspoon soy sauce
1 clove garlic, minced or pressed
¼ teaspoon ground ginger
4 large shoulder (round bone or blade) lamb chops, cut about ¾ inch thick

In a small bowl, stir together mustard, honey, soy, garlic, and ginger. Trim excess fat from chops; slash through remaining edge fat to, but not into, meat at 1-inch intervals.

Place chops on a rack in a broiler pan (see "How to Broil Meat," page 49). Generously spread chops with about half the mustard mixture. Broil about 3 inches below heat for 5 minutes; turn chops and spread with remaining mustard mixture. Broil for about 5 more minutes or until chops are browned and meat near bone is still pink when slashed. Makes 4 servings.

Pan-broiled Lamb Steaks

6 tablespoons butter or margarine, softened
½ teaspoon grated lemon peel
1 tablespoon lemon juice
¼ cup finely chopped parsley
½ teaspoon dry tarragon (optional)
6 lamb steaks, cut ¾ to 1 inch thick

At least 2 hours before serving, place butter, lemon peel, lemon juice, parsley, and tarragon (if used) in a small bowl; stir together until well blended. Cover and refrigerate.

Trim excess fat from steaks. Slash through remaining edge fat to, but not into, meat at 1-inch intervals. Place a wide frying pan over medium-high heat; swirl a piece of the trimmed fat over pan bottom to grease lightly, then discard fat. Add steaks and cook, turning once, until well browned but still pink in thickest portion when slashed (3 to 4 minutes on each side).

To serve, top each steak with about 1 tablespoon of the flavored butter. Makes 6 servings.

Lamb: Braised

Shoulder, shank, or neck of lamb—like the same cuts of beef—benefit from braising since their considerable proportion of connective tissue needs moist-heat cooking. When braised, the meat from these cuts becomes tender and releases its juices to make a delicious gravy.

Springtime Lamb Stew

(Pictured on facing page)

To make this good-looking party stew, we've used an innovative French technique that calls for some new rules. As a first step, instead of browning the meat in oil, you "sweat" out the meat's natural juices. Next you boil the juices away, then you neatly brown the meat in the rendered drippings. This technique turns out tender braised meat accompanied by a silken sauce.

    3   pounds boneless lamb stew meat (neck or
        shoulder), cut into 1 to 2-inch chunks
    2   tablespoons soy sauce
    ½   cup Madeira or port
    4   teaspoons mustard seeds
    1   teaspoon thyme leaves
    ¼   teaspoon black peppercorns
    2   bay leaves
    1½ cups regular-strength chicken broth
    1   cup dry red or white wine
    1½ to 2 pounds small red or white thin-skinned
        potatoes, halved
    8   to 12 slender carrots, peeled
    3   to 6 small turnips, peeled and halved
    6   to 12 small white boiling onions, peeled
    ¾   pound green beans, cut in half, ends and
        strings removed
    ½   pint (1 cup) whipping cream
    1   tablespoon Dijon mustard
        Watercress

Place meat in a 5 or 6-quart Dutch oven. Stir in soy sauce. Cover and bring to a boil over medium heat; reduce heat and let meat simmer in its accumulated juices for 30 minutes. Remove lid and turn heat to high to boil juices down completely (about 10 minutes). When meat starts to sizzle in its own fat, stir frequently until meat is richly browned. Add Madeira and stir well; then add mustard seeds, thyme, peppercorns, bay leaves, broth, and wine.

Lay potatoes, carrots, turnips, and onions on meat. Bring to a boil; cover, reduce heat, and let simmer for about 1 hour or until meat and vegetables are fork-tender.

After about 50 minutes, bring 1 inch water to a boil in a 2 to 3-quart pan. Drop in beans and cook, uncovered, until fork-tender (5 to 8 minutes). Drain.

With a slotted spoon, lift vegetables and meat from broth and mound individually in a wide, shallow, ovenproof serving container. Arrange beans alongside other vegetables. Cover loosely with foil and keep hot in a 150° oven for as long as 20 minutes.

Meanwhile, remove bay leaves from pan juices; add cream and Dijon mustard. Boil on highest heat until sauce is golden, thickened slightly, and reduced to 1¾ cups (8 to 10 minutes). Pour sauce into a serving container. Garnish meat and vegetables with watercress. Let guests serve themselves, spooning sauce onto individual portions. Makes 6 to 8 servings.

Herbed Lamb Shanks

    2   tablespoons salad oil
    4   lamb shanks (about 1 lb. *each*), cracked
    2   cloves garlic, minced or pressed
    2   large onions, sliced
    1   large green pepper, seeded and sliced
    ¾   teaspoon *each* thyme leaves and savory
        leaves
    1   teaspoon salt
    ¼   teaspoon pepper
    1   can (12 oz.) tomato juice
    ½   cup dry red wine or water
    3   tablespoons *each* all-purpose flour and water

Heat oil in a 5 to 6-quart kettle over medium-high heat; add shanks, two at a time, and cook until browned on all sides. Remove from pan. Add garlic, onions, and green pepper to pan and cook until vegetables are lightly browned. Add shanks, thyme, savory, salt, pepper, tomato juice, and wine. Bring to a boil; cover, reduce heat, and simmer until meat is very tender when pierced (2 to 2½ hours). If made ahead, you may cool, cover, and refrigerate until next day.

Skim and discard fat from pan juices. Stir together flour and water and stir into juices. Cook over medium-high heat, stirring, until liquid boils and thickens. Makes 4 servings.

Composing a lamb stew (Recipe on facing page)

1 "Sweating" technique is first step in this braised stew. As chunks of lamb simmer in covered pan, they release natural juices.

2 Next, uncover pan and boil away juices. In rendered drippings that remain (you can hear fat sizzle), quickly and neatly brown the meat.

3 Lay carrots, onions, potatoes, and turnips over meat. Simmer to luscious tenderness in wine and chicken broth. (Boil green beans separately to keep their bright color.)

4 While stew keeps warm in oven, you prepare sauce. Add whipping cream and mustard to pan juices. Cook to a golden color and consistency of heavy cream.

5 Arrange this party stew in a shallow serving container. Let guests serve themselves to tender meat, flavorful vegetables, and silken sauce.

VEAL

Because it comes from very young beef calves, veal is tender and lean, with no marbling and very little external fat. Its delicacy demands special care in cooking.

For roasting, choose a shoulder or leg of veal; you can also use the loin, but it's harder to find and quite expensive. Chops and pounded boneless veal, called "cutlets" or "scallops," are best when quickly pan-fried. But otherwise, slow, moist-heat cooking makes the most of this lean, exquisitely flavored meat.

Generally, you cook veal over low or medium heat; using a high temperature for a long period will toughen veal's lean fibers. Because it's more delicately flavored than most meats, you may want to complement veal with a subtle, well-seasoned sauce.

Spicy Veal Chops

    4 to 6 shoulder or loin veal chops, cut about 1 inch thick
      Pepper
    ¼ cup olive oil
    1 medium-size onion, finely chopped
    2 cloves garlic, slivered
    ½ teaspoon marjoram leaves
    1 can (1 lb.) tomatoes
    ¼ cup tomato paste
    ½ cup dry white wine
      Salt
      Chopped parsley

Sprinkle chops with pepper. Heat oil in a wide frying pan over medium-high heat; add chops and cook until browned on both sides; remove and set aside.

Add onion to pan and cook until soft and golden. Stir in garlic, marjoram, tomatoes (break up with a spoon) and their liquid, tomato paste, and wine. Return chops to pan, spooning sauce over meat. Bring to a boil; cover, reduce heat, and simmer until veal is tender when pierced (20 to 25 minutes). Lift out chops; arrange on a platter and keep warm. Increase heat to high and bring sauce to a boil; cook, stirring, until liquid is reduced by about a fourth. Season to taste with salt. Spoon sauce over chops. Sprinkle with parsley. Makes 4 to 6 servings.

Roast Shoulder of Veal with Carrots & Potatoes

    3 to 3½-pound boneless veal shoulder, rolled and tied
      Lemon-soy butter (recipe follows)
    6 to 8 small carrots
    6 to 8 small thin-skinned potatoes, peeled

Place veal, fat side up, on a rack in a shallow roasting pan. Insert a meat thermometer into thickest part. Prepare lemon-soy butter and brush over veal. Reserve remaining butter. Roast, uncovered, in a 325° oven for 1 hour.

Remove from oven and remove rack from pan. Place veal directly in pan and add carrots and potatoes, turning vegetables in drippings to coat all sides. Continue roasting, uncovered, for 1 to 1½ more hours or until thermometer registers 170° and vegetables are tender when pierced; baste meat and vegetables often with remaining butter and drippings.

Arrange meat and vegetables on a platter. Pour drippings from pan into a small bowl and pass at the table. Makes 6 to 8 servings.

Lemon-soy butter. Melt ⅓ cup **butter** or margarine in a small pan over medium heat. Remove from heat and stir in 2 cloves **garlic,** minced or pressed; 2 tablespoons **soy sauce;** 1 tablespoon **lemon juice;** 1½ teaspoons **thyme leaves;** and ½ teaspoon grated **lemon peel.**

Veal Stroganoff

    1½ pounds boneless veal stew meat, cut into 1½-inch cubes
    2 tablespoons salad oil
    3 mild Italian sausages, cut into 1-inch slices
    1 medium-size onion, chopped
    ½ pound mushrooms, quartered
    1 cup regular-strength beef broth
    1 red or green bell pepper, seeded and chopped
    ½ cup dry sherry or additional beef broth
    ½ pint (1 cup) sour cream
    2 tablespoons all-purpose flour
      Ground nutmeg, salt, and pepper

Trim and discard any excess fat or membrane from meat. Heat oil in a wide frying pan over medium-high heat. Add veal and sausages, a portion at a time, and cook until well browned on all sides; lift out and set aside. Add onion and mushrooms to pan and cook, stirring, until onion is soft. Return meat to pan. Stir in broth, bell pepper, and sherry. Bring to a boil; cover, reduce heat, and simmer until veal is tender when pierced (about 1 hour). Increase heat to high and cook, uncovered, until liquid is reduced to about 1 cup. Meanwhile, in a bowl, stir together sour cream and flour until thoroughly blended.

Reduce heat to medium and stir in sour cream mixture. Season to taste with nutmeg, salt, and pepper. Cook, stirring, until sauce boils and thickens slightly. Makes 6 servings.

Veal Stew with Artichokes

2	pounds boneless veal stew meat, cut into 1-inch cubes
2	tablespoons olive oil or salad oil
1	large onion, chopped
2	cloves garlic, minced or pressed
1	can (14½ oz.) regular-strength chicken broth
½	cup dry white wine
1	teaspoon *each* dry basil and dry rosemary
1	package (about 9 oz.) frozen artichoke hearts, thawed
½	cup whipping cream
	About 3 cups hot cooked buttered noodles
	Grated Parmesan cheese

Trim and discard any excess fat or membrane from meat. Heat oil in a 5-quart kettle over medium-high heat. Add veal, a portion at a time, and cook until well browned on all sides; lift out and set aside. Add onion and garlic to pan and cook, stirring, until onion is soft. Return meat to pan. Stir in broth, wine, basil, and rosemary. Bring to a boil; cover, reduce heat, and simmer until veal is tender when pierced (about 1 hour).

Add artichokes and cook, covered, until artichokes are tender when pierced (5 to 8 minutes). Stir in cream; cook over high heat until slightly thickened (about 3 minutes).

To serve, spoon stew over noodles and pass cheese at the table. Makes about 6 servings.

USING A STEEL

With a bit of care, a good knife can last a lifetime—as long as you keep it properly sharpened. And sharp knives are safer; dull ones can cause more cut fingers.

A steel doesn't actually sharpen a knife; what it does is to reset the blade edge, remove and smooth out minuscule burrs, and realign the almost invisible teeth that form the cutting edge. (Serrated knives, with their big teeth, never need resetting.)

For safety, choose a steel that has a handle guard to protect your fingers. To use the steel, hold it in front of you; then position the heel of the knife at the top of the steel, with the cutting edge at about a 20-degree angle to the steel. With your wrist relaxed, draw the blade from heel to tip toward you across the steel (see *Illustration 1*). Use light pressure and keep the 20-degree angle constant; if you press too hard or let the knife veer to a wider angle, you may nick its edge.

Reset the other side of the knife blade on the underside of the steel. Using the same angle, gently glide the knife, from tip to heel, away from you (see *Illustration 2*). You'll probably need to make only a total of 10 to 12 strokes, alternating from side to side. Then carefully wipe the steel and blade clean.

Use the steel often, especially before any significant amount of cutting or carving.

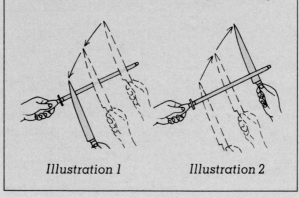

Illustration 1   Illustration 2

How to pan-fry veal cutlets (Recipe on facing page)

1 Place cutlets, one at a time between 2 sheets of wax paper. With flat side of a mallet, gently pound until ¼ inch thick. (Hard pounding tears meat fibers.)

2 Dredge each cutlet in flour, shaking off excess. Dip in beaten egg, then in crumbs. Lay cutlet on a flat surface and press crumbs in with your hands.

3 Cook cutlets, without crowding, in hot oil until browned on one side. Turn and cook until browned on other side. Drain briefly on paper towels.

4 Tender fried veal cutlets are juicy inside, golden and crisp outside. Accent with a squeeze of lemon.

Pounded boneless veal

Many markets offer pounded boneless veal cutlets, but you can pound them yourself (see photo 1 on facing page). Use any piece of veal from the leg, loin, rib, or shoulder that's ⅓ to ½ inch thick and cut like a steak or chop. Cut away any bone and trim fat and membrane before pounding.

Veal Piccata

- ¾ **pound boneless veal cutlets, cut ⅓ inch thick and pounded ¼ inch thick (see photo 1)**
- 1 **tablespoon all-purpose flour**
- ½ **teaspoon salt**
- ⅛ **teaspoon pepper**
- 3 **tablespoons butter or margarine**
- ⅓ **cup dry white wine**
- 1 **teaspoon grated lemon peel**
  Lemon slices

Cut meat into strips about 1½ inches wide and 3 inches long. In a pie pan, mix flour, salt, and pepper. Lightly dust meat with flour mixture. Melt 2 tablespoons of the butter in a wide frying pan over medium-high heat. When butter sizzles, add veal, without crowding, and cook until browned on both sides (about 2 minutes on each side). Remove veal; arrange on a platter and keep warm until all are cooked. Add wine to pan; bring to a boil, scraping browned particles free from pan. Stir in lemon peel and the remaining 1 tablespoon butter; heat until melted. Spoon sauce over veal and garnish with lemon slices. Makes 2 or 3 servings.

Pan-fried Veal Cutlets

(Pictured on facing page)

- 2 **or 3 lemons**
- 1½ **pounds boneless veal cutlets, cut ⅓ inch thick and pounded ¼ inch thick (see photo 1)**
  Salt and pepper
- ¼ **cup all-purpose flour**
- 2 **eggs, lightly beaten**
- 1 **cup fine dry bread crumbs**
  Salad oil
  Parsley (optional)

Cut one lemon into thin slices and remaining lemons into wedges; refrigerate.

Sprinkle veal with salt and pepper; set aside.

In separate pie pans, place flour, eggs, and bread crumbs. Dredge cutlets in flour, (shaking off excess); dip in egg, then in bread crumbs, shaking off excess. Lay cutlets on a flat surface and, with your hands, press in crumbs. If made ahead, cover and refrigerate for up to 4 hours.

Pour oil into a wide frying pan to a depth of ¼ inch; place over medium-high heat. Drop in a pinch of flour—if it floats and sizzles, fat is hot. Add veal in a single layer, without crowding, and cook until golden brown on both sides (about 2 minutes on each side). Drain briefly on paper towels; arrange on a platter and keep warm until all are cooked.

Garnish with lemons and parsley, if desired. Serve immediately. Makes 4 to 6 servings.

White Veal Scaloppine

- 1 **pound boneless veal cutlets, cut ⅓ inch thick and pounded ⅛ to ¼ inch thick (see photo 1)**
- ¼ **cup all-purpose flour**
- 2 **tablespoons salad oil**
- 2 **tablespoons butter or margarine**
- 1 **cup chopped onion**
- ¼ **pound mushrooms, sliced**
- 1 **or 2 cloves garlic, minced or pressed**
- ½ **cup *each* dry white wine and regular-strength chicken broth**
- 2 **teaspoons lemon juice**
- ¼ **teaspoon thyme leaves**
- 1 **teaspoon all-purpose flour**
- ½ **cup sour cream**

Dust cutlets with the ¼ cup flour, shaking off excess. Heat oil and 1 tablespoon of the butter in a wide frying pan over medium-high heat. When fat is hot, add veal in a single layer, without crowding, and cook until browned on both sides (about 1 to 2 minutes on each side). Remove from pan and set aside.

Melt remaining 1 tablespoon butter in pan. Add onion, mushrooms, and garlic; cook, stirring, until onions are soft. Stir in wine, broth, lemon juice, and thyme. Return meat to pan and bring to a boil; cover, reduce heat, and simmer for 15 minutes. Lift out veal; arrange on a platter and keep warm. Stir the 1 teaspoon flour into sour cream; add to pan, blending well. Cook, stirring, until sauce boils and thickens slightly. Spoon over veal. Makes 4 servings.

POULTRY

Star attraction of a traditional Sunday dinner, a festive holiday table, or even an ordinary weekday meal, poultry carries the day for all-around reliable goodness.

For one thing, few other foods offer such succulence and natural richness of flavor as do chicken, turkey, and dainty game hens. And usually such birds rank among the best dinner bargains. Low in cost, they're also considerably lower in fat than most meats, providing top-quality protein at modest calorie and cholesterol levels.

Types of poultry

Frying chickens. Though you may think from the name that there's just one way to cook them, fryers are also suitable for roasting, baking, braising, poaching, broiling, and barbecuing. The most widely available chickens, they average from 3 to 4 pounds. Smaller birds (2 to 3 pounds) are sometimes sold as broilers or broiler-fryers.

Roasting chickens. Because of their size (4 to 6 pounds each), roasters look almost as impressive as turkey—and they're a perfect entrée for a special occasion. If you can't find one in your market, you can roast a large fryer.

Stewing hens. Weighing from 3 to 5 pounds, stewing hens need long, slow simmering to make them tender and to bring out their rich flavor.

Rock Cornish game hens. Delicately flavored, these tiny birds weigh from 1 to 1½ pounds. Cook them whole for individual servings or split a large one in half to serve two.

DONENESS TEST FOR POULTRY

The cooking method you use determines how you'll check your bird for doneness. When sautéing, frying, baking, or braising cut-up chicken, cut a gash in the thickest part of one piece—the meat should not be pink and the juices should run clear yellow. If you're cooking both breasts and thighs, test the thighs for doneness, as they take longer to cook.

There are several ways to test roasted whole birds. Jiggle a leg—it should move freely. Or prick the meat near the thigh joint with a fork; when the juices run clear yellow, the bird is done.

The most accurate way to test roasted chicken or turkey is to use a meat thermometer. Insert it into the thickest portion of the thigh, without touching bone, and roast until the thermometer registers 185°. Also use a thermometer when you're roasting a turkey breast (cook to 170°) or a hindquarter (cook to 185°).

Turkey. Choose between hen turkeys, averaging from 10 to 14 pounds, and tom turkeys, averaging from 16 to 20 pounds. During holiday seasons, you can find even larger tom turkeys, some as heavy as 30 pounds. Since the heavier the bird, the higher the ratio of meat to bone, it's most economical to buy the largest hen or tom you can use.

Buying & storing poultry

When shopping for poultry, look for smooth, unbruised skin. There should be little or no liquid in the package. Depending on what the chickens were fed, their skin may be yellow or bluish white —color is not an indication of quality. As for how much to buy, allow about a pound of chicken or turkey (bone in) for each serving.

Like fish, fresh poultry is perishable and should be cooked within 2 days. Remove the giblets from whole birds before you refrigerate them. If you're not planning to cook the giblets with the bird, freeze the heart and gizzard in one container and the liver in another, collecting more of each until you accumulate enough for a meal or other purposes.

Ideally, you should thaw frozen poultry in the refrigerator for maximum retention of its juices. But before a holiday meal, your refrigerator may be crowded to capacity. To thaw a turkey quickly outside the refrigerator, keep it in a cool place, in its original wrapping, until partially thawed. Then unwrap and finish thawing it under cool running water. Remove the giblets from the cavity as soon as you can pry them loose.

POULTRY ROASTING TIME & TEMPERATURE CHART

To roast a Rock Cornish game hen, chicken, or turkey, follow these simple steps. Remove the giblets from the body cavity. Rinse the bird inside and out; pat dry with paper towels. If you wish, stuff the bird (see pages 97 and 99).

To estimate the total cooking time, multiply the weight of the bird by the minutes per pound (see below). You'll notice that larger birds require less time per pound than smaller ones do. Use the same roasting time whether the bird is stuffed or not.

Place the prepared bird, breast side up, on a rack in a shallow roasting pan. Generously smear its skin with softened butter, or follow the instructions in your recipe. If it's a large bird, insert a meat thermometer into the thickest part of the thigh, without touching bone.

During the last half of the roasting time, baste with the pan juices to keep the bird moist—every 15 minutes for a game hen or chicken, every 30 minutes for a turkey. Check the thermometer toward the end of the estimated time; when it registers 185°, the bird is done. For small chickens or game hens, cook until the juices run clear yellow when the meat near the thighbone is pricked with a fork. Or jiggle the drumstick to see if it moves freely. If the bird finishes browning before it is done, place a piece of foil loosely over it.

Remove the cooked bird from the oven and let it rest for 15 minutes before carving.

To test doneness when you're roasting a turkey part, insert a thermometer in the thickest part of the meat, without touching bone. Cook to 170° for breast meat, 185° for dark meat.

All of our testing was done with poultry taken directly from the refrigerator and roasted in a conventional electric or gas oven.

Bird	Approximate weight (lbs.)	Approximate cooking time (minutes per lb.)	Oven temperature (°F)	Meat Thermometer reading (°F)
Frying chicken	3–4	20–25	375°	185°
Roasting chicken	4–6	20–25	375°	185°
Rock Cornish game hen	1–1½	45–60	375°	—
Hen turkey	10–14	15	325°	185°
Tom turkey	16–30	12	325°	185°
Turkey breast Half, bone in	2–4	15–20	350°	170°
Half, boneless	2–4	20–25	350°	170°
Turkey thigh	½–1½	60	350°	185°
Turkey hindquarter	2½–4	60	350°	185°

Roasting a trussed chicken

What is trussing? It's simply securing the wings and legs of poultry to its body with string. You can truss or not, depending on your personal preference—some cooks always roast birds without trussing. But trussing has several advantages. It ensures moist, tender meat by preventing the skin from splitting at the joints, and it provides a compact, well-shaped bird that's easy to carve.

Though there are many ways to truss poultry, here we show you how to do it with a trussing needle. You can purchase this needle at gourmet cookware shops or in the housewares section of many department stores. The needle must be long enough to penetrate the bird's body and extend about an inch from both wings. For a chicken weighing 3 to 4 pounds, you'll need an 8-inch trussing needle.

Use only white cotton string; colored string will bleed onto the meat, and polyester string may shrink during baking, tearing the bird's skin.

Roast Chicken

(Pictured on facing page)

> 1 frying chicken (3 to 4 lbs.)
> About 2½ cups bread stuffing (optional), page 97
> 2 tablespoons butter or margarine, softened
> Fresh fruit (optional)

Remove giblets from chicken and reserve for other uses; pull off and discard lumps of fat from chicken. Cut off wing tips, if desired.

Stuff body cavity with bread stuffing, if you wish. If trussing is desired, thread trussing needle with white cotton string. Lay chicken on its side. Push needle through flesh between wing joints (see photo 1 on facing page), exiting needle between wing joints on opposite side of body. Flip bird onto other side. Insert needle between thigh and leg joint (photo 2), pushing through. Turn bird breast side up. Bring tail skin up over breast skin; fold tail skin under. Using about 3 sewing stitches, secure tail to breast skin, closing cavity (photo 3).

Push needle through opposite thigh and leg joint. Turn bird on its side and cut ends of string, leaving about 4 inches on each end. Tie ends together tightly (photo 4).

If not trussing, use metal skewers to fasten tail skin to breast and neck skin to back (see photo 2 on page 99).

Place chicken, breast side up, on a rack in a shallow roasting pan. If desired, bring legs together at bottom and tie (photo 5). With your fingers, rub chicken with butter.

Bake, uncovered, in a 375° oven for 1 to 1½ hours or until juices run clear when meat near thighbone is pricked with a fork, or a meat thermometer inserted in thickest part of thigh, without touching bone, registers 185°. Baste with pan drippings every 15 minutes during last half of cooking time. Transfer bird to a platter. Remove string or skewers. Let stand for 10 minutes before carving. Garnish with fresh fruit, if desired. Makes 4 servings.

Roast Chicken with Herbs

> 1 frying chicken (3 to 4 lbs.)
> 3 cloves garlic, halved
> 2 bay leaves
> 3 tablespoons butter or margarine, melted
> ½ teaspoon each salt and pepper
> ¼ teaspoon each ground sage, dry basil, and thyme, oregano, and marjoram leaves

Remove giblets from chicken and reserve for other uses; pull off and discard lumps of fat from chicken.

Rub skin of chicken with 1 cut clove garlic; then put all garlic and bay leaves into body cavity. In a small bowl, stir together butter, salt, pepper, sage, basil, thyme, oregano, and marjoram. Spoon 1 tablespoon of the butter mixture into body cavity.

If trussing is desired, follow trussing directions in preceding recipe. Or use metal skewers to fasten tail skin to breast skin and neck skin to back (see photo 2 on page 99).

Brush skin generously with butter mixture. Place chicken, breast side up, on a rack in a shallow roasting pan. Bake, uncovered, in a 375° oven for 1 to 1½ hours or until juices run clear when meat near thighbone is pricked with a fork, or a meat thermometer inserted into thickest part of thigh, without touching bone, registers 185°. Baste occasionally with any remaining butter mixture or pan drippings during last half-hour of roasting time. Transfer bird to a platter. Remove string or skewers. Let stand for 10 minutes before carving. Makes 4 servings.

How to truss & roast chicken (Recipe on facing page)

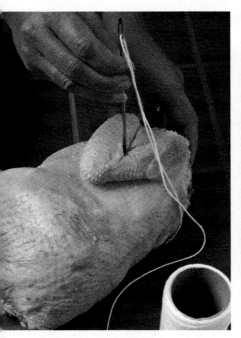

1 Insert threaded trussing needle through flesh between wing joints; push needle through body cavity, exiting between wing joints on other side. Pull string through.

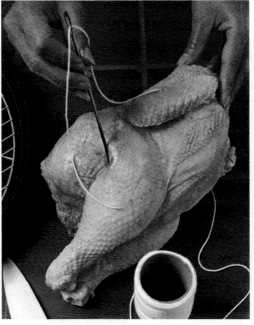

2 Insert needle at an angle between thigh and leg joint, and push toward body cavity. Tucking end under, fold tail skin over breast skin.

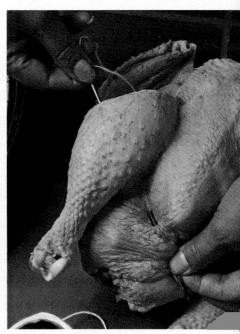

3 Exit needle through tail; stitching in and out about 3 times, secure tail, closing cavity. Push needle through opposite thigh and leg joint.

4 Turn bird on its side; cut string, leaving about 4 inches on each end. Pull string taut from both ends; tie securely and trim excess string.

5 Bring legs together and tie securely with another length of string; trim excess.

6 After roasting, snip long string once and pull out; then cut and remove leg string. Beautifully compact, golden chicken is star attraction at any meal.

Baked chicken

Pop a panful of chicken pieces into the oven, set the timer for an hour, and you're home free. Many baked chicken recipes are just about that easy. Baking works well, too, if you need to double a recipe to accommodate a crowd. Coated, glazed, or marinated, baked chicken is a sure winner.

When you plan to bake chicken pieces—or cook them by any of the other methods detailed in this chapter—you'll save money if you buy a whole bird and cut it up yourself. With the step-by-step instructions illustrated below, you can learn to cut up a chicken quickly. When whole fresh chickens are a good buy, you may wish to cut up several. That way you'll have enough legs and thighs for one meal and breasts for another.

When you cut up a bird yourself, don't throw anything away. The giblets can flavor gravy, the livers make delicious pâté (page 93), and the bones make a flavorful broth (page 85).

Plum-glazed Chicken

  1 **can (1 lb.) purple plums**
  2 **tablespoons butter or margarine**
  1 **medium-size onion, finely chopped**
  ⅓ **cup firmly packed brown sugar**
  ¼ **cup tomato-based chili sauce**
  2 **tablespoons soy sauce**
  1 **teaspoon ground ginger**
  2 **teaspoons lemon juice**
  1 **frying chicken (3 to 3½ lbs.), cut into pieces**
     Salt and pepper

Drain plums, reserving syrup. Remove pits from plums. In a blender or food processor, whirl plums and syrup until puréed.

Melt butter in a wide frying pan over medium heat. Add onion and cook until soft. Stir in plum

CUTTING UP A WHOLE BIRD

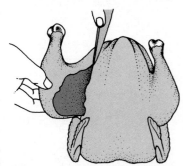

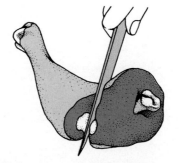

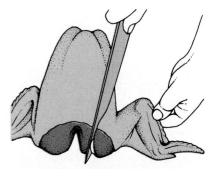

1 To remove leg and thigh, grasp leg and pull away from body. Cut through skin, exposing joint. Bend thigh back from body; cut close to body through hip joint. Repeat with other leg.

2 To separate leg from thigh, cut through skin between joints. Then bend leg back from thigh to expose joint; cut through joint and bottom skin.

3 To remove wing, pull away from body. Cut through skin to expose shoulder joint; sever at joint. To remove wing tip, cut at joint. Repeat with other wing.

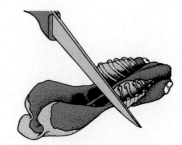

4 To separate back from breast, cut along each side of backbone between rib joints.

5 Bend back piece in half at joint (natural break); cut to separate.

6 To split breast, place breast skin side up; cut through skin and meat along one side of breastbone. (To bone breast, see page 92.)

purée, brown sugar, chili sauce, soy, ginger, and lemon juice. Cook, uncovered, stirring often, until slightly thickened (about 15 minutes).

Sprinkle chicken with salt and pepper. Arrange, skin side down, in a lightly greased baking pan. Bake, uncovered, in a 350° oven for 30 minutes, basting with plum sauce every 15 minutes. Turn chicken skin side up and bake, basting with sauce occasionally, for 30 more minutes or until meat near thighbone is no longer pink when slashed. Heat remaining sauce and pass at the table. Makes 4 servings.

Parmesan Baked Chicken

- 1 **cup dry bread crumbs**
- ½ **cup grated Parmesan cheese**
- ½ **teaspoon** *each* **paprika and garlic salt**
- ¼ **teaspoon pepper**
- 1 **frying chicken (3 to 3½ lbs.), cut into pieces**
- 4 **tablespoons butter or margarine, melted**

In a shallow pan, combine bread crumbs, cheese, paprika, garlic salt, and pepper. Dip chicken pieces in butter, then roll in crumb mixture. Arrange, skin side up, without touching, in a lightly greased baking pan. Bake, uncovered, in a 350° oven for 1 hour or until meat near thighbone is no longer pink when slashed. Makes 4 servings.

PICNIC-STYLE CHICKEN

In a bowl, stir together ⅓ cup **mayonnaise** and ½ teaspoon *each* **salt, garlic salt,** and crushed **dry rosemary.** Brush chicken with mayonnaise mixture, then roll in 1½ cups **cornflake crumbs.** Bake as directed for Parmesan Baked Chicken.

NUT-CRUSTED CHICKEN

Whirl 1⅓ cups **almonds** or roasted peanuts in a blender or food processor until coarsely ground. In a bowl, stir together ½ cup **mayonnaise,** 1 teaspoon *each* **dry mustard** and **thyme leaves,** 2 tablespoons grated **Parmesan cheese,** and ¼ teaspoon **pepper.** Brush chicken with mayonnaise mixture, then roll in nuts. Bake as directed for Parmesan Baked Chicken.

Teriyaki Chicken

- 4 *each* **chicken legs and thighs**
- ⅓ **cup soy sauce**
- 2½ **tablespoons honey**
- 1 **teaspoon grated fresh ginger or ½ teaspoon ground ginger**
- 2 **tablespoons dry sherry**
- ¼ **cup salad oil**
- 1 **clove garlic, minced or pressed**
- 2 **green onions (including tops), thinly sliced**

Place chicken in a plastic bag. Combine soy, honey, ginger, sherry, oil, garlic, and onions; pour over chicken. Seal bag and refrigerate, turning occasionally, for 4 hours or until next day.

Pour off and discard marinade. Place chicken, skin side up, on a rack in a roasting pan. Bake, uncovered, in a 350° oven for 1 hour or until meat near thighbone is no longer pink when slashed. Makes 4 servings.

MAKING CHICKEN BROTH

One obvious economy of cutting up a chicken at home is that nothing need go to waste. For our richly flavored broth, save wing tips, backs, necks, and even the breastbones and skins from boned chicken breasts. Collect them in a gallon-size freezer bag and store them in the freezer until you have 3 to 4 pounds.

To make chicken broth, place 3 to 4 pounds **chicken bones** in an 8-quart kettle. Add 1 large **onion,** quartered; 1 **carrot,** cut into chunks; 1 stalk **celery;** 2 sprigs **parsley;** 1 **bay leaf;** ¼ teaspoon **thyme leaves;** and 2 quarts **cold water.** Bring to a boil over high heat; then reduce heat and simmer, partially covered, for 2 to 3 hours. Strain; discard vegetables and bones. Season to taste with **salt** and **pepper.** Skim off fat.

If made ahead, cool, cover, and refrigerate for up to 3 days; freeze for longer storage. Makes about 1 quart.

How to make Southern Fried Chicken (Recipe on facing page)

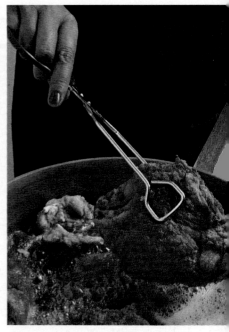

1 To test temperature of fat, drop a pinch of flour into pan—if flour floats and sizzles, fat is hot enough to begin frying chicken pieces.

2 Arrange chicken, skin side down, in fat; allow enough space between pieces for fat to bubble and sizzle—this assures even cooking and browning.

3 With tongs, turn pieces over to cook other side. Then lift out and drain on paper towels.

4 After making a *roux* from drippings and flour, gradually pour in milk, stirring constantly.

5 Cook gravy, stirring constantly with a wire whisk, until gravy boils. (Constant stirring prevents lumps from forming.)

6 Offer crusty pieces of golden-brown Southern Fried Chicken with hot milk gravy.

Fried chicken

A time-honored family favorite, fried chicken satisfies every preference. Crisp and golden on the outside, tender and juicy inside, it's delicious either hot or at room temperature—with fork or with fingers.

Though everyone loves the results, some cooks dislike the spattering that comes from cooking the chicken in a fair amount of fat. The secret to spatter-free cooking is to use a heavy, wide frying pan that's at least 2 inches deep.

If you remove the browned bits from the cooking fat, you can recycle it to fry chicken another time. Let the fat cool, then pour it through a strainer lined with several thicknesses of cheesecloth, into a wide-mouthed jar. Refrigerate until needed; discard the fat when it darkens or starts to smell rancid.

Easy Fried Chicken

    1   **frying chicken (about 3 lbs.), cut into pieces**
    2   **tablespoons dry sherry**
    ½   **cup all-purpose flour**
    1   **teaspoon *each* garlic salt and salt**
    ½   **teaspoon paprika**
    ¼   **teaspoon *each* pepper, rubbed sage, thyme leaves, and dry basil**
        About 2½ cups salad oil

Place chicken in a shallow pan and sprinkle with sherry; let stand for 10 minutes. Meanwhile, in a plastic bag, combine flour, garlic salt, salt, paprika, pepper, sage, thyme, and basil. Into a heavy, wide frying pan with a lid, pour oil to a depth of ½ inch. Without drying, place chicken, a few pieces at a time, in bag and shake to coat. Arrange chicken without crowding, skin side down, in *unheated* oil.

Cover pan and place over medium-high heat. When chicken begins sizzling loudly (about 7 minutes), begin timing—cook for 15 minutes. With tongs, turn pieces over and continue cooking, uncovered, until meat near thighbone is no longer pink when slashed (about 10 more minutes). Lift out chicken and let drain briefly on paper towels. Serve hot or let cool to room temperature. Makes 4 servings.

Southern Fried Chicken with Milk Gravy

(Pictured on facing page)

There's a secret to the crispness of these golden brown chicken morsels: you refrigerate the floured pieces for an hour before frying them.

    1   **egg**
         All-purpose flour
    1   **frying chicken (about 3 lbs.), cut into pieces**
         Solid shortening
    ¼   **cup all-purpose flour**
    2½   **cups milk**
         Salt and pepper

Beat egg lightly in a shallow bowl. Place about ½ cup flour in another shallow bowl. Dip chicken pieces, one at a time, in egg until evenly moistened; then roll in flour, shaking off excess. Place on a baking sheet and refrigerate, uncovered, for 1 hour.

In a heavy, wide frying pan over medium-high heat, melt enough shortening to reach a depth of ¼ inch. Meanwhile, recoat chicken with flour, shaking off excess.

To test temperature of fat, drop a pinch of flour into pan; flour should float and sizzle on hot fat. (If flour sinks to bottom of pan and disperses, fat is not hot enough for frying.)

When fat is hot, add chicken pieces, skin side down in a single layer. (Arrange legs and thighs in center of pan where heat is concentrated; dark meat pieces take longer to cook.) Allow enough space between pieces for fat to bubble and sizzle; this assures even cooking and browning.

Cook chicken pieces for 15 minutes. With tongs, turn pieces over and continue cooking until meat near thighbone is no longer pink when slashed (15 to 20 more minutes). Lift out chicken and let drain on paper towels.

Pour off and reserve drippings, leaving browned particles on bottom of pan. Return 5 tablespoons of drippings to pan (discard remainder); scrape browned particles free. Blend in the ¼ cup flour and cook, stirring, over medium-high heat until bubbly. Gradually pour in milk and continue cooking and stirring until sauce boils and thickens. Season to taste with salt and pepper.

Arrange chicken pieces on a serving platter. Pass gravy at the table. Makes 4 servings.

Braised chicken

A moist-heat method used to tenderize tough cuts of meat, braising plays a different role with chicken. Today's plump frying chickens arrive at the market naturally moist and tender, so we braise them only to effect delicious flavor variations. With each change of braising liquid and seasoning, chicken turns into an exciting new experience. As a bonus, the braising liquid becomes the base for a flavorful sauce, perfect to spoon over noodles or rice.

Chicken with Wine

> 3 strips bacon, coarsely chopped
> 1 frying chicken (3 to 3½ lbs.), cut into pieces
> 8 to 10 small boiling onions
> ½ pound small mushrooms
> 1 can (14½ oz.) regular-strength beef broth
> 1 cup dry red wine
> 2 tablespoons *each* Dijon mustard and chopped parsley
> 1 teaspoon cornstarch mixed with 2 teaspoons water

In a wide frying pan over medium heat, cook bacon until crisp. Remove with a slotted spoon, drain, and set aside. Add chicken to pan, increase heat to medium-high, and cook in drippings, turning, until browned on all sides. Remove chicken and set aside. Add onions to pan, reduce heat to medium, and cook until well browned. Remove onions and set aside. Stir in mushrooms and cook until soft; remove mushrooms and set aside.

Add broth to pan and bring to a boil, scraping browned particles free from pan; cook until reduced to about 1 cup. Stir in wine and mustard. Return chicken, onions, and mushrooms to pan. Bring to a boil; cover, reduce heat, and simmer until meat near thighbone is no longer pink when slashed (40 to 45 minutes). With a slotted spoon, lift out chicken and vegetables; arrange on a platter and keep warm. Skim off and discard fat. Stir bacon, parsley, and cornstarch mixture into pan juices; cook, stirring, until sauce boils and thickens slightly. Pour over chicken and vegetables. Makes 4 servings.

Chicken Cacciatore

> 2 tablespoons olive oil or salad oil
> 2 tablespoons butter or margarine
> 1 frying chicken (3 to 3½ lbs.) cut into pieces
> ½ pound mushrooms, sliced
> 1 medium-size onion, chopped
> 2 green peppers, seeded and chopped
> 2 cloves garlic, minced or pressed
> 2 tablespoons chopped parsley
> ½ cup water
> ½ cup dry white wine or regular-strength chicken broth
> 1 can (6 oz.) tomato paste
> 1½ teaspoons salt
> ¼ teaspoon *each* marjoram, oregano, and thyme leaves

Heat oil and butter in a wide frying pan over medium-high heat. Add chicken and cook, turning, until browned on all sides. Remove chicken and set aside. Pour off and discard all but 3 tablespoons drippings.

Add mushrooms, onion, green peppers, and garlic to pan; reduce heat to medium and cook, stirring, until onion is soft. Stir in parsley, water, wine, tomato paste, salt, marjoram, oregano, and thyme. Return chicken to pan. Bring to a boil; cover, reduce heat, and simmer until meat near thighbone is no longer pink when slashed (40 to 45 minutes). Makes 4 servings.

A GUIDE TO PERFECT BRAISED CHICKEN

- To keep sauce lean, trim excess fat under edges of chicken skin on breasts and thighs before cooking.
- For even browning, pat chicken pieces dry with paper towels before coating or before placing in cooking fat.
- Don't crowd pieces as you brown them —otherwise you'll have chicken that's more stewed than sautéed.
- When you return browned pieces to pan for braising, arrange breasts on top; they cook faster and need to stay relatively removed from heat source.
- If made ahead, reheat braised chicken slowly in a covered pan over lowest heat.

Garlic Chicken

- 4 strips bacon
- 1 frying chicken (3 to 3½ lbs.), cut into pieces
- 2 medium-size onions, chopped
- 5 cloves garlic, minced or pressed
- 1 cup dry white wine
- ¼ cup dry vermouth
- 2 tablespoons dry basil
- 1 teaspoon poultry seasoning
  Salt and pepper
- 1 tablespoon cornstarch mixed with 2 tablespoons water

In a wide frying pan over medium heat, cook bacon until crisp. Remove bacon from pan, drain, crumble, and set aside. Add chicken to pan, increase heat to medium-high, and cook in drippings, turning, until browned on all sides. Remove chicken and set aside.

Add onions and garlic to pan; reduce heat to medium and cook until onions are soft. Return chicken and bacon to pan. Add wine, vermouth, basil, and poultry seasoning; season to taste with salt and pepper. Bring to a boil; cover, reduce heat, and simmer until meat near thighbone is no longer pink when slashed (40 to 45 minutes).

With a slotted spoon, lift out chicken, arrange on a platter and keep warm. Stir cornstarch mixture into pan juices and cook, stirring, until sauce boils and thickens slightly. Spoon over chicken or pass at the table. Makes 4 servings.

Applejack Chicken

- 1 frying chicken (3 to 3½ lbs.), cut into pieces
  Salt and pepper
- 2 tablespoons butter or margarine
- 1 medium-size onion, chopped
- 1 can (6 oz.) frozen apple juice concentrate, thawed
- 1 Newtown pippin apple
- ¼ pound mushrooms, sliced
- ¼ cup half-and-half (light cream)
- 1 tablespoon cornstarch
- 3 tablespoons brandy or dry sherry
  Chopped parsley

Sprinkle chicken lightly with salt and pepper. Melt butter in a wide frying pan over medium-high heat. Add chicken and cook, turning, until browned on all sides. Remove chicken and set aside.

Add onion to pan, reduce heat to medium, and cook, stirring, until soft. Return chicken to pan; pour over apple juice concentrate. Bring to a boil; cover, reduce heat, and simmer for 20 minutes.

Meanwhile, peel, core, and dice apple. Add apple and mushrooms to chicken, cover, and continue cooking until meat near thighbone is no longer pink when slashed (20 to 25 more minutes). With a slotted spoon, lift out chicken, vegetables, and apple; arrange on a platter and keep warm. Combine half-and-half, cornstarch, and brandy. Stir into pan juices and cook, stirring, until sauce boils and thickens slightly. Pour over chicken and sprinkle with parsley. Makes 4 servings.

Yogurt-Orange Chicken

- 1 frying chicken (3 to 3½ lbs.), cut into pieces
  Salt and pepper
- 2 tablespoons butter or margarine
- 1 large onion, chopped
- 2 cloves garlic, minced or pressed
- 2 large oranges
- ½ teaspoon *each* ground coriander, ground cumin, and salt
- 1 tablespoon sugar
- 1 tablespoon cornstarch mixed with 1 cup unflavored yogurt

Sprinkle chicken lightly with salt and pepper. Melt butter in a wide frying pan over medium-high heat. Add chicken and cook, turning, until browned on all sides. Remove chicken and set aside.

Add onion and garlic to pan, reduce heat to medium, and cook, stirring, until onion is soft. Meanwhile, grate 1 orange to make 1 teaspoon grated peel; ream juice from both oranges to make ¾ cup (if necessary, add water to make ¾ cup liquid). Return chicken to pan; add orange juice, orange peel, coriander, cumin, the ½ teaspoon salt, and sugar. Bring to a boil; cover, reduce heat, and simmer until meat near thighbone is no longer pink when slashed (40 to 45 minutes).

With a slotted spoon, lift out chicken; arrange on a platter and keep warm. Stir cornstarch-yogurt mixture into pan juices and cook, stirring, until sauce boils and thickens slightly. Pour over chicken. Makes 4 servings.

Boned chicken breast entrées

Boned chicken breasts make neat serving-size pieces for quick but elegant entrées. We start you off with two made from breast meat that has been pounded thin and wrapped around a savory filling. Because these dishes can be assembled a day ahead, they're good choices for company meals. The chicken breast recipes on pages 92 and 93 can be table-ready in less than 30 minutes.

Easy Baked Chicken Kiev

(Pictured on facing page)

    4   whole chicken breasts (about 4 lbs. *total*),
        boned, split, and skinned (page 92)
    ½   cup *each* fine dry bread crumbs and grated
        Parmesan cheese
    1½ teaspoons oregano leaves
    ½   teaspoon garlic salt
    ¼   teaspoon pepper
    4   tablespoons butter or margarine, softened
    1   tablespoon chopped parsley
    4   ounces jack cheese, cut into 8 strips
        (*each* ½ inch thick and 1½ inches long)
    5   tablespoons butter or margarine, melted

Place chicken breasts, one at a time, between 2 sheets of wax paper or plastic wrap. With flat side of a mallet, gently pound breasts until each is about ¼ inch thick; set aside.

In a rimmed plate or pie pan, combine bread crumbs, Parmesan cheese, 1 teaspoon of the oregano, garlic salt, and pepper; set aside. In a small bowl, stir together the 4 tablespoons softened butter, parsley, and remaining ½ teaspoon oregano.

Spread about ½ tablespoon of the herb-butter mixture across each breast about an inch from lower edge; lay a strip of jack cheese over butter mixture. Fold lower edge of breast over filling (see photo 1 on facing page), then fold in sides and roll up to enclose filling (photo 2).

Dip each bundle in the melted butter and drain briefly; then roll in bread crumb mixture until evenly coated (photo 3). Place bundles, seam side down, without touching, in a 9 by 13-inch baking pan. Drizzle with any remaining butter. Cover and refrigerate for at least 4 hours or until next day.

Bake, uncovered, in a preheated 425° oven for 20 minutes or until chicken is no longer pink when lightly slashed (cut just a small slash so filling doesn't ooze out). Makes 4 to 8 servings.

Crab-stuffed Chicken Breasts

    4   whole chicken breasts (about 4 lbs. *total*),
        boned, split, and skinned (page 92)
    4   tablespoons butter or margarine
    ½   cup thinly sliced green onions (including
        tops)
    ¼   pound mushrooms, thinly sliced
    3   tablespoons all-purpose flour
    ¼   teaspoon thyme leaves
    ½   cup *each* milk, dry white wine, and regular-
        strength chicken broth
        Salt and pepper
    ½   pound crabmeat
    ⅓   cup *each* finely chopped parsley and fine dry
        bread crumbs
    1½ cups (6 oz.) shredded Swiss cheese

Place chicken breasts, one at a time, between 2 sheets of wax paper or plastic wrap. With flat side of a mallet, gently pound breasts until each is about ¼ inch thick; set aside.

Melt butter in a wide frying pan over medium heat. Add onions and mushrooms and cook, stirring, until onions are soft. Stir in flour and thyme and continue cooking and stirring until bubbly. Gradually pour in milk, wine, and broth; cook, stirring, until sauce boils and thickens. Season to taste with salt and pepper.

In a small bowl, stir together ¼ cup of the sauce, crab, parsley, and bread crumbs. Spread an equal amount of filling over each chicken breast, to within ¼ inch of edges. Fold lower edge over filling; then fold in sides and roll up to enclose. Place bundles, seam side down, in a greased 9 by 13-inch baking pan.

Pour remaining sauce over bundles and sprinkle with cheese. If made ahead, cover and refrigerate until next day. Bake, covered, in a 400° oven for 30 minutes (40 minutes, if refrigerated) or until chicken is no longer pink when lightly slashed (cut just a small slash so filling doesn't ooze out). Makes 4 to 8 servings.

How to make Chicken Kiev (Recipe on facing page)

1 Spread herb-butter mixture across breast about an inch from lower edge; cover with strip of cheese. Fold lower edge of breast over filling.

2 Fold in sides to enclose filling; then roll breast up into a bundle.

3 Dip each bundle in melted butter and let drain briefly; then roll in crumb mixture until evenly coated. Place seam side down, without touching, in baking pan.

4 Crisp and juicy Chicken Kiev— one slice reveals a filling of melted cheese flecked with savory herbs.

...Boned chicken breast entrées

Italian-style Chicken Scallops

- 3 **whole chicken breasts (about 3 lbs.** *total***), boned, split, and skinned**
- 1 **egg**
- 3 **tablespoons milk**
- ¼ **cup finely chopped onion**
- 2 **cloves garlic, minced or pressed**
- ½ **cup** *each* **cornflake crumbs, all-purpose flour, and grated Parmesan cheese**
- 1 **teaspoon Italian herb seasoning or ¼ teaspoon** *each* **dry basil and oregano, thyme, and marjoram leaves**
- ¼ **teaspoon** *each* **pepper and ground coriander**
- 3 **tablespoons butter or margarine**
- 3 **tablespoons salad oil**
- 6 **slices (1 oz.** *each***) mozzarella cheese**

Place chicken breasts, one at a time, between 2 sheets of wax paper or plastic wrap. With flat side of a mallet, gently pound breasts until each is about ⅜ inch thick; set aside.

In a blender or food processor, whirl egg, milk, onion, and garlic until smooth; pour into a shallow bowl. In a rimmed plate or pie pan, stir together cornflake crumbs, flour, Parmesan cheese, Italian seasoning, pepper, and coriander. Dip chicken pieces in egg mixture, then roll in crumb mixture; with your fingers, press crumbs into meat.

Heat butter and oil in a wide frying pan over medium-high heat. When fat sizzles, add half the chicken pieces and cook for about 1½ minutes on each side; place in a single layer on a baking sheet. Repeat with remaining chicken. Top each

HOW TO BONE A CHICKEN BREAST

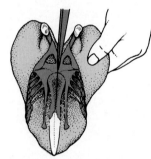

1 Lay breast skin side down; run a sharp knife down center to sever thin membrane and expose keel bone (dark spoon-shaped bone) and thick white cartilage.

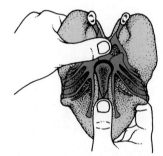

2 Placing one thumb on tip end of keel bone and other at base of rib cage, grasp breast firmly in both hands. Bend breast back with both hands until keel bone breaks through.

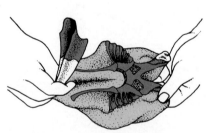

3 Run finger under edge of keel bone and thick cartilage, then pull out and discard.

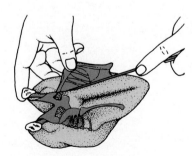

4 Insert knife under long first rib. Resting knife against bones, scrap meat away from bones. Cut rib away, and sever and remove shoulder joint. Repeat with other side of breast.

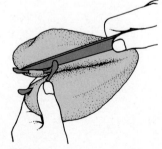

5 With fingers, locate wishbone. Cutting close to bone, remove wishbone.

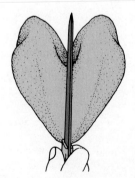

6 Lay breast meat flat on a cutting board and cut breast in half; remove white tendon from bottom side of each half. Pull off skin, if suggested in recipe.

piece with a slice of the mozzarella cheese. Broil about 6 inches below heat just until cheese is melted (2 to 3 minutes). Makes 3 to 6 servings.

Chicken in Tarragon Cream

- ½ **cup sour cream**
- ¼ **teaspoon dry tarragon**
- 2 **teaspoons sugar**
- 1 **teaspoon cornstarch**
- 2 **whole chicken breasts (about 2 lbs. *total*), boned, split, and skinned**
  Salt and pepper
  All-purpose flour
- 1 **tablespoon butter or margarine**
- 1 **tablespoon salad oil**
- ½ **cup dry white wine**
- 1 **tablespoon lemon juice**
- 1 **green onion (including top), thinly sliced**
- 1 **clove garlic, minced or pressed**

In a small bowl, stir together sour cream, tarragon, sugar, and cornstarch; set aside.

Sprinkle chicken breasts with salt and pepper; dredge in flour, shaking off excess. Heat butter and oil in a wide frying pan over medium-high heat. When fat sizzles, add chicken breasts and cook until golden (about 3 minutes on each side). Add wine, lemon juice, onion, and garlic. Cover, reduce heat, and simmer until meat in thickest part is no longer pink when slashed (10 to 15 minutes).

Remove from heat; lift out chicken and arrange on a platter. Stir sour cream mixture into pan juices. Return to low heat and cook, stirring, until sauce bubbles and thickens slightly. Pour over chicken. Makes 2 to 4 servings.

Chicken Breasts Mediterranean

- 3 **tablespoons olive oil or salad oil**
- 2 **whole chicken breasts (about 2 lbs. *total*), boned and split**
- 1 **small onion, finely chopped**
- ½ **cup pitted ripe or green olives**
- ½ **teaspoon thyme leaves**
- 1 **cup dry white wine**
- 4 **thin lemon slices**
- ⅓ **cup finely chopped parsley**

Heat oil in a wide frying pan over medium-high heat; add chicken breasts and cook until well browned (about 5 minutes on each side). Lift out chicken and set aside.

Add onion, olives, and thyme to pan drippings; cook, stirring, until onion is golden (about 5 minutes). Add wine and chicken breasts, topping each breast with a lemon slice. Cover, reduce heat, and simmer until meat in thickest part is no longer pink when slashed (about 10 minutes). Lift out chicken and arrange on a platter; keep warm.

Increase heat to high and boil sauce, stirring often, until reduced to about ¼ cup; stir in parsley. Pour sauce over chicken. Makes 2 to 4 servings.

CHICKEN LIVER PÂTÉ

Offer this creamy pâté with crackers as a before-dinner appetizer. Or for a first course, serve small wedges of it on a lettuce-lined plate, along with slices of crusty bread.

Melt 3 tablespoons **butter** or margarine in a wide frying pan over medium heat. Add ¼ cup chopped **onion** and cook, stirring, until soft. Add 1 cup (½ lb.) **chicken livers,** cut in half, and continue cooking, stirring occasionally, until liver is no longer pink when slashed (about 7 minutes).

Place liver mixture in a blender or food processor. Add 3 tablespoons **dry sherry** and 6 tablespoons **butter** or margarine, softened. Whirl until smooth. Spoon into a bowl and season to taste with **salt** and **pepper.**

Cover and refrigerate for at least 4 hours or up to 3 days. Let stand at room temperature for 20 minutes before serving. Makes about 1 cup.

Showmanship with Flaming Game Hens (Recipe on facing page)

1 Baste hens during last half-hour of roasting time. Use bulb baster and tip pan slightly to retrieve drippings from under roasting rack.

2 Gradually pour cornstarch-water mixture into cherry sauce and stir constantly until sauce comes to a boil.

3 Sauce is done when it thickens slightly and turns from opaque to clear. Whole cherries, lemon juice and peel, and pan juices enrich sauce.

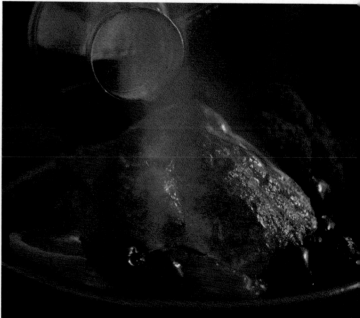

4 Arrange hens on individual plates and spoon hot cherry sauce over each. Then heat brandy in a small container. At the table, ignite, and pour over hens.

Rock Cornish game hens

Plump with white meat only, these dainty birds are exquisite company fare. For a hearty portion, you can offer a 1-pound game hen whole for each serving. A larger hen (1½ pounds) will serve two nicely when paired with a savory stuffing.

Game Hens with Flaming Cherry Sauce

(Pictured on facing page)

2 **Rock Cornish game hens** (about 1 lb. *each*)
   Salt and pepper
2 tablespoons **butter or margarine,** melted
¼ teaspoon *each* **ground ginger, paprika, and salt**
   Cherry sauce (recipe follows)
   Orange slices
3 tablespoons **brandy** (optional)

Rinse hens and pat dry. Sprinkle cavities with salt and pepper. Place hens, breast side up, on a rack in a roasting pan. In a small pan, combine butter with ginger, paprika, and the ¼ teaspoon salt; brush over hens. Bake, uncovered, in a 375° oven for 45 to 60 minutes or until leg joint moves easily; during last half-hour, baste occasionally with pan drippings.

Meanwhile, prepare cherry sauce. When hens are roasted, skim and discard fat from pan juices and stir juices into sauce. Arrange hens on individual plates and garnish with orange slices. Spoon cherry sauce over hens. If desired, warm brandy in a small pan; set aflame (*not* beneath an exhaust fan or flammable items) and pour over birds. Makes 2 servings.

Cherry sauce. Drain 1 small can (about 8 oz.) pitted **dark sweet cherries,** reserving ⅓ cup of the syrup. Set cherries aside. In a small pan, combine reserved syrup with ⅔ cup regular-strength **chicken broth;** 1 small **onion,** cut into wedges; 8 **whole cloves;** and ¼ teaspoon **ground cinnamon.** Bring to a boil, stirring; reduce heat and simmer, uncovered, for 10 minutes. Strain, discarding cloves and onion.

Return sauce to pan. In a measuring cup, stir together 1½ tablespoons **cornstarch** and 3 tablespoons **water** until smooth; stir into sauce and cook over medium heat, stirring, until sauce boils and thickens slightly. Stir in cherries, ¼ teaspoon **grated lemon peel,** and 1 tablespoon **lemon juice.**

GLAZED GAME HENS

Prepare **Game Hens with Flaming Cherry Sauce,** but omit cherry sauce. Increase **butter** or margarine in basting sauce to 4 tablespoons. Place 1 tablespoon basting sauce inside of each hen; brush remaining sauce over hens before roasting. Heat 3 tablespoons strained **apricot jam** over low heat. During last 15 minutes of roasting, brush birds several times with jam. Serve birds whole or, if large, cut in half with kitchen scissors.

Game Hens with Spinach-Rice Stuffing

   Spinach-rice stuffing (recipe follows)
3 **Rock Cornish game hens** (20 to 24 oz. *each*)
4 tablespoons **butter or margarine**
1 **green onion** (including top), minced
1 tablespoon finely chopped **parsley**
¼ teaspoon *each* **dry mustard and fines herbes**

Prepare spinach-rice stuffing. With kitchen scissors, cut hens in half lengthwise. Rinse and pat dry. Press ¾ cup of the stuffing onto cut side of each hen half. Holding stuffing in place with your hand, arrange hens, skin side up, in a greased shallow baking pan.

Melt butter in a small pan over low heat; stir in onion, parsley, mustard, and fines herbes. Brush over hens. Bake, uncovered, in a 375° oven for 45 to 60 minutes or until leg joint moves easily; during last half-hour, baste occasionally with pan drippings. Makes 6 servings.

Spinach-rice stuffing. Cut ¾ pound **spinach** into ¼-inch-wide strips. Heat 2 tablespoons **salad oil** in a wide frying pan over medium-high heat. Add spinach; 1 can (8 oz.) **water chestnuts,** sliced; 3 **green onions** (including tops), sliced; and 1 stalk **celery,** finely chopped. Cover and cook for 2 minutes; uncover and continue cooking for 1 more minute. Remove from heat and stir in 2 cups cold **cooked rice** and ¼ teaspoon **dry rosemary.** Season to taste with **salt** and **pepper.**

Turkey

Turkey, either in parts or ground, is widely available and attractively modest both in cost and in calories.

Braised Turkey Legs

- ½ **cup all-purpose flour**
- 1 **teaspoon** *each* **salt and oregano leaves**
- ½ **teaspoon pepper**
- 4 **turkey drumsticks (about 5 lbs.** *total***)**
- ¼ **cup olive oil or salad oil**
- 2 **large onions, chopped**
- 2 **cloves garlic, minced or pressed**
- 1 **cup regular-strength chicken broth**
- ½ **cup dry red wine**
- 1 **bay leaf**
- ½ **teaspoon** *each* **thyme leaves and dry rosemary**

In a rimmed plate or pie pan, combine flour, salt, oregano, and pepper. Dredge drumsticks in flour mixture; set remaining flour mixture aside.

Heat oil in a wide frying pan over medium heat; add turkey and cook until browned on all sides. Transfer to a 4 to 6-quart casserole or roasting pan. Add onions and garlic to pan drippings and cook until onions are soft. Stir in broth, wine, bay leaf, thyme, and rosemary, scraping browned particles free from pan. Pour broth mixture over turkey, cover, and bake in a 350° oven for 2 to 2½ hours or until fork-tender.

Lift out turkey and arrange on a platter. Measure reserved flour mixture and blend with an equal amount of cold water. Stir into pan juices. Cook, stirring, until gravy boils and thickens. Spoon some of the gravy over turkey; pass remaining gravy at the table. Makes 4 servings.

Turkey Piccata

- 2 **to 3 pounds boneless uncooked turkey breast, skinned**
- ½ **teaspoon** *each* **garlic powder, pepper, and dry basil**
  All-purpose flour
- 2 **tablespoons butter or margarine**
- 2 **tablespoons olive oil or salad oil**
- 1 **cup regular-strength beef broth**
- 3 **tablespoons lemon juice**
- 1 **lemon, thinly sliced**
- 2 **tablespoons capers, drained**

Cut turkey breast with the grain into ¼ to ⅜-inch slices. Pound any end chunks to about ¼ inch thick. In a small bowl, combine garlic powder, pepper, and basil; rub into turkey slices. Dredge turkey in flour until evenly coated, shaking off excess. Heat butter and oil in a wide frying pan over medium-high heat; add turkey slices, a few at a time, and cook until lightly browned on both sides (about 4 minutes total). Lift out and set aside.

Add broth and lemon juice to pan drippings; cook for about 1 minute, scraping browned particles free from pan. Return turkey to pan and arrange lemon slices on top; cover and simmer until meat is no longer pink when slashed (about 3 minutes). Transfer turkey and sauce to a platter. Sprinkle with capers. Makes 6 to 8 servings.

Hot Turkey Meatball Salad

- 1 **pound ground turkey**
- 1 **egg, lightly beaten**
- ⅓ **cup chopped green onions (including tops)**
- 4 **teaspoons soy sauce**
- 2 **tablespoons golden sherry**
- ¼ **cup fine dry bread crumbs**
- 1 **can (8 oz.) water chestnuts, chopped**
  Brown sauce (recipe follows)
- 1 **head iceberg lettuce, finely shredded**
- ¼ **cup thinly sliced green onions (including tops)**
- 1 **lemon, cut into wedges**

In a bowl, combine turkey, egg, the ⅓ cup chopped onions, soy, sherry, bread crumbs, and water chestnuts. Mix well; cover and refrigerate for 2 hours or until firm enough to shape. Shape into 1-inch balls and place about 1½ inches apart on 2 greased rimmed baking sheets. Bake, uncovered, in a 450° oven for about 8 minutes.

Meanwhile, prepare brown sauce. Spread lettuce on a platter. Spoon meatballs on top; sprinkle with the ¼ cup sliced onions and garnish with lemon wedges. Serve immediately. Pass brown sauce at the table. Makes 4 servings.

Brown sauce. In a small pan, combine 1 teaspoon **sugar** and 1 tablespoon **cornstarch.** Add 1 tablespoon **golden sherry,** 2 teaspoons **soy sauce,** ½ teaspoon **vinegar,** and 1½ cups regular-strength **chicken broth;** stir until smooth. Cook over medium heat, stirring, until sauce boils and thickens.

Poultry stuffings

For this versatile stuffing recipe, use day-old bread—stuffing made with soft, fresh bread becomes mushy with cooking. If you have only fresh bread on hand, place slices in a 150° oven for a few minutes until dried throughout.

You can prepare the stuffing up to a day in advance, then cover and refrigerate it. But to ensure against food poisoning, *do not* stuff your bird until just before roasting. And after the bird is cooked, spoon out all the stuffing and refrigerate any leftovers.

As the bird cooks, the stuffing will expand, so be sure to pack the stuffing into the cavities with a light hand. Place any stuffing you can't fit into the bird in a lightly greased baking dish; cover and cook it alongside the bird during the last hour of roasting. For a crunchy texture, uncover the stuffing after 30 minutes.

Old-fashioned Bread Stuffing

    ¾ cup (¼ lb. plus 4 tablespoons) butter or
       margarine
    3 large onions, chopped
  1½ teaspoons marjoram leaves
    ¾ teaspoon *each* pepper, ground sage, and
       thyme leaves
   12 cups day-old whole wheat or white bread
       (or a combination of the two), cut into ½-inch
       cubes
    2 cups chopped celery
    ½ cup chopped parsley
       Salt

Melt ½ cup of the butter in a wide frying pan over medium heat. Add onions and cook, stirring occasionally, until golden (about 15 minutes). Add remaining 4 tablespoons butter, marjoram, pepper, sage, and thyme. Remove from heat.

In a 5-quart container, combine bread cubes, celery, and parsley; add onion mixture. With 2 spoons, toss until bread cubes are slightly moistened. Season to taste with salt. If made ahead, cover and refrigerate for up to a day; let stand at room temperature for about 20 minutes before stuffing poultry. Makes about 14 cups.

GIBLET STUFFING

Place **giblets** (except livers) in a 1½-quart pan; cover with water. Bring to a boil over high heat; cover, reduce heat, and simmer until tender when pierced (about 1½ hours). Drain, then chop and add to **Old-fashioned Bread Stuffing** before tossing.

MUSHROOM STUFFING

Prepare **Old-fashioned Bread Stuffing,** but add 1 pound **mushrooms,** thinly sliced, to pan with onions; cook until all the liquid has evaporated. Reduce bread cubes to 10 cups.

OYSTER STUFFING

Prepare **Old-fashioned Bread Stuffing,** but use only 10 cups bread cubes. Add 2 jars (8 to 10 oz. *each*) **oysters,** drained and chopped, to bread cube mixture.

WATER CHESTNUT STUFFING

Prepare **Old-fashioned Bread Stuffing,** but use only 10 cups bread cubes. Add 2 cans (about 8 oz. *each*) **water chestnuts,** drained and chopped, to bread cube mixture.

HOW MUCH STUFFING TO ALLOW FOR POULTRY

Whether you're roasting chicken, game hens, or turkey (up to 14 pounds), allow about ¾ cup stuffing for each pound of poultry; for turkeys over 14 pounds, allow ½ cup stuffing for each pound.

Roast turkey with giblet gravy

The size turkey you roast depends on your guest list and on your fondness for leftovers. Generally, figure on about a pound of turkey (bone in) per person.

Preparing turkey. Remove neck and giblets; reserve for giblet gravy (below) or stuffing (page 97). Rinse bird inside and out; pat dry with paper towels.

To roast without stuffing, rub inside with salt, truss (see below), and roast as directed on page 81.

To stuff and truss, prepare stuffing (page 97). **Do not** stuff turkey until just before roasting. Lay turkey breast side down. Lightly stuff neck cavity (see photo 1 on facing page). Bring neck skin up and over cavity to enclose filling. With a metal skewer, fasten neck skin to back, pushing skewer in and out 3 times (photo 2).

Turn bird over; lightly stuff body cavity (photo 3). Place a heel of bread in cavity to secure stuffing. Tuck tail and legs under wire clamp (photo 4) or, if turkey has no clamp, use 3 or 4 metal skewers to close cavity (see *Illustration 1*); using white cotton string, lace up like a boot and tie securely (see *Illustration 2*).

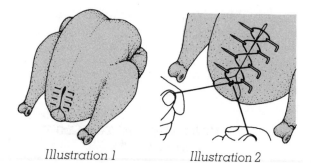

Illustration 1   Illustration 2

Place turkey, breast side up, on a rack in a shallow roasting pan. Insert a meat thermometer into thickest part of thigh meat, without touching bone. (Do this even if turkey has a pop-up thermometer; our testing indicates that sometimes the bird is overcooked before thermometer pops up.) Bend wing tips under neck (photo 5). Rub body with 2 tablespoons softened butter or margarine. Roast on lowest oven rack as directed on page 81.

Making giblet gravy. While turkey is roasting, place **neck** and **giblets** (except liver) in a 2-quart pan and cover with 4 cups **water.** Bring to a boil over high heat. Cover, reduce heat, and simmer until tender (about 1½ hours). Strain and reserve

stock; discard neck. Chop giblets, cover, and refrigerate.

Remove cooked turkey to a platter, lightly cover with foil, and let stand for 15 minutes before carving. Add 1 cup of the reserved **stock** to **pan drippings.** Place over medium heat, and scrape browned particles free from pan; pour mixture into a large measuring cup. Fat will rise to top of mixture.

Determine amount of gravy you want—for each cup liquid, you'll need 2 tablespoons *each* **fat** (from drippings) and **all-purpose flour.** Spoon fat off mixture in measuring cup; measure desired amount of fat and pour into a pan (if you don't have enough turkey fat, add butter); discard any remaining fat. Add enough of the reserved stock to drippings in cup to reach desired amount of liquid; set aside.

Heat fat over medium heat. Stir in flour (equal to amount of fat) and cook, stirring, until bubbly. Remove from heat. Gradually pour in stock mixture, stirring constantly. Return to heat and cook, stirring, until gravy boils and thickens. For thinner gravy, add more broth. Stir in giblets and season to taste with **salt** and **pepper.**

Carving the bird. Before carving, lightly cover turkey with foil and let stand for 15 minutes. To remove thighs and legs, pull leg down and sever thigh from body at thigh joint. Locate joint between drumstick and thigh; pull down on leg and sever drumstick. Thinly slice thigh and leg meat. Cut off wings at shoulder joint. Make a horizontal cut under ribs near neck, cutting through to bone (see *Illustration 3*). Slice meat down at right angle to cut, following contour of bones (see *Illustration 4*).

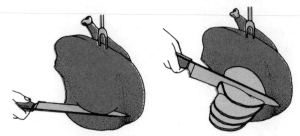

Illustration 3   Illustration 4

Stuffing a turkey (Directions on facing page)

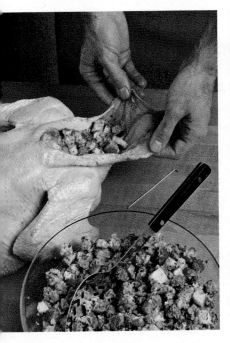

1 Place turkey on counter, breast side down; lightly fill neck cavity with stuffing.

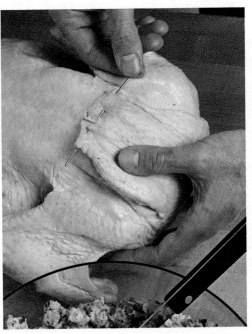

2 Bring neck skin up over cavity. With a metal skewer, fasten neck skin to back, pushing skewer in and out 3 times through neck and back skin.

3 Turn turkey over and loosely pack body cavity with stuffing. Secure stuffing with heel of bread.

4 Slip tail and legs under wire clamp or sew cavity closed (see *Illustrations 1* and *2* on facing page). Bake remaining stuffing with turkey.

5 Bend wing tips under body (tips support neck and help keep turkey level).

6 Roasted turkey with all the trimmings—sumptuous fare that includes moist, savory stuffing concealed inside bird and under crisp brown skin at neck.

FISH & SHELLFISH

FISH

Fish today is a high-fashion food—an answer to the contemporary cook's concern for the lean and natural. Once chosen primarily to vary the weekly menu and ease the budget, fish now symbolizes light, delicious, and elegant dining. One of the easiest and most impressive company entrées, fish also makes an excellent hurry-up meal.

Markets offer a wide selection of good fish buys, despite rising prices and some shortages in the case of particularly popular fish. Varieties once sold only near the source of the catch are now shipped virtually everywhere in the country. At the same time, we're discovering the good taste of new varieties once overlooked by commercial fishermen.

You can buy fish cut into steaks or fillets *(see illustration)*, or you can buy fish whole. Expect about half the weight of whole fish to be edible; steaks and boneless fillets are almost entirely edible. No matter what form you select, start with the freshest fish you can find. The flesh of whole fish should spring back when gently pressed, and the eyes should be clear and full, not sunken. When shopping for fillets and steaks, look for moist, firm flesh. Keep your fresh fish refrigerated and cook it within 2 days.

In many areas, fresh fish is simply not available. Though it's true that freshly caught fish tastes best, keep in mind that processed-at-sea frozen fish may be fresher than a catch that has waited for you in the market for several days.

Always thaw frozen fish in the refrigerator, because freezing and thawing breaks down fish fibers, increasing the possibility of spoilage. For this reason, you should also plan to cook frozen fish the same day it is thawed, and never refreeze partially or completely thawed fish. **If you plan to prepare thawed frozen fish with a coating, first pat the fish dry with paper towels.**

Besides whole frozen fish, 1-pound packages of sole, cod, perch, and haddock fillets are widely available, too. This chapter gives directions for cooking these blocks of frozen fish without thawing.

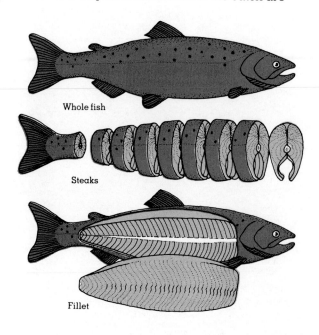

Whole fish

Steaks

Fillet

How long to cook fish

If fish were shaped like building blocks, cooking times would be a snap to calculate. Very large fish are cut into steaks of even thickness, but most whole fish and fish fillets have irregular shapes. To estimate a cooking time, lay the fillet, steak, or whole fish flat on a counter and measure its thickest portion—either by eyeballing or by actually standing a ruler beside the fish.

A good rule of thumb for *pan-frying or poaching* is to allow 8 to 10 minutes of cooking per inch of thickness. If the thickness is more or less than an inch, you adjust the cooking time to maintain this ratio of 8:1 or 10:1. For example, a ½-inch-thick fillet will cook in 4 to 5 minutes. This rule doesn't apply to *baked* fish, because a sauce or topping will affect the cooking time.

Baked fish

A little short on time and energy? Try baking your fish. This simple approach requires little last-minute activity. But remember to set your timer so you'll know when to test the fish for doneness.

Cheesy Fish Sticks

- 1 **cup fine dry bread crumbs**
- 1 **cup (4 oz.) shredded sharp Cheddar cheese**
- ¼ **cup salad oil**
- ½ **teaspoon salt**
- 1 **clove garlic, minced or pressed**
- 2 **pounds firm-textured white fish fillets (halibut, rockfish, sea bass, swordfish), *each* ¾ to 1 inch thick**

Preheat oven to 450°. In a blender or food processor, whirl bread crumbs and cheese together (a portion at a time, if necessary) until mixture looks like cornmeal. Turn out onto a piece of wax paper.

In a bowl, combine salad oil, salt, and garlic. Cut fillets crosswise into 1½-inch-wide strips. Dip each strip into seasoned oil, then coat on both sides with cheese mixture. Arrange in a single layer, without crowding, in a lightly greased baking pan. Bake, uncovered, for 6 to 8 minutes or until fish tests done (see above). Makes 6 servings.

TESTING FISH FOR DONENESS

For years, recipes have recommended cooking fish until it flakes easily when prodded in the thickest portion with a fork. ("Flaking" means that the flesh slides apart along natural divisions.)

Our testing indicates that cooking to this stage is usually a touch too much, since fish continues to cook from its own internal heat during the interval between cooking and serving. A better method is to cook the fish until the flesh inside is just slightly opaque. If you do this, the fish will flake by the time it arrives at the table.

As fish cooks, its translucent flesh changes to opaque white (or pink, in the case of salmon). *Near the end of the estimated cooking time, make this test for doneness: Cut a slit in the center of the thickest portion of the fish. When the flesh inside is just slightly opaque and has lost its wet look, take the fish off the heat.*

Baked Fish Provençal

- 3 **tablespoons butter or margarine**
- ¼ **pound mushrooms, thinly sliced**
- 2 **small tomatoes, peeled and chopped**
- 2 **cloves garlic, minced or pressed**
  Salt and pepper
- 2 **pounds fish steaks (halibut, ling cod, salmon, sea bass, swordfish), *each* about 1 inch thick**
- ⅓ **pound small cooked shrimp**
  Tomato wedges, ripe olives, parsley sprigs, and lemon wedges

Preheat oven to 400°. Melt butter in a wide frying pan over medium heat. Add mushrooms and cook until soft; stir in tomatoes and garlic. Season to taste with salt and pepper and heat through.

Arrange fish in a single layer in a greased shallow baking pan. Sprinkle fish lightly with salt and pepper. Arrange shrimp over fish, and spoon hot mushroom mixture over shrimp.

Bake, uncovered, for 12 to 15 minutes or until fish tests done (see above). Transfer to a platter. Garnish with tomato wedges, olives, parsley sprigs, and lemon wedges. Makes 6 servings.

Pan-frying your favorite fish fillets (Recipe on facing page)

1 Assemble flour, egg mixture, and fish before heating pan and oil. Coat fish just before placing in hot oil.

2 Don't crowd pan—you'll need room to turn pieces over easily. Use brown-ahead, bake-later technique, as shown, or cook fish completely.

3 Make almond butter sauce just before serving. When butter is foamy, stir in almonds and cook until golden, then add lemon juice and wine.

4 Cook-ahead approach frees you to take care of other details for a company meal. Just top fish with the flavorful sauce and serve.

...Baked fish

Baked Fish Florentine

- 1 **pound mild-flavored white fish fillets (red snapper, sea bass, turbot), *each* about ¾ inch thick**
  Salt and pepper
- ¾ **cup sour cream**
- ⅓ **cup mayonnaise**
- 2 **tablespoons *each* all-purpose flour and lemon juice**
- ¼ **teaspoon dill weed**
- 2 **bunches spinach (about 1½ lbs. *total*), stemmed and well rinsed**
  Paprika

Preheat oven to 400°. Arrange fish fillets in a single layer in a greased 9 by 13-inch baking pan. Sprinkle fish lightly with salt and pepper. With a wire whisk, blend sour cream, mayonnaise, flour, lemon juice, and dill until smooth; spread over fish. Bake, uncovered, for about 10 minutes or until fish tests done (see page 101).

Meanwhile, put spinach (with water that clings to leaves) in a wide frying pan over medium-high heat. Cover and cook, stirring occasionally, until spinach wilts (2 to 4 minutes); drain.

Arrange spinach in a single layer on a platter; place cooked fish on top. Spoon any extra sauce from baking dish over fish and sprinkle with paprika. Makes 4 servings.

Pan-fried fish

Pan-frying is a quick and easy method of turning fish fillets, fish steaks, or small whole fish into glorious golden entrées of crisp-coated, buttery tenderness. The French counterpart of pan-frying is termed *à la meunière*, or butter-sautéing.

Because they cook so quickly, thin fillets brown better if they're first dusted with flour or dipped in a coating. Firmer, thicker pieces don't need coating to brown well, but you may enjoy the flavor boost.

If the fish is moist, dry it with paper towels before coating and cooking.

Fish Fillets with Almond Butter

(Pictured on facing page)

You can complete the cooking on top of the range, or use the brown-ahead, bake-later technique.

- 3 **eggs**
- 2 **tablespoons grated Parmesan cheese**
- 1 **tablespoon chopped parsley**
- ½ **teaspoon salt**
- ¼ **teaspoon pepper**
  About ½ cup all-purpose flour
  About 3 tablespoons olive oil
- 2 **to 2½ pounds firm-textured white fish fillets, each ¾ to 1 inch thick**
- ½ **cup butter**
- ¼ **cup sliced almonds**
- 3 **tablespoons lemon juice**
- 2 **tablespoons dry white wine**

In a rimmed plate or pie pan, beat eggs until well blended. Stir in cheese, parsley, salt, and pepper. Have flour ready on another plate. Heat 2 tablespoons of the oil in a wide frying pan over medium heat until oil ripples when pan is tilted.

While oil is heating, dredge a piece of fish in flour on all sides; shake off excess. Dip into egg mixture; drain briefly, then place in hot pan. Continue coating fish as needed to fill pan. Cook until fish is golden brown and tests done (see page 101) —takes 3 to 5 minutes on each side, depending on thickness. Transfer fish to a platter, cover loosely, and keep warm. Repeat, adding oil as needed, until all fish are cooked.

Melt butter in a clean pan over medium heat. When butter foams, stir in almonds and cook just until they begin to brown. Turn off heat and stir in lemon juice and wine. Spoon sauce over fish and serve immediately. Makes 6 to 8 servings.

Brown-ahead, bake-later technique. Fish pieces should be at least ¾ inch thick. Follow directions for coating and pan-frying, but increase heat to medium-high and fry fish just until golden brown (about 1 minute on each side). Arrange fish in an ovenproof serving dish; cover loosely and set aside at room temperature for up to 1 hour. Bake, uncovered, in a preheated 375° oven for 10 minutes or until fish tests done (see page 101). Spoon sauce over fish.

...Pan-fried fish

FISH FILLETS WITH MUSHROOM BUTTER

Pan-fry fish fillets as directed on page 103, but omit almond butter. Melt 2 tablespoons **butter** or margarine in a wide frying pan over medium-high heat. Add ¼ pound **mushrooms,** sliced; 2 **shallots** or green onions, chopped; 1 clove **garlic,** minced or pressed; ¼ teaspoon **dry tarragon;** and a dash of **pepper.** Cook, stirring, until mushrooms are lightly browned. Turn off heat and stir in 1 tablespoon *each* **lemon juice** and minced **parsley.** Pour sauce over fish.

FISH FILLETS WITH TOMATO-CAPER SAUCE

Pan-fry fish fillets as directed on page 103, but omit almond butter. Melt 4 tablespoons **butter** or margarine in a wide frying pan over medium heat. Add 1 medium-size **onion,** chopped, and 1 clove **garlic,** minced or pressed. Cook, stirring, until onion is soft. Add 1 can (about 1 lb.) Italian-style **tomatoes** (break up with a spoon) and their liquid, and 2 teaspoons **capers.** Stirring occasionally, simmer, uncovered, until sauce thickens. Stir in 1 tablespoon **lemon juice** and 2 tablespoons minced **parsley.** Keep hot or, if made ahead, reheat. Spoon over fish.

Hemingway's Trout

6 whole cleaned trout (about 8 oz. *each*)
1 cup milk
3 green onions (including tops), chopped
1 tablespoon chopped parsley
2 tablespoons lemon juice
¼ teaspoon pepper
  Salt
6 strips bacon
½ cup all-purpose flour
2 tablespoons yellow cornmeal
  Lemon wedges (optional)

Arrange fish in a single layer in a baking dish; pour milk over fish and let stand for 10 minutes. In a small bowl, combine onions, parsley, lemon juice, and pepper. Remove fish from milk; sprinkle cavity of each trout with salt and spread with onion mixture.

In a wide frying pan over medium heat, cook bacon until crisp. Remove bacon from pan, drain,

and set aside. Leave 3 tablespoons drippings in pan; reserve remaining drippings.

Combine flour and cornmeal on a piece of wax paper; dredge trout in mixture until coated on both sides. Heat the 3 tablespoons bacon drippings in pan over medium heat; arrange half the fish in pan. Cook, turning once, until fish tests done (see page 101)—takes 4 to 5 minutes on each side. Transfer fish to a platter, cover loosely, and keep warm. Cook remaining fish, adding reserved drippings as needed. Slip a bacon strip into cavity of each fish. Garnish with lemon wedges, if desired. Makes 6 servings.

Sole with Grapes

1 to 1½ pounds fillet of sole or skinless flounder, *each* fillet ½ to ¾ inch thick
  Salt
  Ground nutmeg
  All-purpose flour
  About 2 tablespoons butter or margarine
  About 2 tablespoons salad oil
1 cup seedless grapes
½ cup whipping cream

Sprinkle fish lightly with salt and nutmeg. Dust with flour; shake off excess.

Heat half the butter and salad oil in a wide frying pan over medium heat until it foams. Add fish, without crowding, and cook, turning once, until fish is golden and tests done (see page 101)—

DO'S AND DON'TS OF PAN-FRYING

● *Do* use a frying pan that distributes heat evenly. A heavy pan is best.
● *Don't* use butter alone for the cooking fat; it burns easily. Half butter and half salad or olive oil (or all olive oil) provides the best flavor without chance of burning.
● *Don't* dredge fish ahead of time. Doing it at the last minute ensures a crisp crust.
● *Don't* start with a cold pan. Heat butter-oil combination until it foams; heat oil until it ripples.
● *Do* give fish plenty of pan space. If necessary, cook in two batches so you have room to turn fish without breaking it.

takes 4 to 7 minutes total, depending on thickness. Transfer fish to a platter, cover loosely, and keep warm. Repeat, adding butter and oil as needed, until all fish are cooked.

When last fish is removed, add grapes to pan, increase heat to high, and swirl grapes just until warm and bright green. Pour over fish.

Add cream to pan and boil over high heat, stirring and scraping to blend with pan drippings, until cream is light golden; drizzle over fish and grapes. Serve immediately. Makes 3 or 4 servings.

Fish Steaks with Rosemary

1	to 1½ pounds halibut, salmon, or swordfish steaks, *each* about 1 inch thick
	Salt and pepper
	All-purpose flour
⅓	cup olive oil
¼	cup white wine vinegar
2	tablespoons water
3	cloves garlic
½	teaspoon fresh or dry rosemary

Lightly sprinkle fish with salt and pepper. Dust with flour, shaking off excess. Heat oil in a wide frying pan over medium heat until oil ripples when pan is tilted. Add fish, without crowding, and cook, turning once, until fish tests done (see page 101)—takes 4 to 5 minutes on each side. Transfer to a platter, cover loosely, and keep warm.

Add vinegar and water to pan drippings. When sizzling stops, add garlic and rosemary. Boil rapidly, scraping browned particles free from pan, until sauce is reduced by half. Discard garlic. Spoon sauce over fish and serve immediately. Makes 3 or 4 servings.

Poached fish

Poaching is unmatched as a way of preparing seafood. The fish simmers in a seasoned broth that adds its own delicate flavor. Any variety of fish can be poached, but the method is best suited to varieties with low fat content, such as sole and turbot; to fatter fish, such as salmon; or to mild-flavored fish, such as trout. All forms of fish—fillets, steaks, whole fish, or even packages of frozen fish fillets—lend themselves to poaching.

Pan Poaching to Suit Any Fish

In the classic method of poaching, fish is completely immersed in seasoned liquid. After the fish cooks, the liquid is reduced (cooked down), then combined with butter and flour to make a sauce.

But in the short-cut method that follows, you poach with less liquid, then boil the pan juices alone for just a few minutes to make a naturally thickened sauce.

Our directions include two poaching broths. The onion-wine broth suits fish with a mild to moderate flavor, such as ling cod, halibut, snapper, and sole. The herb-tomato broth (page 106) is best with moderate to more richly flavored fish, such as rockfish, salmon, and swordfish.

Have ready 1 to 1½ pounds **fish** fillets, steaks, or small whole cleaned fish, or a 1-pound package of frozen fish fillets. Prepare a **poaching broth** (recipes follow) in a wide frying pan and bring to a slow boil. Arrange fish in a single layer in pan, or place frozen block of fish in pan. Cover pan; reduce heat to keep broth simmering.

Simmer thin fillets (¼ to ⅓ inch thick) without turning until they test done (see page 101)—takes 3 to 4 minutes. Simmer ½ to 1-inch-thick pieces, or whole fish up to 1½ inches thick, until they test done—takes 4 to 10 minutes, depending on thickness. Simmer block of frozen fish in the hot liquid for 15 to 18 minutes (spread frozen fillets flat in pan when they're thawed) or until they test done.

With a wide spatula, remove fish to a warm plate; cover and keep warm. Boil juices in pan over high heat until reduced to a medium-thick sauce. Season to taste with **salt, pepper,** and **lemon juice;** pour over fish. Garnish with **chopped parsley** or avocado slices, if desired. Makes 3 or 4 servings.

Onion-wine broth. Melt 1 tablespoon **butter** or margarine in a wide frying pan over medium heat. Add 2 or 3 **green onions,** thinly sliced, or 2 shallots, finely chopped; and 1 clove **garlic,** minced or pressed. Cook, stirring, until soft (about 3 minutes). Stir in ¼ cup *each* **dry white wine** and regular-strength **chicken broth,** or ½ cup chicken broth only.

...Poached fish

Tomato-herb broth. Melt 1 tablespoon **butter** or margarine in a wide frying pan over medium heat. Add 1 medium-size **onion,** chopped; and 1 clove **garlic,** minced or pressed. Cook, stirring, until soft (about 3 minutes). Stir in 1 large **tomato** (peeled and diced) or 1 cup canned tomatoes (break up with a spoon) and their liquid, ¼ cup **dry white wine** or regular-strength chicken broth, ½ teaspoon *each* **dry basil** and **oregano leaves,** and a dash of **pepper.** Bring to a boil; cover, reduce heat, and simmer for 5 minutes.

Poached Fish in Cheese Sauce

- 1½   tablespoons lemon juice
- 1   bay leaf
- ¼   cup dry white wine
- 3   black peppercorns
- 3   sprigs parsley
- ¼   teaspoon salt
- 1   package (1 lb.) frozen fish fillets (unthawed)
- 6   *each* small red or white thin-skinned potatoes and small white boiling onions (cut in half, if larger than 1½ inches in diameter)
- 1   cup frozen peas (unthawed)
- 2   tablespoons butter or margarine
- 1½   tablespoons all-purpose flour
- ¼   cup milk or half-and-half (light cream)
- ¼   teaspoon dry mustard
- ⅔   cup shredded Swiss cheese
    Dash of ground nutmeg

In a wide frying pan, combine lemon juice, bay leaf, wine, peppercorns, parsley, and salt. Add fish, potatoes, and onions; then add water just to cover fish. Bring to a boil; cover, reduce heat, and simmer until fish is almost opaque throughout (about 15 minutes).

Add peas; cover and simmer until fish tests done (see page 101)—takes 4 to 6 more minutes. With a slotted spatula, transfer fish and vegetables to a rimmed platter; cover and keep warm. (If potatoes are not done, cover and continue cooking them alone until tender.) Boil poaching liquid, uncovered, until reduced to ¾ cup. Strain liquid into bowl; set liquid aside and discard seasonings.

Melt butter in a pan over low heat. Stir in flour and cook until bubbly; remove from heat. Gradually whisk in reserved poaching liquid along with milk and mustard. Return to heat and cook, stir-

ring, until thickened. Add Swiss cheese and nutmeg; continue stirring, until cheese is melted. Pour over fish and vegetables. Makes 3 or 4 servings.

Rolled Sole Fillets with Dill Sauce

(Pictured on facing page)

- 2   tablespoons butter or margarine
- 1   *each* carrot and celery stalk, cut into julienne strips
    White part of 1 leek, cut into julienne strips, or 1 small onion, cut in half and sliced lengthwise
- 8   sole fillets, *each* ¼ to ⅜ inch thick
    Salt and pepper
    Dill weed
    About ½ cup *each* water and dry white wine
- ½   cup half-and-half (light cream)
- 3   tablespoons butter or margarine
- 3   tablespoons all-purpose flour
- ½   teaspoon Dijon mustard

Melt the 2 tablespoons butter in a wide frying pan over medium heat. Stir in carrot, celery, and leek; cook for 2 minutes. Cover pan, reduce heat to low, and continue cooking until vegetables are tender (about 5 minutes). Let cool slightly.

Place a fillet, skinned side down, on work surface. Sprinkle lightly with salt, pepper, and dill. Place a small bundle of butter-steamed vegetable strips across one end of fillet, and roll fillet into a cylinder. Repeat until all fillets are filled and rolled. Without crowding, arrange fish rolls, seam side down, in a pan at least 3 inches deep. If done ahead, cover and refrigerate for as long as 4 hours.

Pour enough water and wine over fish so poaching liquid is ½ inch deep. Heat, uncovered, over high heat, just until small bubbles form. Immediately reduce heat to low, cover pan, and simmer until fish tests done (see page 101)—takes 10 to 15 minutes. With a slotted spatula, transfer rolls to a platter; cover loosely and keep warm.

Measure 1 cup of poaching liquid (discard remainder) and combine with half-and-half. To make a *roux*, melt the 3 tablespoons butter in a pan over medium heat; stir in flour and cook, stirring, until bubbly (about 1 minute); remove from heat. Gradually stir in half-and-half mixture. Return to heat and cook, stirring, until thickened. Stir in mustard, salt, pepper, and dill to taste. Spoon sauce over fish. Makes 4 servings.

Poaching Rolled Sole Fillets (Recipe on facing page)

1 Roll up strips of butter-steamed vegetables in sole fillets. No need to skewer them closed; fish rolls seal themselves during poaching.

2 Simmer gently in mixture of wine and water. Stop the cooking as soon as fish tests done (see page 101). Fish will continue to cook from its own heat while you prepare dill sauce.

3 Remove pan from heat before pouring poaching liquid and half-and-half into butter-flour *roux*. Return to heat; then cook and stir until sauce boils and thickens.

4 Celebrate the joys of the season with steamed asparagus and sole fillets bathed in creamy dill sauce. Rice & Vermicelli Pilaf (page 121) completes the meal.

SHELLFISH

Crusty little creatures of the ocean, shellfish live a shadowy existence until they reach a good cook's kitchen. Then they hit the gourmet limelight—and you'll know why when you try some of these recipes.

Clams

With canned clams in your cupboard, you can turn out a memorable meal in minutes. Live hard-shell clams need a bit more attention. They should be refrigerated, cleaned completely, and eaten within a day after purchase.

Scrub the shells thoroughly under cold water with a stiff-bristled brush. Before cooking, check to be sure no clams are dead—with hard-shell clams, a gaping shell that refuses to close when touched indicates the clam is dead and must be discarded. The reverse is true after cooking—discard any clams that haven't opened.

New England Clam Chowder

- 4 strips bacon, diced
- 1 *each* medium-size onion, carrot, and celery stalk, chopped
- 3 medium-size (about 1½ lbs.) potatoes, peeled and cut into ½-inch cubes
- 2 cups water
- 1 teaspoon *each* salt and Worcestershire
- ¼ teaspoon pepper
- 4 drops liquid hot pepper seasoning
- 1 pint (2 cups) half-and-half (light cream) or milk
- 3 cans (6½ oz. *each*) chopped or minced clams
- 2 tablespoons chopped parsley

In a 3 or 4-quart pan over medium heat, cook bacon, stirring occasionally, until crisp. Spoon out all but 3 tablespoons of the drippings. To the remaining drippings and bacon, add onion, carrot, and celery; cook until onion is soft. Add potatoes, water, salt, Worcestershire, pepper, and hot pepper seasoning; bring to a boil. Reduce heat; cover and simmer for 15 minutes or until potatoes are fork-tender. Stir in half-and-half, clams and their liquid, and parsley. Heat just until piping hot; do not boil. Makes about 8 cups.

Steamed Clams

- 2 tablespoons olive oil or salad oil
- 1 large onion, chopped
- 2 cloves garlic, minced or pressed
- 1 teaspoon *each* dry basil and oregano leaves
- 3 tablespoons chopped parsley
- 1 cup dry white wine or regular-strength chicken broth
- 1 bottle (8 oz.) clam juice
- 20 to 30 small, live, hard-shell clams, well scrubbed
- 2 tomatoes, seeded and chopped
- 2 cups cooked rice (¾ cup uncooked rice)

Heat oil in a 5 or 6-quart kettle over medium heat. Add onion and garlic and cook, stirring, until onion is soft. Stir in basil, oregano, parsley, wine, and clam juice. Cover, reduce heat, and simmer for 5 minutes.

Add clams; cover and simmer until clams open (10 to 12 minutes). Discard any unopened clams. Stir in tomatoes and rice. Cover and cook until heated through. Ladle clams and broth into individual bowls. Makes 2 servings.

STEAMED CLAMS, LATIN-STYLE

Prepare **Steamed Clams,** but substitute ¼ teaspoon *each* **liquid hot pepper seasoning** and **ground cumin** for the basil, and reduce oregano to ½ teaspoon. Substitute 1 bottle (16 oz.) **seasoned clam and tomato-flavored cocktail** for wine and clam juice. Omit tomatoes and rice.

THE SECRET OF TENDER SHELLFISH

Clams, crabs, oysters, scallops, shrimp... each kind of shellfish has its own cooking time. But one rule prevails: shellfish should be cooked quickly to preserve the sweet, delicate flavors. When a recipe calls for precooked shellfish (such as canned clams for chowder or cooked crab for a casserole), assemble the dish as directed, then plan your time so you will heat it through just once and serve it as soon as it's bubbly.

Crab

Most whole crabs on the market today are already cooked. You can tell because the shells are usually tinged with red. If you live close to the source, you can buy cooked crab that has not been frozen. Farther afield, whole cooked crab may have been frozen and thawed—not quite so fresh, of course, but very tasty.

Though cooked, whole crab still needs to be cleaned and cracked (see illustrations below). Store it in the refrigerator until serving time, and use any crab—fresh or thawed—within a day after purchase. Four pounds of crab in the shell yield about 1 pound (4 servings) of crabmeat.

If you prefer to sidestep the effort of shelling crab, look for fresh or frozen cooked crabmeat; it has a more natural taste than canned crab.

Cracked Crab Fest

We call it "fest" because it's fun and delicious— and it's eaten with your fingers.

> Cooked whole crab in shell (allow 1 lb. of crab in shell per person; soft-shell crabs are not recommended)
> Hot piquant sauce (recipe follows)
> Tartar sauce (recipe follows)

Clean and crack cooked crab as shown in illustrations below. Mound on a tray; cover and chill until serving time. Pass one or both sauces in separate bowls at the table (each recipe makes enough for 4 to 6 servings). Provide nutcrackers and small forks for removing meat from shells.

Hot piquant sauce. In a 1-quart pan, combine ¼ cup *each* **tomato-based chili sauce** and **lemon juice,** 4 tablespoons **butter** or margarine, and 2 tablespoons *each* **Worcestershire** and **sugar.** Place on high heat and bring to a boil, stirring. Serve hot. Makes about ¾ cup.

Tartar sauce. In a small bowl, combine ½ cup *each* **mayonnaise** and **sour cream,** ¼ cup *each* chopped **dill pickle** and **green onion,** and 1 tablespoon **capers.** Makes about 1½ cups sauce.

Continental Crab

- ¼ **pound mushrooms, sliced**
- ¼ **cup seeded and chopped green pepper**
- 2 **tablespoons butter or margarine**
- 1½ **tablespoons all-purpose flour**
- ½ **cup half-and-half (light cream)**
- ¼ **cup dry white wine**
- 1 **tablespoon lemon juice**
- ¼ **teaspoon dill weed**
- ¼ **cup grated Parmesan cheese**
- ½ **pound crabmeat**
  Hot cooked rice
- 2 **green onions (including tops), thinly sliced**

In a wide frying pan over medium-high heat, cook mushrooms and green pepper in butter until mushrooms are soft and their juices have evaporated. Blend in flour and cook, stirring, until bubbly. Remove pan from heat and gradually stir in half-and-half and wine. Return to heat and cook, stirring constantly, until sauce boils and thickens. Stir in lemon juice, dill, and cheese; reduce heat to low and cook, uncovered, for 3 minutes. Stir in crab and cook just until heated through. Spoon over hot cooked rice and sprinkle with green onions. Makes 2 servings.

HOW TO CLEAN & CRACK COOKED CRAB

1 Remove claws and legs by twisting where they join body.

2 Holding each leg and claw on edge, crack shell with mallet.

3 Pull crab's back shell off. Discard gills, spongy parts. Rinse body.

4 Tap back of heavy knife with mallet to cut crab body in half.

Making a Crab Quiche (Recipe on facing page)

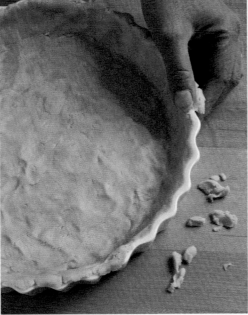

1 Press Butter Pastry dough evenly over bottom and up sides of quiche dish or pie pan. This pastry can take a lot of handling without becoming tough.

2 With thumb on top edge of dough and index finger on outside edge of dish, trim pastry even with top of pan.

3 Place foil in shell and partially fill with uncooked beans or rice. Bake for 10 minutes, lift off foil and beans, and bake shell for 5 more minutes. Save beans to use again for this purpose.

4 Layer crab and cheese filling. Pour egg-milk mixture over filling, taking care not to pour any of it between baked shell and pan—otherwise quiche will be difficult to remove after baking.

5 For ease in cutting neat wedges, let quiche stand for 10 minutes—this gives custard and cheese time to set. Garnish with parsley sprig.

...Crab

Crab Quiche

(Pictured on facing page)

Butter Pastry (page 167)
½ pound crabmeat or 1 can (9 oz.) chunk-style tuna, drained and flaked
1 cup (4 oz.) shredded Swiss cheese
¼ cup *each* grated Parmesan cheese and chopped green onions
1 jar (2 oz.) diced pimento, drained
3 eggs
1 cup milk
½ teaspoon salt
⅛ teaspoon pepper
¼ teaspoon ground nutmeg
Parsley sprigs

Preheat oven to 425°. Press pastry over bottom and up sides of a 1½-inch-deep, 9-inch quiche dish or pie pan. (Or, on a lightly floured board, roll out pastry to about ⅛-inch thickness and fit into dish or pan.) Place a piece of foil inside pastry shell and partially fill with uncooked beans or rice. Bake in a 425° oven for 10 minutes. Lift off foil and beans; return pastry to oven for 5 more minutes or until lightly browned. Remove from oven and let cool slightly. Reduce oven temperature to 350°.

In even layers, distribute crab, Swiss cheese, Parmesan cheese, green onion, and pimento in pastry shell. In a bowl, beat eggs, milk, salt, pepper, and nutmeg; pour over layers in shell. Bake for 45 minutes or until a knife inserted in center comes out clean. Let stand for 10 minutes before cutting. Garnish with parsley. Makes 6 servings.

Oysters

Before you buy a jar of shucked (shelled) oysters, be sure they're fresh. Look on the lid for an expiration date, and inspect the liquor (juices) surrounding the oysters—at least two-thirds of it should look clear rather than milky.

Oysters are graded by size and packed in jars marked to indicate weight (ounces) or volume (quarts, pints). As a rule of thumb, count on about 4 ounces (¼ pint) shucked oysters per person.

Do not wash oysters before cooking; the liquor contributes to the flavor. And despite its appearance, every bit of the oyster is edible.

Sautéed Oysters with Basil

8 ounces (½ pint) shucked fresh oysters, drained
All-purpose flour
2 tablespoons butter or margarine
½ teaspoon dry basil
2 tablespoons dry white wine

If oysters are large, cut them in half. Pat dry with paper towels. Dredge in flour and shake off excess. Melt butter in a medium-size frying pan over medium-high heat. When butter sizzles, add oysters and sprinkle with basil. Sauté just long enough to brown the flour coating and to heat oysters through (about 1½ minutes on each side); transfer oysters to a serving dish.

Pour wine into pan and cook, scraping browned particles free from pan, until sauce is reduced to 1 tablespoon. Spoon sauce over oysters. Makes 2 servings.

Oyster Crisp

Simple but spectacular, this quick casserole makes the most of oysters; it has sprightly hints of bacon, cheese, and crunchy crackers.

16 ounces (1 pint) shucked fresh oysters, with their liquor
¼ teaspoon salt
⅛ teaspoon *each* pepper and ground nutmeg
6 strips bacon, crisply cooked, drained, and crumbled
1 cup (4 oz.) shredded Swiss cheese
½ pint (1 cup) whipping cream
14 saltine crackers, coarsely crushed
2 tablespoons butter or margarine

Preheat oven to 400°. Pour oysters and their liquor into a greased shallow 1½-quart baking dish. If oysters are large, cut them into bite-size pieces. Sprinkle salt, pepper, and nutmeg over oysters, then scatter bacon over them, and top with cheese. Pour cream over all, cover with cracker crumbs, and dot with butter. Bake, uncovered, for 15 minutes or until edges of oysters begin to curl. Makes 4 servings.

Scallops

Two varieties of scallops are available, distinguished mainly by size. The smaller—and more delicately flavored—is the bay scallop; the larger and more common variety is the sea scallop. The two can be used interchangeably in recipes.

If scallops are frozen, thaw them in the refrigerator. If they appear sandy, rinse them with cold water before cooking, then pat dry with paper towels. One pound of scallops makes 3 or 4 servings.

Scallops & Mushrooms au Gratin

- 1 cup regular-strength chicken broth
- 1 pound scallops, cut into bite-size pieces
- 4 tablespoons butter or margarine
- ½ pound mushrooms, sliced
- 1½ teaspoons lemon juice
- 1 small onion, finely chopped
- 3 tablespoons all-purpose flour
- ¼ cup whipping cream
  Dash of nutmeg
- 1 tablespoon chopped parsley
- ¾ cup (3 oz.) shredded Swiss cheese
  Salt

In a wide frying pan over medium-high heat, bring broth to a boil. Add scallops; cover, reduce heat, and simmer for about 3 minutes or until scallops are barely opaque. With a slotted spoon, lift scallops from pan and set aside. Pour poaching liquid into a measuring cup—you should have 1 cup; if not, boil to reduce or add water to increase to 1 cup.

In same pan over medium-high heat, melt 1½ tablespoons of the butter. Add mushrooms and lemon juice and cook until mushrooms are lightly browned and juices have evaporated; remove mushrooms from pan and reserve.

In same pan, place onion and the remaining 2½ tablespoons butter and cook, stirring, until onion is soft. Stir in flour and cook until bubbly. Remove pan from heat and gradually stir in reserved poaching broth. Return to heat and cook, stirring, until sauce boils and thickens. Stir in reserved mushrooms, cream, and nutmeg. Remove from heat and stir in parsley, ¼ cup of the cheese, and scallops. Season to taste with salt. Divide mixture evenly among three 1½-cup ramekins or 6 purchased scallop shells and sprinkle remaining ½ cup cheese evenly over mixture in each. If made ahead, cool, cover, and refrigerate until next day.

Bake, uncovered, in a preheated 400° oven for 12 to 15 minutes or until hot and bubbly. Makes 6 appetizer servings or 3 main-dish servings.

Tarragon Scallop Sauté

- 6 tablespoons butter or margarine
- ½ teaspoon tarragon leaves
- 3 tablespoons chopped shallots or white part of green onions
- ½ pound mushrooms, sliced
- 1 pound scallops, cut into bite-size pieces
- 2 tablespoons dry white wine
  Chopped parsley
  Lemon wedges

Melt butter in a wide frying pan over medium-high heat. Add tarragon, shallots, and mushrooms; cook, stirring frequently, until mushrooms are soft. Push mushrooms to one side of pan and add scallops. Cook, turning with a wide spatula, just until scallops are opaque throughout (about 4 minutes). Sprinkle wine over scallops and cook for 1 more minute. Garnish each serving with parsley and lemon wedges. Makes 3 or 4 servings.

Broiled Ginger-Honey Scallops

- 3 tablespoons lemon juice
- 2 tablespoons salad oil
- 1 tablespoon *each* honey and soy sauce
- ¼ teaspoon ground ginger
- 1 small clove garlic, minced or pressed
- 1 pound scallops, cut into bite-size pieces

In a bowl, combine lemon juice, oil, honey, soy, ginger, and garlic. Add scallops and mix until well coated. Cover and refrigerate for 3 to 6 hours.

Lift scallops from marinade (reserve marinade) and thread on 4 skewers. Broil about 3 inches below heat, turning occasionally and basting with reserved marinade, just until scallops are opaque throughout (3 to 5 minutes). Makes 3 or 4 servings.

SESAME-COATED SCALLOPS

Toast ¼ cup **sesame seeds** in a heavy frying pan over medium heat, shaking pan occasionally, until they turn golden and begin to pop (about 2 minutes). Spread seeds on a plate. Prepare **Broiled Ginger-Honey Scallops.** After broiling, turn each skewer over in seeds to coat scallops evenly.

Seviche

A popular Mexican appetizer, seviche is made from raw scallops. But after marinating in lemon juice, the scallops look and taste as though they'd been poached.

> ¾ **pound scallops, thinly sliced across the grain**
> ½ **cup lemon juice**
> 2 **to 4 tablespoons diced canned green chiles**
> ¼ **cup minced onion**
> 1 **large tomato, peeled, seeded, and chopped**
> ½ **teaspoon salt**
> ¼ **teaspoon oregano leaves**
> 2 **tablespoons olive oil or salad oil**
> ½ **avocado**

In a bowl, combine scallops and lemon juice; cover and refrigerate for 2 to 4 hours. Stir in diced chiles, onion, tomato, salt, oregano, and olive oil. Dice avocado and stir in. Spoon scallops and marinade into cocktail or sherbet glasses. Makes 6 appetizer servings.

Shrimp

Shrimp come in many sizes. The tiny ones (150 to 180 per pound) are always sold cleaned and cooked and are a perfect choice for salads and seafood cocktails. Larger sizes are sold raw (in the shell) or cooked (in the shell or shelled).

When you plan to use one of the larger sizes, raw shrimp in the shell are the best buy. See the photos on page 115 for how to clean shrimp.

Use any shrimp—fresh, or frozen and thawed—within a day after purchase; and, of course, store them in the refrigerator. To estimate servings, expect 2 pounds of raw shrimp in the shell to yield 1 pound of shelled, deveined meat.

HOW TO COOK RAW SHRIMP

Shrimp cook well in or out of their shells, but they're easier to devein before cooking. Just remove the shell, make a shallow cut lengthwise down the back, and rinse out the sand vein. Or, cut the shell along the back with scissors and rinse out the vein.

In a deep pot, bring 4 cups **water** to a boil with 1 tablespoon **salt,** 2 tablespoons **lemon juice,** 1 sliced **onion,** and 1 **bay leaf.** Drop in 1 to 2 pounds **raw shrimp,** reduce heat, and simmer for 4 to 6 minutes or until shrimp turn pink; don't overcook. Drain immediately and serve hot; or let cool, cover, and refrigerate.

Mexican Shrimp Appetizer

> ½ **cup catsup**
> ¼ **teaspoon grated lime peel**
> ¼ **cup *each* lime juice and dry white wine**
>   **Salt**
> 3 **or 4 drops liquid hot pepper seasoning**
> 1½ **pounds medium-size shrimp, shelled, deveined, and cooked (directions above)**
>   **Guacamole (recipe follows)**
>   **Tortilla chips**

In a bowl, combine catsup, lime peel, lime juice, wine, salt to taste, and hot pepper seasoning. Add shrimp and toss to coat completely. Cover and chill for at least 4 hours or until next day.

Prepare guacamole; mound in center of a round serving plate. Drain chilled shrimp and arrange around edge of plate. To eat, dip shrimp and tortilla chips in guacamole. Makes 10 to 12 appetizer servings.

Guacamole. Cut 2 large ripe **avocados** in half, remove pits, and, with a spoon, scoop pulp into a bowl. With a fork, mash pulp coarsely while blending in 2 to 3 tablespoons **lemon or lime juice.** Add **salt** to taste and 1 to 2 tablespoons chopped **fresh cilantro** (coriander) or about ½ teaspoon ground coriander. For a touch of heat, stir in 1 minced **green onion** and 2 to 4 tablespoons canned **diced green chiles,** or add liquid hot pepper seasoning to taste. Makes about 1⅔ cups.

...Shrimp

Scampi

(Pictured on facing page)

Scampi are actually a type of shrimp available only to Italy and her Adriatic neighbors, but this recipe produces something very similar.

        About ¾ pound medium-size raw shrimp, shelled and deveined
    6   tablespoons butter or margarine
    1   tablespoon minced green onion
    1   tablespoon olive oil or salad oil
    4 to 5 cloves garlic, minced or pressed
    2   teaspoons lemon juice
    ¼   teaspoon salt
    2   tablespoons minced parsley
    ¼   teaspoon grated lemon peel
        Dash of liquid hot pepper seasoning

Pat shrimp dry with paper towels; set aside. Melt butter in a wide frying pan over medium heat. Stir in green onion, oil, garlic, lemon juice, and salt; cook until bubbly.

Add shrimp to pan and cook, stirring occasionally, until shrimp turn pink (4 to 5 minutes). Stir in parsley, lemon peel, and hot pepper seasoning. Makes 2 servings.

Szechwan Shrimp

Stir-fried shrimp has an especially savory nip to it. Here's an excellent Chinese rendition.

    1   teaspoon salt
    1   pound medium-size raw shrimp, shelled and deveined
         Cooking sauce (directions follow)
    2½   tablespoons salad oil
    3   large cloves garlic, minced
    1   teaspoon minced fresh ginger
    ¼   teaspoon crushed red pepper
    4   green onions (including tops), thinly sliced

With your hands, rub salt into shrimp. Let shrimp stand for 15 minutes, then rinse well, drain, and pat dry with paper towels.

Prepare cooking sauce and set aside.

Heat 1½ tablespoons of the oil in a wide frying pan or wok over medium heat. When oil is hot, add shrimp and stir-fry until shrimp turn pink (3 to 4 minutes). Remove from pan and set aside.

Heat the remaining 1 tablespoon oil. Add garlic, ginger, and red pepper and stir-fry for 5 seconds. Return shrimp to pan, add green onions, and stir once. Stir cooking sauce, add to pan, and cook, stirring, until sauce bubbles and thickens. Makes 3 servings.

Cooking sauce. In a bowl, combine 1 tablespoon each **Worcestershire** and **dry sherry**, 2 tablespoons **catsup**, ¼ cup **water**, 2 teaspoons **sugar**, ½ teaspoon **salt**, and 1½ teaspoons **cornstarch**.

Shrimp Creole

The popularity of this Louisiana classic has spread well beyond New Orleans.

    1   large onion, coarsely chopped
    2   cloves garlic, minced or pressed
    1   medium-size green pepper, seeded and chopped
    2   stalks celery, chopped
    ⅓   cup salad oil
    2   teaspoons paprika
    1   can (about 1 lb.) tomatoes
    2   cups water
    1   teaspoon salt
    ⅛   teaspoon pepper
    ¼   teaspoon liquid hot pepper seasoning
    1   bay leaf
    1½   pounds medium-size raw shrimp, shelled and deveined
    2   tablespoons cornstarch mixed with ¼ cup water
    3 to 4 cups hot cooked rice

In a 5 or 6-quart kettle over medium-high heat, cook onion, garlic, green pepper, and celery in oil until vegetables are soft and just beginning to brown (about 10 minutes). Stir in paprika and cook for 1 minute. Add tomatoes (break up with a spoon) and their liquid, water, salt, pepper, hot pepper seasoning, and bay leaf; bring to a boil. Reduce heat; cover and simmer for 20 minutes.

Add shrimp and continue simmering until shrimp turn pink (6 to 8 minutes). Stir cornstarch mixture and add to pan; cook, stirring, until sauce bubbles and thickens slightly. Remove bay leaf. Serve in bowls over hot cooked rice. Makes 5 or 6 servings.

How to prepare shrimp for Scampi (Recipe on facing page)

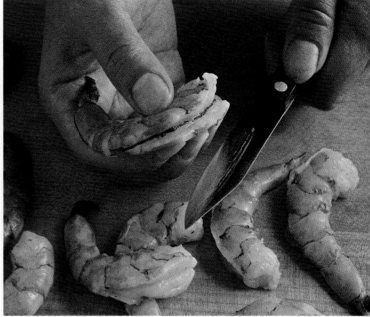

1 To shell raw shrimp, remove legs first. Split shell open down belly of shrimp, then gently tug tip of tail-shell free and pull shell away from body.

2 To remove sand vein, make a shallow cut down back of shrimp, then rinse out sand vein. To devein unshelled shrimp, cut along back with scissors and remove vein.

3 To make Scampi, give shrimp a quick cooking in lemon-garlic butter. As shrimp cook, their color changes from white to pink.

4 Serve Scampi with every spoonful of its delicious sauce. Dip artichokes and French bread into garlicky sauce too.

PASTA, BEANS & GRAINS

PASTA

Pasta's popularity is easy to understand: it's fun, it's creative, and it's wonderful to eat. The entire parade of pasta shapes—from whimsical corkscrews to straightforward tubes—can be dressed with many types of sauces, some rich and zesty, some light and delicate.

To get you started, here are some very special combinations to fill your kitchen with alluring aromas and establish your reputation as a cook. You can make them all with packaged fresh or dried pasta from the supermarket, but for the extra fun of more unusual shapes, you might enjoy exploring an Italian delicatessen.

Some of these recipes, such as Fettuccine Verde, take only minutes to prepare. They taste best when served right away, so have family or guests seated as the noodles go into the boiling water. No one will mind waiting briefly to applaud your virtuoso pasta performance. On the other hand, a dish such as lasagne requires more time, but you can prepare it in advance, then refrigerate it to reheat before serving.

How to cook pasta

The cooking time for pasta varies with the pasta's size and shape, but the doneness test is the same for all: boil it *al dente*. Literally this Italian term means "to the tooth"—tender but firm to bite—and that's the way pasta tastes best.

Start with a pot that will comfortably hold the amount of boiling water you'll need. For each 8 ounces (½ pound) dried pasta, bring 3 quarts water to a rapid boil. Add 1 tablespoon salt. For a pound of dried pasta, double the water only.

Add pasta to the boiling water. (For spaghetti that is too long for the pot, hold a bunch of it by one end and gently push the other end into the boiling water until the strands soften enough to submerge.) Stir only if pasta needs to be separated. Keep the water boiling continuously and cook pasta, uncovered, according to the times suggested on the package. As soon as the pasta

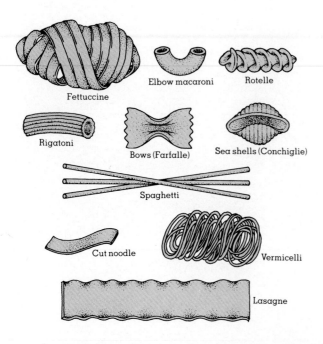

Fettuccine

Elbow macaroni

Rotelle

Rigatoni

Bows (Farfalle)

Sea shells (Conchiglie)

Spaghetti

Cut noodle

Vermicelli

Lasagne

is *al dente*, drain it and dress with sauce. Rinse with cold water only if you want to use it in a salad or need to cool lasagne noodles so you can handle them.

To estimate pasta quantities, use this general guideline: 2 ounces dried pasta makes about 1 cup cooked pasta or 1 serving.

German-style Macaroni & Cheese

> 8 ounces elbow macaroni, rotelle, sea shells, rigatoni, or bows
> Boiling salted water
> About 12 ounces (¾ lb.) garlic sausages or kielbasa (Polish sausage), thinly sliced
> 4 tablespoons butter or margarine
> 2 large onions, chopped
> ¼ cup all-purpose flour
> 2 cups milk
> 4 teaspoons prepared German-style or other spicy mustard
> ½ teaspoon caraway seeds
> ¾ teaspoon salt
> ¼ teaspoon white pepper
> 3 cups (12 oz.) shredded Swiss cheese

Following package directions, cook macaroni in boiling salted water until *al dente;* then drain thoroughly.

In a wide frying pan over medium heat, brown sausage slices in 1 tablespoon of the butter. Remove sausage from pan and set aside.

Add the remaining 3 tablespoons butter and onions to pan and cook, stirring, until onions are soft. Stir in flour and cook until bubbly. Remove pan from heat and stir in milk. Return to heat and, stirring, cook until sauce is smooth and thickened. Remove from heat and stir in mustard, caraway, salt, pepper, and drained macaroni; stir until well coated.

Place half the macaroni mixture in a buttered shallow 2½ to 3-quart baking dish. Distribute half the sausage, then half the cheese on top. Then layer on remaining macaroni mixture, then sausage, and then cheese. If made ahead, let cool, cover, and refrigerate.

Bake, uncovered, in a 400° oven for 25 to 35 minutes or until cheese is bubbly and center of casserole is hot. Makes 6 to 8 servings.

Lasagne Belmonte

A wonderful cook-ahead casserole for entertaining, this version of lasagne follows the traditional style of southern Italy. For a spicier flavor, substitute Italian sausage for part of the beef.

> 1 medium-size onion, chopped
> 3 tablespoons olive oil or salad oil
> 1½ pounds lean ground beef or 1 pound lean ground beef and ½ pound mild Italian sausages
> 1 clove garlic, minced or pressed
> 2 cans (8 oz. *each*) tomato sauce
> 1 can (6 oz.) tomato paste
> ½ cup *each* dry red wine and water
> 1 teaspoon *each* salt and oregano leaves
> ½ teaspoon *each* pepper and sugar
> 8 ounces lasagne noodles
> Boiling salted water
> 2 cups (1 lb.) ricotta cheese or 1 pint small curd cottage cheese
> 8 ounces mozzarella cheese, thinly sliced
> ½ cup grated Parmesan cheese

In a wide frying pan over medium-high heat, cook onion in oil until onion is soft; add beef and garlic and cook, stirring, until meat is browned and crumbly. (If using sausages, remove casings; chop sausage and brown with beef.) Spoon off and discard excess fat. Stir in tomato sauce, tomato paste, wine, water, salt, oregano, pepper, and sugar. Cover pan and simmer for about 1½ hours.

Meanwhile, following package directions, cook lasagne noodles in a large kettle of boiling salted water until *al dente.* Drain, rinse with cold water, and drain again.

Butter a 9 by 13-inch baking dish. Spread a thin layer of sauce over the bottom. Arrange ⅓ of the noodles in an even layer over sauce. Spread ⅓ of the sauce over noodles; dot with ⅓ of the ricotta, then cover with ⅓ of the mozzarella. Repeat this layering two more times. Sprinkle Parmesan cheese over top. If made ahead, cover and refrigerate.

Bake, uncovered, in a 350° oven until hot and bubbly (40 to 50 minutes). Cut into squares to serve. Makes 8 servings.

Making Fettuccine Verde (Recipe on facing page)

1 Boil pasta rapidly, uncovered, until *al dente*—tender but firm to bite. Wooden spaghetti rake scoops up noodle strands so you can easily test for doneness.

2 Lift out inner colander of spaghetti cooker to drain pasta; or pour pasta into a standing colander to drain. Shake gently. Any excess water will blend with sauce.

3 Reduce sauce by boiling rapidly. As water in whipping cream evaporates, sauce thickens slightly.

4 Add hot drained pasta to pan and toss gently. Sprinkle with a third of the cheese and toss until noodles are evenly coated. Toss with another third of the cheese.

5 Sprinkle nutmeg and remaining cheese over fettuccine just before serving. Serve immediately—noodles are like sponges and soak up cream if allowed to stand.

...Pasta

Fettuccine Verde

(Pictured on facing page)

    12 ounces fresh fettuccine, or 8 ounces dried
        fettuccine or medium-wide noodles
        Boiling salted water
     6 tablespoons butter or margarine
     1 cup sliced green onions (including tops)
     2 cloves garlic, minced or pressed
    ½ pint (1 cup) whipping cream
        About 1½ cups grated Parmesan cheese
        Salt and pepper
    ⅛ teaspoon ground nutmeg

Following package directions, cook fresh or dried
noodles in a large kettle of boiling salted water
until *al dente;* then drain.

While noodles are cooking, melt butter in a
wide frying pan over medium-high heat. Add
green onions and garlic and cook, stirring, for 2
minutes. Add cream and boil rapidly until slightly
thickened and large shiny bubbles form (about
2 minutes). Add hot drained noodles to pan and
toss gently. Add ½ cup of the cheese and toss until
noodles are evenly coated. Add another ½ cup
cheese and salt and pepper to taste; toss again.
Sprinkle nutmeg and remaining ½ cup cheese
over the top just before serving. Makes 4 servings.

Carbonara

The secret of this delicate sauce is the effect of the
beaten raw eggs. By coating the spaghetti, they
help the cheese and meat to cling to it evenly—
intensifying the rich flavor.

    ¼ pound mild Italian sausages
    ¼ pound prosciutto or cooked ham, thinly sliced
     4 tablespoons butter
     8 ounces spaghetti
        Boiling salted water
    ½ cup chopped parsley
     3 eggs, well beaten
    ½ cup grated Parmesan cheese
        Dash of freshly ground black pepper
        Grated Parmesan cheese

Remove casings from sausages and crumble or
chop meat. Finely chop prosciutto or ham. In a
wide frying pan over medium-low heat, melt

2 tablespoons of the butter. Add sausage and
prosciutto to pan and cook, stirring, for about 10
minutes or until sausage is lightly browned.

Following package directions, cook spaghetti
in a large kettle of boiling salted water until *al
dente;* then drain. Add spaghetti to hot meat mixture; then add the remaining 2 tablespoons butter
and parsley. Mix well. At once pour in eggs and
quickly lift and mix spaghetti to coat well with
eggs. Sprinkle in the ½ cup cheese and pepper;
mix again. Serve with more cheese, if desired.
Makes 4 servings.

Marinara Spaghetti

     1 medium-size onion, finely chopped
     1 large carrot, finely chopped
     1 large green pepper, seeded and finely
        chopped
     4 cloves garlic, minced or pressed
     2 tablespoons olive oil or salad oil
     1 can (1 lb.) tomato purée
     3 cans (8 oz. *each*) tomato sauce
    ½ cup dry red wine
     2 teaspoons salt
     1 tablespoon sugar
    ¼ teaspoon pepper
     1 teaspoon *each* dry rosemary, oregano leaves,
        and dry basil
     1 bay leaf
     2 pounds lean boneless pork shoulder, cut into
        ½-inch cubes
    ¼ pound mushrooms, sliced
     1 pound spaghetti or rigatoni
        Boiling salted water
        Grated Parmesan cheese

In a 6 to 8-quart kettle over medium heat, cook onion, carrot, green pepper, and garlic in oil until
vegetables are tender. Add tomato purée, tomato sauce, wine, salt, sugar, pepper, rosemary,
oregano, basil, bay leaf, and pork; bring to a boil.
Reduce heat; cover and simmer until pork is fork-
tender (about 1½ hours). Add mushrooms and
simmer, uncovered, for 10 more minutes. Remove
bay leaf.

Following package directions, cook spaghetti
in a large kettle of boiling salted water until *al
dente;* then drain. Toss with cheese to taste. Arrange spaghetti on a serving dish, ladle some
sauce over it, and serve. Freeze any remaining
sauce. Makes 6 to 8 servings.

DRIED BEANS

Low in cost, high in nutrition, and rich in good, earthy flavors, dried beans are one of the best food bargains going. Cooking beans is easy and requires little attention, but you do need to plan ahead because all dried beans require presoaking. Rinse and sort beans, then soak them by one of the following methods:

Quick soaking. In a kettle, combine 1 pound **dried beans** with 2 quarts **hot water** and 2 teaspoons **salt.** Heat to boiling and cook for 2 minutes. Turn off heat. Cover and let stand for 1 hour. Drain; discard water.

Long soaking. In a kettle, combine 1 pound **dried beans** with 2 quarts **cold water** and 2 teaspoons **salt.** Soak overnight. Drain; discard water.

To cook beans. After draining soaked beans, add 2 quarts **fresh water** and bring to a boil. Reduce heat and simmer, partially covered, until beans are tender (1 to 2 hours, depending on kind of beans used). When beans are tender, add **salt** to taste (up to 1 teaspoon). Beans double in size during cooking; 1 pound dry beans yields about 4 cups cooked beans.

Chile con Carne

- 1 tablespoon salad oil
- 1 medium-size onion, chopped
- 1 pound lean ground beef
- 1 can (about 1 lb.) tomatoes
- ¾ teaspoon salt
- 1½ teaspoons chili powder
- 1 teaspoon oregano leaves
- ½ teaspoon ground cumin
  About 4 cups cooked kidney, pinto, or red beans, plus ½ cup cooking liquid; *or* 1 large can (1 lb. 11 oz.) kidney beans, not drained
- 2 green onions
- 1 small avocado
- 1 lime

Heat oil in a 5 or 6-quart pan over medium-high heat; add onion and cook until soft. Add beef and cook, stirring, until meat is browned and crumbly. Spoon off and discard excess fat. Stir in tomatoes (break up with a spoon) and their liquid, salt, chili powder, oregano, and cumin. In a blender or food processor, whirl a third of the beans until smooth, adding their liquid as needed; stir into meat mix-

ture. Then add remaining whole beans, along with any remaining liquid, to meat. Simmer, uncovered, stirring occasionally, for 30 minutes.

Meanwhile, cut green onions into thin slices. Pit, peel, and slice avocado. Cut lime into eighths. Serve chile in bowls and garnish with green onions, avocado, and lime wedges. Makes 4 servings.

Black Bean Soup

- 4 tablespoons olive oil or salad oil
- 2 medium-size onions, finely chopped
- 2 medium-size green peppers, seeded and chopped
- 4 cloves garlic, minced or pressed
  About 3 cups regular-strength chicken broth
- 1½ teaspoons *each* ground cumin and oregano leaves
- 2 tablespoons vinegar
  About 6 cups cooked black or red beans, drained
  Salt
  Garnishes: Chopped green or red onion, chopped hard-cooked eggs, lemon wedges, hot cooked rice, chopped canned green chiles

Heat oil in a 5-quart pan over medium heat. Add onions, green peppers, and garlic; cook, stirring, until soft. Add broth, cumin, oregano, vinegar, and beans. Cover and simmer for 30 minutes, adding more broth, if desired, for thinner consistency. Add salt to taste. Ladle into bowls and garnish as desired. Makes 6 servings.

Refried Beans

  About 4 cups cooked pinto or pink beans, plus ½ cup cooking liquid
- ⅔ to 1 cup bacon drippings or lard
  Salt

Mash beans with a potato masher or electric mixer, or whirl until smooth in a food processor. Heat bacon drippings in a wide frying pan over medium heat. Add beans and mix well. Cook, stirring frequently, until beans are thickened and fat is absorbed. Add salt to taste. Serve hot or reheat. Makes 4 cups.

GRAINS

In menu planning, grains play a multiple role. With richly sauced entrées, rice or wheat acts as a neutral background and provides a base to soak up flavors. With simple, unadorned entrées, well-seasoned grains can stand on their own—maybe even steal the show.

In this section, we focus on the most widely available grains—long and short-grain rice (both brown and white) and cracked wheat (bulgur). As a rule of thumb, you can expect 1 cup of uncooked grain to expand to 3 cups during cooking. For basic steaming recipes, check package directions. For times when you want to go beyond the basics, here are some ideas.

Mexican Rice

    1 small onion, finely chopped
    3 tablespoons butter or margarine
    1 cup long-grain white rice
    1 clove garlic, minced or pressed
    2 medium-size tomatoes, peeled, seeded, and chopped
  1½ cups regular-strength chicken broth
    1 or 2 canned green chiles, chopped
       Salt and pepper
    2 tablespoons chopped fresh coriander (cilantro), optional
    ½ cup pimento-stuffed green olives, sliced

In a 2-quart pan over medium heat, cook onion in butter until soft. Add rice and garlic; cook, stirring occasionally, until rice is golden (about 5 minutes). Add tomatoes, broth, chiles, and salt and pepper to taste. Cover and bring to a boil; reduce heat and simmer until rice is *al dente* and all liquid is absorbed (about 20 minutes).

Turn off heat and stir in coriander (if used) and olives. Let stand, covered, for 10 minutes. Makes 4 to 6 servings.

MEXICAN RICE WITH PEAS & HAM

Prepare **Mexican Rice,** but add ½ pound diced cooked **ham** when adding broth. About 10 minutes before rice is finished cooking, add 1 cup **frozen peas.** Omit coriander and olives.

Rice Pilaf

    1 small onion, finely chopped
    4 tablespoons butter or margarine
    1 cup long-grain white rice
    1 can (14½ oz.) regular-strength chicken or beef broth
       Salt and pepper
    1 tablespoon chopped parsley (optional)

In a 2-quart pan over medium heat, cook onion in butter until soft. Add rice and cook, stirring occasionally, until rice is golden (about 5 minutes). Add broth and salt and pepper to taste. Cover and bring to a boil; reduce heat and simmer until rice is *al dente* and all liquid is absorbed (20 to 25 minutes). Fluff up rice with a fork and toss gently with parsley, if used. Makes 4 to 6 servings.

RICE & VERMICELLI PILAF (Pictured on page 107)

Prepare **Rice Pilaf,** but substitute ½ cup broken **vermicelli** for onion. Cook with rice for only 1 minute before adding broth.

CRACKED WHEAT PILAF

Prepare **Rice Pilaf,** but substitute 1 cup **cracked wheat** (bulgur) for rice.

MUSHROOM PILAF (Pictured on page 134)

Prepare **Rice Pilaf,** but substitute ¼ pound **mushrooms** (sliced) for onion, cooking them in the butter until soft; then substitute 1 cup **cracked wheat** (bulgur) for rice.

DONENESS TEST FOR GRAINS

As with vegetables, each grain has its optimum cooking time, and each requires a different amount of cooking liquid. While most vegetables are cooked to the crisp-tender stage, the test for grains is like the test for pasta: *al dente*—tender but firm to bite. At this point, each grain has a slightly resilient core, and the cooking liquid has been absorbed.

...Grains

Fruited Rice Pilaf

> 1 **cup long-grain brown rice**
> 2 **cups regular-strength chicken broth**
> 2 **tablespoons butter or margarine**
> ¼ **cup cashews**
> ¼ **cup *each* raisins and coarsely chopped dried apricots and pitted dates**
> **Salt**

In a 2-quart pan, combine rice and broth. Cover and bring to a boil over high heat; reduce heat to low and simmer until rice is *al dente* and all liquid is absorbed (about 45 minutes).

Meanwhile, melt butter in a small frying pan over medium-low heat. Add nuts and cook until golden. Remove from pan with a slotted spoon and set aside. Add raisins, apricots, and dates to pan and cook, stirring, for 2 minutes.

When rice is cooked, stir in dried fruits; cover and let stand for 5 minutes. Stir in nuts and salt to taste just before serving. Makes 4 to 6 servings.

Confetti Rice

> 1 **cup long-grain white rice**
> 3 **tablespoons butter or margarine**
> 1 **cup regular-strength chicken or beef broth**
> ½ **cup water**
> ¼ **teaspoon *each* salt and dry basil**
> ½ **cup *each* shredded carrot and finely chopped celery**
> ¼ **cup sliced green onions (including tops)**
> ¼ **cup shelled sunflower seeds or sliced almonds**

In a 2-quart pan over medium heat, cook rice in butter, stirring occasionally, until golden (about 5 minutes). Add broth, water, salt, and basil. Cover and bring to a boil; reduce heat and simmer until rice is almost tender and most of liquid is absorbed (about 15 minutes).

Stir in carrot, celery, onions, and sunflower seeds. Cover and continue cooking until rice is *al dente* and all liquid is absorbed (about 10 minutes); vegetables should be crisp-tender. Makes 4 to 6 servings.

Risotto

(Pictured on facing page)

Risotto is rice, Italian-style. It cooks to a creamy, flowing consistency—unlike the separate, fluffy grains that are customary in American cooking. If you want to splurge, use the saffron, but this dish is wonderful with or without it.

> 4 **tablespoons olive oil**
> 6 **tablespoons butter or margarine**
> 1 **large onion, finely chopped**
> 1 **large clove garlic, minced or pressed**
> 2 **cups short-grain (pearl) rice or long-grain white rice**
> ⅛ **teaspoon saffron (optional)**
> 4 **cans (14½ oz. *each*) regular-strength chicken or beef broth**
> 1 **cup grated Parmesan cheese**

Place olive oil and 4 tablespoons of the butter in a heavy 3 or 4-quart pan over medium heat. When butter is melted, add onion and cook, stirring, until soft and golden. Add garlic and rice and stir until rice looks milky and opaque (about 3 minutes). Stir in saffron (if used) and mix in broth. Cook, uncovered, stirring occasionally, until mixture comes to a boil.

Adjust heat so rice boils gently; then cook, uncovered, until rice is *al dente* and most of the liquid is absorbed (20 to 25 minutes). Toward end of cooking time, stir rice occasionally to prevent sticking. Turn off heat and stir in cheese and the remaining 2 tablespoons butter. Makes 8 servings.

ASPARAGUS RISOTTO

Prepare **Risotto,** but decrease broth to about 6 cups and add ⅛ teaspoon **white pepper.** While risotto is cooking, snap off tough ends of 1 pound **asparagus.** Cut stems into ½-inch slanting slices; set tips aside. About 10 minutes before rice is done, mix in sliced asparagus stems; about 5 minutes later, mix in tips. When rice is almost *al dente,* stir in ½ pint (1 cup) **whipping cream.**

How to make Risotto (Recipe on facing page)

1 Cook onion in butter and oil; then cook rice in butter-oil mixture, too. This step cooks floury coating on rice and prevents grains from sticking together.

2 Rice simmers in chicken broth in an open pan so you can watch its progress. When most of the liquid has been absorbed, turn off heat and add Parmesan.

3 Gently stir in cheese and remaining butter. If there is a short delay in serving, cover pan to keep risotto warm.

4 Golden, saffron-flavored risotto is so distinctive it pairs best with simple accompaniments such as grilled Italian sausage and Swiss chard brightened with cherry tomatoes.

VEGETABLES

Have you ever wandered through a vegetable garden on a carefree summer afternoon and nibbled on tender kernels of fresh-picked corn, so sweet they needed no cooking? Or plucked a plump red tomato right off the vine? Or sampled a few sweet green peas?

No? Well, you're not alone. All too many of us grew up with overcooked canned or frozen vegetables—poor reflections of their original garden-fresh condition.

But times and trends are changing. Vegetables are playing a more central role in family and company meals, and people are rediscovering vegetables' vibrant flavors and crisp textures.

When you buy your vegetables, focus on those that are in season. That's when they're not only the best buy but also are at their peak of flavor and quality. Cooked briefly, just to the right degree of tenderness, they'll retain more of their flavor, color, texture, and nutritional value. Look for cooking times and preparation information in the vegetable chart on pages 127–130. But the real test, of course, is your own taste.

Storing to maintain freshness

Store the following vegetables, dry and unwashed, in plastic bags in the refrigerator: *artichokes, asparagus, beets, broccoli, Brussels sprouts, cabbage, carrots, cauliflower, Chinese pea pods, corn (in husks), eggplant, green beans,* *green peppers, parsnips, peas (in pods), rutabagas, summer squash, tomatoes, and turnips. Mushrooms* do better when stored in a paper bag, which allows air circulation.

Celery, green onions, leeks, and greens (such as kale, spinach, and Swiss chard) need some moisture during storage, but they shouldn't be wet. Rinse them under cool running water and drain thoroughly. Wrap in paper towels, then place in plastic bags before refrigerating.

Watercress and fresh herbs should be rinsed, then put in a container with their stems in water. Slip a plastic bag over the tops, secure the bag to the container, and refrigerate.

Yellow, white, and red onions, garlic, potatoes, sweet potatoes, and winter squash should be stored in a cool (about 50°), well-ventilated dry place out of direct sunlight. Once winter squash is cut, wrap it in plastic and refrigerate it.

Vegetable cutting techniques

A French knife is an indispensable tool for cutting vegetables. By learning to use it well, you can save a great deal of time and enjoy cooking more. To get started, look at the illustrations on the facing page. As you cook, try each technique with a hands-on approach. It takes practice to chop and slice with speed, but once you learn the skills, you'll never forget them.

Chopping. Hold top of knife blade at both ends. Chop with steady up-and-down movements, scraping chopped vegetables into a heap, as necessary, with knife blade.

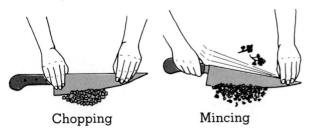

Chopping   Mincing

Mincing. Push chopped vegetables into a heap. Keeping tip of knife blade on cutting board, and using it as a pivot, lift heel of knife in up-and-down movements to finely chop vegetables.

Slicing. To slice a round vegetable such as an onion or potato, cut it in half and lay halves, cut side down, on a cutting board. Gripping one half with your fingers, and curling your finger tips under toward your palm, cut straight down through vegetable at a right angle to board.

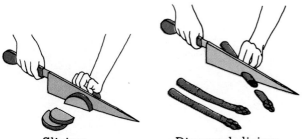

Slicing   Diagonal slicing

Diagonal slicing. To diagonally slice long vegetables, cut them crosswise on the diagonal. With long thin vegetables, such as asparagus or green beans, you can diagonally slice several at a time.

Cutting into julienne strips. To cut vegetables such as zucchini, carrots, turnips, or potatoes into julienne strips (similar in size to wooden match-

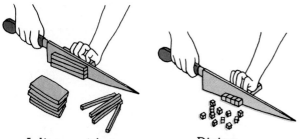

Julienne strips   Dicing

sticks), first cut vegetable, if necessary, into 2 to 3-inch lengths. Cut a thin lengthwise strip off one side and lay vegetable on flat side. Cut into ⅛-inch-thick slices, stack 2 or 3 slices at a time, and cut slices into ⅛-inch-thick strips.

Dicing. Cut as directed for julienne strips, but cut strips, a handful at a time, crosswise into dice. For larger dice, start with ¼ or ½-inch-thick slices, then cut crosswise to make ¼ or ½-inch cubes.

WHY & HOW TO BLANCH VEGETABLES

The technique of blanching (parboiling) vegetables has many uses. You blanch tomatoes briefly to loosen their skins for peeling (see photo, page 126). Most vegetables are blanched before they're frozen, to capture peak color and flavor. And vegetables to be served cold, such as broccoli or asparagus, are blanched before they're marinated in a vinaigrette dressing (page 25).

Many vegetables, such as carrots, cauliflower, green beans, and turnips, just taste especially good when they're blanched first, then lightly sautéed in butter. This method is convenient for entertaining, because you can partially cook the vegetable ahead and have only the final step left to do.

To blanch vegetables that will be served cold or sautéed in butter, immerse them (whole or cut) in a large quantity of rapidly boiling water (6 quarts water for 2 pounds vegetables). Boil, uncovered, for the minimum time suggested under "Cooking instructions" in the vegetable chart (pages 127–130) or until crisp-tender. Drain immediately, plunge into a large quantity of cold water to stop the cooking, then drain again. Spread on paper towels and pat dry.

Marinate vegetables you intend to serve cold; those you plan to serve hot can be refrigerated for up to 8 hours, then reheated. To reheat, melt 2 to 4 tablespoons butter or margarine in a heavy frying pan over medium-high heat. Add 1 to 2 pounds blanched vegetables to the hot butter and shake the pan just until the vegetables are heated through and lightly browned. Season with salt and pepper to taste.

Preparing vegetables: Special techniques

To peel tomatoes, blanch by dipping in boiling water for 30 seconds; rinse in cold water to cool. Slide tip of knife under skin and strip off skin. Cut out core from stem end.

To seed tomatoes, cut in half crosswise. Gently squeeze each half to remove seeds and juice. You can then chop or slice tomatoes.

To cut raw corn off cob, slice down length of cob with sharp knife, leaving kernel bases attached. For creamy corn, also scrape cob with back of knife to remove corn pulp and milk.

To prepare spaghetti squash, bake first (see chart, page 130), then cut in half and remove seeds. Use fork to remove spaghetti-like strands. Season with butter, salt, and pepper.

To shred cabbage, cut in half lengthwise. Cut out v-shape core. Place cabbage, flat side down, on cutting board. Thinly slice crosswise with French knife.

To prevent loss of color from beets during cooking, boil them without peeling. After cooking, let cool slightly; trim off roots and stems, then slip off skins.

PREPARING & COOKING VEGETABLES

Use the following chart as a guide for preparing and cooking your favorite vegetables. **The amount suggested for each vegetable will yield about 4 servings.** The chart covers boiling, steaming, and baking; to stir-fry vegetables, see page 135.

Remember that uniform size and shape of whole or cut vegetables ensure even cooking. You may find that cooking times will vary slightly, depending on size and freshness of the produce.

Cooking instructions. General cooking instructions for the vegetables are as follows:

To boil: Bring designated amount of water to a boil over high heat, then add vegetable. When water returns to a boil, cover pan (if specified), reduce heat so water will boil gently throughout the cooking time, and begin timing.

To steam: Choose a wide frying pan or any other pan large enough to hold a steaming rack that will accommodate your whole vegetables in a single layer or cut-up vegetables in an even layer not more than 1½ to 2 inches deep.

Bring 1 to 1½ inches water to a boil over high heat; place vegetables on rack above boiling water. Cover pan, adjust heat so water continues to boil throughout cooking time, and begin to time. If necessary, add more boiling water to pan to maintain water level throughout cooking.

To bake: Place vegetable in ovenproof baking dish, shallow baking pan, or rimmed baking sheet as directed; baking potatoes can be placed directly on oven rack, if desired. Do not crowd vegetables—leave ample room for heat to circulate.

When are vegetables done? Test vegetables after minimum cooking time recommended in chart. Most cooked vegetables should be tender-crisp when pierced with a fork (pierce vegetables such as artichokes, broccoli, Brussels sprouts, and cauliflower in the stem end or stalk). Potatoes should be tender throughout when pierced. Greens should appear wilted but retain their bright color.

Serving instructions. Drain vegetables immediately, saving liquid for soup, stock, or sauces, if desired. To serve vegetables hot, season them to your taste with one or more of the "compatible seasonings." On pages 132–133, you'll find recipes for specific sauces suggested. Recipes for Flavored Butters are on page 137.

Vegetable (amount for 4 servings)	Preparation	Cooking instructions	Compatible seasonings
Artichokes—4 medium to large			
Whole	Cut off stem; cut off top ⅓ of artichoke. Remove small coarse outer leaves. Using scissors, cut off thorny tips of remaining leaves. Rinse well. Plunge into vinegar-water or lemon-water.	*To boil:* In a 5 to 6-quart kettle, cook, covered, in 3 to 4 quarts water with 2 tablespoons vinegar or lemon juice for 30 to 45 minutes. If desired, add to water 1 bay leaf, 1 clove garlic (peeled), and 6 to 8 whole black peppercorns. *To steam:* On a rack above boiling water, cook, covered, for 25 to 35 minutes.	Melted butter, garlic butter, mayonnaise, hollandaise sauce
Asparagus—1½ to 2 pounds			
Spears	Snap or cut off tough ends. If desired, peel stalks to remove scales. Rinse well.	*To boil:* In a wide frying pan, cook, covered, in 1 inch water for 7 to 10 minutes. *To steam:* On a rack above boiling water, cook, covered, for 8 to 12 minutes.	Butter, lemon juice, tarragon, vinaigrette dressing, hollandaise sauce
Slices (½ to 1 inch)	Same as above, then slice diagonally.	*To boil:* In a wide frying pan, cook, covered, in ½ inch water for 2 to 5 minutes. *To steam:* On a rack above boiling water, cook, covered, for 5 to 7 minutes.	Same as above
Beans, green or wax—1 pound			
Whole	Rinse well. Snap off ends.	*To boil:* In a 3-quart pan, cook, covered, in 1 inch water for 5 to 10 minutes. *To steam:* On a rack above boiling water, cook, covered, for 10 to 15 minutes.	Butter, chives, dill weed, thyme, almonds, crumbled bacon, cheese sauce, dill sauce
Slices (1 to 2 inches)	Same as above, then slice diagonally or crosswise.	*To boil:* In a 3-quart pan, cook, covered, in 1 inch water for 4 to 7 minutes. *To steam:* On a rack above boiling water, cook, covered, for 8 to 12 minutes.	Same as above

(Continued on next page)

...Preparing & cooking vegetables

Vegetable (amount for 4 servings)	Preparation	Cooking instructions	Compatible seasonings
Beets—1 to 1½ pounds (2 to 3-inch diameter)			
Whole	Scrub well. Leave roots, 1 to 2 inches of stem, and skin intact. Do not peel before cooking. After cooking, cool, then trim off root and stem, and slip off skins.	**To boil:** In a 4 to 5-quart kettle, cook, covered, in water to cover for 20 to 45 minutes. **To bake:** Wrap beets in foil and bake in a 375° oven for 1 to 1¼ hours.	Butter, mustard butter, dill weed, lemon or orange juice or peel, thyme, wine vinegar
Broccoli—1 to 1½ pounds			
Spears or flowerets	Rinse. Cut off flowerets or spears; slash stems. Trim bases of thick stalks, peel, then thinly slice.	**To boil:** In a wide frying pan, cook, covered, in 1 inch water for 7 to 12 minutes. **To steam:** On a rack above boiling water, cook, covered, for 15 to 20 minutes.	Butter, garlic, ginger, rosemary, hollandaise sauce, mornay sauce
Brussels sprouts—1¼ to 1½ pounds			
Whole	Trim off stem ends and discolored leaves. Rinse well. For even cooking, cut a shallow X in each stem end.	**To boil:** In a 3-quart pan, cook, uncovered, in 1 inch water for 3 to 5 minutes; cover and cook for 4 to 5 more minutes. **To steam:** On a rack above boiling water, cook, covered, for 15 to 25 minutes.	Butter, grated Parmesan cheese, buttered bread crumbs, cheese sauce
Cabbage (all varieties)—1 to 1½ pounds			
Wedges	Discard any wilted outer leaves. Slice in half lengthwise and cut out core; rinse. Cut into 2-inch wedges.	**To boil:** In a wide frying pan, cook, uncovered, in 1 inch water for 2 minutes; cover and cook for 6 to 10 more minutes. **To steam:** On a rack above boiling water, cook, uncovered, for 2 minutes; cover and cook for 7 to 12 more minutes.	Butter, caraway seeds, dill weed, grated Parmesan cheese, sour cream
Shredded	Discard any wilted outer leaves. Slice in half lengthwise and cut out core; rinse. Place, cut side down, on cutting board and slice thinly.	**To boil:** In a wide frying pan, cook, uncovered, in ½ inch water for 1 to 2 minutes; cover and cook for 2 to 3 more minutes. **To steam:** On a rack above boiling water, cook, uncovered, for 2 to 3 minutes; cover and cook for 2 to 4 more minutes.	Same as above
Carrots—1 pound			
Whole (medium-size)	Scrub well or peel; cut off ends. Rinse.	**To boil:** In a wide frying pan, cook, covered, in 1 inch water for 10 to 20 minutes. **To steam:** On a rack above boiling water, cook, covered, for 12 to 20 minutes.	Butter, cinnamon, ginger, mint, nutmeg, parsley, thyme
Slices (¼ inch)	Same as above; then slice diagonally or crosswise.	**To boil:** In a wide frying pan, cook, covered, in ½ inch water for 5 to 10 minutes. **To steam:** On a rack above boiling water, cook, covered, for 5 to 10 minutes.	Same as above
Cauliflower—1¼ to 1½ pounds (1 medium-size head)			
Whole	Remove outer leaves. Cut out core. Rinse.	**To boil:** In a 4 to 5-quart kettle, cook, covered, in 1 inch water for 15 to 20 minutes. **To steam:** On a rack above boiling water, cook, covered, for 20 to 25 minutes.	Butter, chives, dill weed, nutmeg, cheese sauce, curry sauce, hollandaise sauce
Flowerets	Same as above, but break into flowerets.	**To boil:** In a wide frying pan, cook, covered, in ½ inch water for 5 to 9 minutes. **To steam:** On a rack above boiling water, cook, covered, for 10 to 18 minutes.	Same as above
Celery—1½ pounds (1 medium-size bunch)			
Slices (1 inch)	Separate stalks. Trim off leaves and base. Rinse well, then slice diagonally or crosswise.	**To boil:** In a wide frying pan, cook, covered, in ½ inch water for 5 to 10 minutes. **To steam:** On a rack above boiling water, cook, covered, for 8 to 10 minutes.	Butter, tarragon, thyme, grated Parmesan cheese
Corn on the cob—4 large ears or 8 small to medium-size ears			
Whole	Remove husks and silk; trim stem, if desired.	**To boil:** In a 4 to 5-quart kettle, cook, covered, in 2 to 3 quarts water for 3 to 5 minutes.	Butter, flavored butters, lime juice

Vegetable (amount for 4 servings)	Preparation	Cooking instructions	Compatible seasonings
Eggplant—1½ pounds (1 large or 2 small to medium-size)			
Slices (½ inch)	Rinse and cut into ½-inch slices. Sprinkle with 1 teaspoon salt; let stand for 30 minutes. Rinse and pat dry. Brush with salad oil.	*To bake:* Arrange in single layer in shallow baking pan. Bake, uncovered, in a 425° to 450° oven for 20 to 30 minutes.	Garlic butter, basil, curry powder, marjoram, grated Parmesan cheese, tomato
Greens (beet, collard, kale, mustard, turnip)—1 to 1½ pounds			
Leaves	Remove tough stems; rinse well in large quantity of water; drain. Coarsely chop leaves, if desired.	*To boil:* In a 4 to 5-quart kettle, cook, covered, in 1 to 1½ inches water for 7 to 9 minutes. *To steam:* On a rack above boiling water, cook, covered, for 7 to 9 minutes.	Butter, crumbled bacon, lemon juice, wine vinegar, sour cream
Leeks—1½ pounds (1-inch diameter)			
Halves	Cut off root bases. Trim tops so only 1½ inches of dark green leaves remain; split leeks lengthwise. Rinse.	*To boil:* In a wide frying pan, cook, covered, in ½ inch water for 5 to 8 minutes. *To steam:* On a rack above boiling water, cook, covered, for 5 to 8 minutes.	Flavored butters, crumbled bacon, grated Parmesan cheese
Okra—1 pound			
Whole	Trim off stem ends. Rinse pods; leave whole.	*To boil:* In a 3-quart pan, cook, covered, in water to cover for 5 to 10 minutes.	Butter, garlic butter, chives, parsley, tomato
Onions, small white boiling—1 pound			
Whole	Cover with boiling water; let stand for 3 minutes, then drain. Trim ends and peel; cut a shallow X in stem end.	*To boil:* In a 3-quart pan, cook, uncovered, in 1½ inches water for 15 to 20 minutes. *To bake:* Place in baking dish; drizzle with butter or margarine. Bake, uncovered, in a 350° oven for 30 to 45 minutes, basting occasionally.	Butter, parsley, sage, thyme, brown or white sugar
Parsnips—1 pound			
Whole	Cut off ends; peel. Rinse.	*To boil:* In a wide frying pan, cook, covered, in 1 inch water for 10 to 15 minutes. *To steam:* On a rack above boiling water, cook, covered, for 15 to 20 minutes.	Butter, brown sugar, honey, lemon juice, Worcestershire
Pea pods, Chinese—¾ pound			
Whole	Snap off both ends and pull off strings. Rinse.	*To boil:* In a 5-quart kettle, cook, uncovered, in 3 quarts water for 30 seconds. *To steam:* On a rack above boiling water, cook, covered, for 3 to 5 minutes.	Butter, toasted sesame seeds, soy sauce
Peas, green—2½ pounds (yields 2½ to 3 cups, shelled)			
	Shell peas; rinse.	*To boil:* In a 3-quart pan, cook, covered, in ½ inch water for 5 to 10 minutes. *To steam:* On a rack above boiling water, cook, covered, for 8 to 12 minutes.	Butter, chives, mint, rosemary, thyme, mornay sauce
Potatoes, baking— 2 to 2½ pounds (4 medium to large)			
Whole	Scrub well. Rub with oil or butter, if desired, and pierce in several places with fork.	*To bake:* Place on a rimmed baking sheet or directly on oven rack; bake, uncovered, in a 400° oven for 1 hour.	Butter, chives, crumbled bacon, paprika, sour cream
Quartered	Peel, cut into quarters, and rinse.	*To boil:* In a 5-quart kettle, cook, covered, in 1 inch water for about 20 minutes.	Butter, gravy, dill sauce
Potatoes, thin-skinned red or white—1½ pounds			
Whole (3-inch diameter)	Scrub well; do not peel.	*To boil:* In a 3-quart pan, cook, covered, in 2 inches water for 20 to 30 minutes. *To steam:* On a rack above boiling water, cook, covered, for 30 to 35 minutes.	Butter, flavored butters, dill weed, parsley, rosemary, crumbled bacon
Slices (½ inch)	Same as above, then slice.	*To boil:* In a 3-quart pan, cook, covered, in 1 inch water for 13 to 15 minutes. *To steam:* On a rack above boiling water, cook, covered, for 8 to 10 minutes.	Same as above

(Continued on next page)

...Preparing & cooking vegetables

Vegetable (amount for 4 servings)	Preparation	Cooking instructions	Compatible seasonings
Potatoes, sweet and yams—2 to 2½ pounds (4 medium to large)			
Whole	**For baking:** Scrub well. Rub with oil, if desired, and pierce in several places with fork. **For boiling:** Scrub well; do not peel.	**To bake:** Place on a rimmed baking sheet; cook, uncovered, in a 400° oven for 45 to 50 minutes. **To boil:** In a 3-quart pan, cook, covered, in 2 inches water for 20 to 40 minutes, depending on size.	Butter, allspice, cinnamon, nutmeg, brown sugar, maple syrup
Rutabagas—1½ to 2 pounds			
Slices (¼ inch)	Peel, rinse, and slice.	**To boil:** In a wide frying pan, cook, covered, in ½ to 1 inch water for 6 to 8 minutes. **To steam:** On a rack above boiling water, cook, covered, for 7 to 9 minutes.	Butter, cinnamon, dill weed, brown sugar, lemon juice
Spinach—1½ pounds (2 bunches)			
Leaves	Discard wilted leaves and remove tough stems. Rinse well in a large quantity of water; drain.	**To boil:** In a 4 to 5-quart kettle, cook, covered, in water that clings to leaves, for 2 to 4 minutes.	Butter, basil, mint, nutmeg, crumbled bacon
Squash, spaghetti—2 pounds			
Whole	Rinse. Do not peel. Leave whole, but pierce all over with fork.	**To bake:** On a rimmed baking sheet, cook, uncovered, in a 350° oven for 1½ hours; turn over after 45 minutes. After baking, cut squash in half; remove seeds. Use a fork to separate spaghetti-like strands.	Butter, flavored butters
Squash, summer (crookneck, pattypan, zucchini)—1 to 1½ pounds			
Whole	Cut off ends; rinse. Do not peel.	**To boil:** In a 3-quart pan, cook, covered, in 1 inch water for 8 to 12 minutes. **To steam:** On a rack above boiling water, cook, covered, for 10 to 12 minutes.	Butter, basil, dill weed, fines herbes, marjoram, onion, cheese sauce
Slices (½ inch)	Same as above; then slice.	**To boil:** In a 3-quart pan, cook, covered, in ½ inch water for 3 to 6 minutes. **To steam:** On a rack above boiling water, cook, covered, for 4 to 7 minutes.	Same as above
Squash, winter (acorn, banana, butternut, Hubbard)—1½ pounds			
Halves or serving-size pieces	Rinse. Cut acorn or butternut squash in half lengthwise; cut banana or Hubbard squash into serving-size pieces. Remove seeds and stringy portions. **For baking:** Same as above, then rub cut edges with butter.	**To boil:** In a wide frying pan, cook, covered, in 2 inches water for 10 to 15 minutes. **To bake:** Place, cut side down, in greased baking pan. Bake, uncovered, in a 400° to 450° oven for 30 to 40 minutes.	Butter, allspice, cinnamon, ginger, nutmeg, brown sugar, crumbled bacon, onion
Slices (½ inch)	Rinse, peel, and slice.	**To boil:** In a wide frying pan, cook, covered, in ½ inch water for 7 to 9 minutes.	Same as above
Swiss chard—1½ pounds			
Leaves	Rinse well; drain. Slice stems into 1-inch pieces; slice leaves crosswise into 1-inch shreds.	**To boil:** In a wide frying pan, cook stems, covered, in ¼ inch water for 2 minutes, then add leaves and cook for 1 to 2 more minutes.	Butter, nutmeg, crumbled bacon, onion
Turnips—1½ to 2 pounds (about 4 medium-size)			
Whole	**For boiling:** Rinse and peel. **For baking:** Rinse; do not peel.	**To boil:** In a 4 to 5-quart kettle, cook, covered, in 2 inches water for 25 to 35 minutes. **To bake:** Arrange in shallow layer in greased baking pan. Dot generously with butter, sprinkle lightly with water, and bake, uncovered, in a 400° oven for 30 to 45 minutes.	Butter, crumbled bacon, soy sauce
Slices (¼ inch)	Rinse, peel, and slice.	**To boil:** In a wide frying pan, cook, covered, in ½ inch water for 6 to 8 minutes. **To steam:** On a rack above boiling water, cook, covered, for 7 to 9 minutes.	Same as above

Preparing vegetables: Special techniques

To remove astringency in eggplant, draw out moisture by sprinkling with 1 teaspoon salt and letting it stand for 30 minutes. Rinse, if desired; pat dry before cooking.

To find hidden dirt in a leek, trim both ends. Insert knife through white part just below leaves, and cut in half lengthwise through leaves. Rinse leek thoroughly.

To roast peppers, broil 1 inch below heat, turning frequently, until blistered and charred. Place in plastic bag; seal. Let sweat for 15 to 20 minutes. Peel, seed, and rinse.

To ensure even cooking in Brussels sprouts (or small white boiling onions), cut a shallow X in each stem end before cooking. Boil or steam as desired.

To prepare Chinese pea pods for cooking, snap or cut off one end and pull off attached string. Repeat at opposite end for the other string.

To prepare broccoli for cooking, cut into flowerets (center) or spears (lower left); slit stems. Trim off bases of thick stalks, peel, then thinly slice or cut into julienne strips.

A complement of vegetable sauces

When properly cooked, vegetables retain so much rich, natural flavor that they need no further enhancement than salt and pepper—and maybe a sprinkling of herbs or a pat of butter. But for more liveliness and diversity in menu planning, you may want to serve vegetables with a sauce.

To get you started, we present the following repertoire of sauces, with suggestions for their use. Though paired here with vegetables, these sauces are basic to many kinds of cooking, and you'll find other uses for them, as well.

Hollandaise Sauce

This classic French emulsion sauce has a bad reputation: it's supposed to be tricky to make and easy to ruin. But like mayonnaise (page 26), it's not as temperamental as you might think. And if you make hollandaise in a blender or food processor, it's practically foolproof.

Blender or processor hollandaise is a very thick, smooth sauce. Cooked hollandaise, on the other hand, is a fluffier, more delicate sauce. With either method, one whole egg or three egg yolks can be used interchangeably. The all-yolk sauce simply has a more golden color and tends to be thicker.

Rich and elegant, this sauce makes the most of freshly cooked artichokes or asparagus; it's also a wonderful choice to crown poached fish or Eggs Benedict (page 39).

    1   whole egg or 3 egg yolks
    1   teaspoon Dijon or other prepared mustard
    1   tablespoon lemon juice or white wine
        vinegar
    1   cup (½ lb.) butter or margarine, melted
        and hot

Blender or food processor hollandaise. Whirl egg, mustard, and lemon juice until well blended. With motor on high, add butter, a few drops at a time in the beginning, but increasing to a slow, steady stream (about ¹⁄₁₆ inch wide) as mixture begins to thicken. Serve immediately. Or, if sauce is to be used within several hours, pour into a jar, cover, and let stand; then warm the sauce (directions follow). If made further ahead, cover and refrigerate for up to a week; bring to room temperature before warming. Makes 1 to 1½ cups.

Cooked hollandaise. Using a wire whisk or portable electric mixer, combine egg, mustard, and lemon juice in the top of a double boiler. Place pan over gently simmering water (water should not boil or touch bottom of pan). Beating constantly, add butter, a few drops at a time in the beginning, but increasing to a slow, steady stream (about ¹⁄₁₆ inch wide) as mixture begins to thicken. After all butter is added, continue to cook, beating, until sauce thickens. A cooked whole-egg sauce should look like cream that is just beginning to thicken when whipped; an all-yolk sauce should be thick enough to hold its shape briefly when dropped from a beater.

As soon as sauce has thickened, remove from heat and serve immediately. Or, if sauce is to be used within several hours, pour into a jar, cover, and let stand; then warm the sauce (directions follow). If made further ahead, cover and refrigerate for up to a week; bring to room temperature before warming. Makes 1 to 1½ cups.

To warm hollandaise. Bring sauce to room temperature and stir to soften. Place jar in water that's hot to touch; stir until sauce is warm, not hot.

MOUSSELINE SAUCE

Prepare **Hollandaise Sauce.** Whip ½ cup **whipping cream** until stiff peaks form; fold into hollandaise (hot or at room temperature). Serve immediately over boiled or steamed vegetables or fish.

FIXING A CURDLED HOLLANDAISE

Don't give up if your hollandaise curdles and separates—you can rescue it. For 1 to 1½ cups sauce (yield from one recipe), pour 1 tablespoon water into a bowl.

If making blender or food processor hollandaise, use a wire whisk or a fork to beat 3 tablespoons curdled sauce into water. Place in blender or processor and whirl at high speed, slowly adding remaining curdled sauce to form sauce again.

If making cooked hollandaise, use a wire whisk or a fork to beat a very thin stream of curdled sauce into water. Beating constantly, continue adding curdled sauce slowly, as when making original sauce, until all curdled sauce is incorporated and sauce is no longer separated.

BÉARNAISE SAUCE

In a small pan, combine 1 tablespoon minced **shallot** or onion, 1 teaspoon **dry tarragon,** and 3 tablespoons **white wine vinegar.** Simmer over medium heat until liquid is reduced to 2 teaspoons. Prepare **Hollandaise Sauce,** but stir shallot mixture (hot or cold) into egg, mustard, and lemon juice before adding butter. Good with green beans, salmon, beef, broiled chicken, lamb, and egg dishes.

MALTAISE SAUCE

Prepare **Hollandaise Sauce,** but stir 2 tablespoons **orange juice** and ½ teaspoon grated **orange peel** into egg mixture before adding butter. Good with asparagus, broccoli, and Brussels sprouts.

White Sauce (Béchamel)

Knowing how to make white sauce is one of the hidden cornerstones of cooking, for the sauce is seldom made as an end in itself. Generally, it performs as part of another dish—as the base for a soufflé; the binding agent for a casserole or a crêpe filling of poultry, fish, or vegetables; the finishing touch for an *au gratin* dish. White sauce is also the starting point for most "creamed" dishes.

Our basic recipe for a medium-thick white sauce takes only about 5 minutes to make. The recipe and its variations make a cup of sauce, but can easily be doubled.

> 2 **tablespoons butter or margarine**
> 2 **tablespoons all-purpose flour**
> 1 **cup milk**
> **Salt and pepper**

In a 1½ to 2-quart pan over medium heat, melt butter. Add flour and cook, stirring, until butter-flour mixture *(roux)* is bubbling and foamy. (The flour must be cooked long enough to eliminate the raw flour taste, but not so long as to color beyond a light gold.) Remove pan from heat and, using a wire whisk, gradually blend in milk. Return pan to heat and cook, stirring, until sauce is smooth, thick, and boiling. Season to taste with salt and pepper. Makes 1 cup.

VELOUTÉ

Prepare **White Sauce,** but use regular-strength **chicken broth** instead of milk. Good with any cooked vegetable and poultry.

CHEDDAR CHEESE SAUCE

Prepare **White Sauce,** but stir ½ cup shredded **Cheddar cheese** into finished sauce and simmer until cheese is melted. Good with broccoli, cauliflower, potatoes, and other vegetables.

MORNAY SAUCE

Prepare **White Sauce,** but stir a dash of **nutmeg** and ¼ to ½ cup grated **Parmesan cheese** into finished sauce and simmer for 2 minutes. Good with broccoli, cauliflower, potatoes, crab, oysters, scallops, fish, poultry, pasta, and eggs.

CURRY SAUCE

Prepare **White Sauce,** but add to butter 1½ teaspoons **curry powder** and ⅛ teaspoon **ground ginger** along with the flour. Good with carrots, cauliflower, shrimp, lamb, poultry, and eggs.

DILL SAUCE

Prepare **White Sauce,** but stir 2 teaspoons **dill weed,** 1 teaspoon chopped **parsley,** and ½ teaspoon **lemon juice** into finished sauce. Good with green beans, carrots, potatoes, and fish.

MUSTARD SAUCE

Prepare **White Sauce,** but stir 1 tablespoon **Dijon mustard** into finished sauce. Simmer for 1 minute. Good with broccoli, Brussels sprouts, cabbage, potatoes, poached or baked fish, and poultry.

MUSHROOM SAUCE

Melt butter for **White Sauce.** In it, cook ¼ pound sliced **mushrooms** until soft. Proceed with recipe, but use 1 cup **half-and-half** (light cream) instead of milk. Stir 2 teaspoons *each* **lemon juice** and **dry sherry** into finished sauce. Good with green beans, potatoes, spinach (in creamed spinach), and ground beef patties.

How to stir-fry vegetables (Recipe on facing page)

1 Cut vegetables into small, uniform pieces so they will cook quickly. Have vegetables, liquid, and seasonings or sauce ready before you start to cook.

2 Stir-frying requires a very hot pan. Heat pan, then heat oil until it ripples. Add firmest vegetables to pan first; stir to coat with oil. Add liquid, if needed; cover pan.

3 Tender vegetables go in near end of cooking time. Stir-fry them uncovered. At point of doneness, cooking liquid should have evaporated, leaving crisp-tender vegetables.

4 Piping hot stir-fried vegetables lend freshness to any entrée. Choose combinations with compatible flavors, contrasting colors. Select vegetables in season.

Stir-fried vegetables for garden fresh flavor

Of all the techniques for cooking vegetables, we think stir-frying is the most versatile—and the most fun. With this method, vegetables retain their crisp textures, bright colors, and natural flavors, and the cooking takes only a few minutes.

The stir-fry steps are more important than the type of equipment you use. You can stir-fry in the traditional dome-shaped wok or in a wide frying pan. Vegetables cook quickly, so have everything ready before you begin.

Basic Stir-fried Vegetables

(Pictured on facing page)

Following this basic recipe and its Oriental stir-fry variation, we list those vegetables most suitable for stir-frying, along with cutting suggestions, amounts of liquid to add, and cooking times.

> **Garnish (optional): 3 tablespoons pine nuts, slivered almonds, cashews, or sunflower seeds**
> 2 **to 2½ tablespoons salad oil**
> 1 **pound cut vegetables**
> 1 **small clove garlic, minced or pressed**
> **Regular-strength chicken broth or water**
> **Chopped fresh herbs or dry herbs (see "Compatible seasonings" column in vegetable chart, pages 127–130)**
> **Salt and pepper**

If using a garnish, cook nuts or seeds in a wide frying pan or wok over medium heat in ½ tablespoon of the oil until golden; set aside.

Increase heat to high. When pan is hot, add 2 tablespoons oil. When oil ripples, add vegetables and garlic and stir-fry for 1 minute. Add liquid; cover and cook until vegetables are crisp-tender.

If you wish to cook several vegetables and the textures are different, add firmest vegetable to pan first and partially cook. Add the more tender vegetables near end of cooking time. Stir in nuts or seeds; season with herbs and salt and pepper to taste. Makes 4 servings.

ORIENTAL STIR-FRIED VEGETABLES

In a bowl, combine ½ cup regular-strength **chicken broth** or water, 1 tablespoon **cornstarch,** and 2 teaspoons **soy sauce.** Prepare **Basic Stir-fried Vegetables,** but add ½ teaspoon minced **fresh ginger** along with garlic. Cook with liquid

until crisp-tender, then stir cooking sauce, add to pan, and cook, stirring, until sauce bubbles and thickens (about 30 seconds). Omit herbs.

Asparagus. Cut into ¼-inch slanting slices. Stir-fry for 1 minute. Add 2 tablespoons liquid; cover and cook for 2 to 3 minutes.

Broccoli. Cut off flowerets and slash their stems. Peel thick stalks, then slice thinly or cut into julienne strips. Stir-fry for 1 minute. Add 2 tablespoons liquid; cover and cook for 3 to 4 minutes.

Cabbage (all varieties). Cut into ¼-inch slices or 1-inch pieces. Stir-fry for 1 minute. Add 1 tablespoon liquid; cover and cook for 2 minutes.

Carrots. Cut into ¼-inch slanting slices. Stir-fry for 1 minute. Add 3 tablespoons liquid; cover and cook for 3 to 4 minutes.

Cauliflower. Break into flowerets, then slice ⅛ inch thick. Stir-fry for 1 minute. Add 3 tablespoons liquid; cover and cook for 3 to 4 minutes.

Celery. Cut into ¼-inch slices. Stir-fry for 1 minute. Add a few drops liquid and cook for 1 minute.

Green beans. Cut into 1-inch lengths. Stir-fry for 1 minute. Add 3 tablespoons liquid; cover and cook for 4 minutes.

Mushrooms. Slice through stems in ¼-inch-thick slices. Stir-fry for 1 minute. Add 1 tablespoon liquid and toss for 2 minutes.

Onions. Cut into wedges or slice; separate layers or rings. Stir-fry for 1 to 2 minutes.

Peppers (green and red bell). Seed; cut into 1-inch squares or ¼-inch slices. Stir-fry for 1 minute. Add 1 tablespoon liquid and cook for 1 minute.

Chinese pea pods. Break off ends and remove strings. Stir fry for 1 minute. Add 1 tablespoon liquid and cook for 1 minute.

Tomatoes. Cut into wedges. Stir-fry for 1 to 2 minutes.

Zucchini (and other summer squash). Cut into ¼-inch slanting slices. Stir-fry for 1 minute. Add 1 tablespoon liquid; cover and cook for 3 minutes.

A seasonal parade of recipes

Even reluctant vegetable eaters will love their greens and yellows when you treat them to a few of the upcoming recipes. These tempting dishes will take you effortlessly, yet deliciously, through the seasons, in an alphabetical parade—from those artichokes you couldn't resist at the roadside stand, to that bumper crop of backyard zucchini.

Artichokes with Sour Cream-Ham Dip

(Pictured on page 139)

> 4 medium-size artichokes (4 inches in diameter)
> 2 tablespoons olive oil or salad oil
> ½ pint (1 cup) sour cream
> ½ cup mayonnaise
> 2 tablespoons minced onion
> ¼ teaspoon *each* Worcestershire and garlic salt
> 1 package (4 oz.) sliced cooked ham, minced
> 4 parsley sprigs

Prepare and boil artichokes (see chart, page 127), but add olive oil to cooking water. When stem ends are fork tender, drain artichokes. Let cool slightly, then pull out center leaves. Using a spoon, scrape out fuzzy centers. Cool, wrap, and refrigerate artichokes for 1 hour or until next day.

Meanwhile, in a bowl, stir together sour cream, mayonnaise, onion, Worcestershire, garlic salt, and all but 2 tablespoons of the ham. Save remaining ham for garnish. Cover and chill for at least 1 hour.

To serve, place artichokes on individual plates. Fan out leaves from heart like petals of a flower. Spoon sour cream mixture into center. Garnish with remaining ham and parsley. Use leaves as scoopers, but serve with forks for eating artichoke hearts. Makes 4 servings.

Asparagus Polonaise

> 2 pounds asparagus
> 4 tablespoons butter or margarine
> 2 tablespoons soft bread crumbs
> 1 hard-cooked egg, chopped
> 1 tablespoon minced parsley

Prepare and boil or steam asparagus spears or slices (see chart, page 127). In a small pan, melt butter over medium heat. Add bread crumbs and cook until lightly browned. Remove from heat and stir in chopped egg and parsley. Spoon over hot, drained asparagus. Makes 4 servings.

Asparagus with Cashew Butter

> 2 pounds asparagus
> 4 tablespoons butter or margarine
> 2 teaspoons lemon juice
> ¼ teaspoon marjoram leaves
> ¼ cup salted cashews, coarsely chopped

Prepare and boil or steam asparagus spears or slices (see chart, page 127). In a small pan, melt butter over low heat. Add lemon juice, marjoram, and cashews and simmer for 2 minutes. Pour over hot, drained asparagus. Makes 4 servings.

Deviled Green Beans

> 2 tablespoons butter or margarine
> 1 medium-size onion, chopped
> 1 clove garlic, minced or pressed
> ½ green pepper, seeded and chopped
> 1 jar (2 oz.) sliced pimentos, chopped
> 2 teaspoons prepared mustard
> 1 can (8 oz.) tomato sauce
> 1 pound green beans
>   Salt and pepper
> 1 cup (4 oz.) shredded Cheddar cheese

Melt butter in a wide frying pan over medium-high heat. Add onion, garlic, and green pepper and cook until onion is soft (about 5 minutes). Remove from heat and stir in pimentos, mustard, and tomato sauce.

Prepare and boil or steam sliced beans (see chart, page 127). Stir drained beans into tomato sauce mixture. Season to taste with salt and pepper. Spoon into a 1-quart casserole and sprinkle with cheese. Bake in a 350° oven for 25 minutes or until cheese is melted. Makes 4 servings.

Beets with Mustard Butter

    4 tablespoons butter or margarine, softened
    1 tablespoon *each* tarragon vinegar and
       prepared mustard
    4 to 6 medium-size beets
    1 to 2 tablespoons water

In a bowl, beat together butter, vinegar, and mustard; set aside. Prepare, boil, and peel beets (see chart, page 128), then cut into ½-inch cubes. Return beets to pan and add water. Cover and cook until beets are heated through and water has evaporated. Add mustard-butter mixture and stir until it melts and coats beets. Makes 4 to 6 servings.

Broccoli with Cheese Topping

    1½ pounds broccoli
     1 cup (4 oz.) shredded Swiss cheese
    ⅓ cup mayonnaise
     2 tablespoons grated onion
    ½ teaspoon prepared mustard
    ¼ teaspoon salt
    ⅛ teaspoon pepper

Prepare and boil or steam broccoli spears and sliced stems (see chart, page 128). Arrange drained broccoli (hot or cold) in a buttered shallow baking dish. In a bowl, combine cheese, mayonnaise, onion, mustard, salt, and pepper; spoon evenly over broccoli. Bake, uncovered, in a 350° oven for about 15 minutes or until broccoli is hot and sauce is bubbly. Makes 4 to 6 servings.

Creamy Cabbage

    2 tablespoons butter or margarine
    1 small head cabbage (1 to 1½ lbs.), quartered,
       cored, and thinly sliced
    2 tablespoons water
    1 small package (3 oz.) cream cheese with
       chives, cut into small cubes
       Salt and pepper

Melt butter in a wide frying pan over medium-high heat. Add cabbage and water. Cover and cook, stirring once halfway through cooking, until cabbage is crisp-tender (about 5 minutes total).

Reduce heat to low and distribute cream cheese over cabbage. Stir lightly until cheese melts into pan juices. Season to taste with salt and pepper. Makes 4 to 6 servings.

HOW TO MAKE FLAVORED BUTTERS

Flavored butters are a type of convenience seasoning you make at home. You can mix one in minutes, then store it in the refrigerator for those times when you want a special topping for vegetables, meat, poultry, or fish. Flavored butters are also very good on hot, toasty French bread.

For storage beyond 2 weeks, shape a flavored butter into a log, wrap it in foil, and freeze. There's no need to thaw. Cut off slices as needed and melt over piping hot food. Each of the following recipes makes ½ cup.

Fines herbes butter. In a bowl, mix until well blended ½ cup **butter** or margarine, softened; white part of 1 **green onion,** minced; 2 tablespoons chopped **parsley,** ½ teaspoon *each* **dry tarragon** and **dry chervil,** and a dash of **pepper.** Melt on corn on the cob, green beans, steamed zucchini; pan-fried sole fillets; sautéed liver; and poached eggs.

Garlic butter. In a bowl, mix until well blended ½ cup **butter** or margarine, softened; 2 or 3 cloves **garlic,** minced or pressed; and 2 tablespoons chopped **parsley.** Spread on French bread; use to season boiled potatoes and steamed vegetables; melt on broiled salmon, lamb chops, and steaks.

Mustard butter. In a bowl, mix until well blended ½ cup **butter** or margarine, softened; 2 teaspoons **dry mustard;** 2 tablespoons chopped **parsley;** ½ teaspoon **Worcestershire;** ¼ teaspoon **garlic salt;** and a dash of **pepper.** Spread on bread for meat or cheese sandwiches. Use to season steamed asparagus, carrots, and zucchini; melt on steaks, hamburgers, and fish.

...Seasonal parade of vegetables

Carrots Vichy

> 8 to 12 slender carrots
> 4 tablespoons butter or margarine
> 2 tablespoons brandy (optional)
> ¼ cup minced parsley
> Salt and pepper

Prepare and boil whole carrots (see chart, page 128). Melt butter in a wide frying pan over medium-high heat. Add brandy, if desired. Add hot drained carrots and cook, shaking pan, until carrots are lightly browned on all sides. Mix in parsley and season to taste with salt and pepper. Makes 4 to 6 servings.

Orange-glazed Carrots

> 1 tablespoon cornstarch
> ½ teaspoon grated orange peel
> ½ cup orange juice
> 1 teaspoon prepared mustard
> 3 tablespoons butter or margarine
> 1 large onion, cut in half and thinly sliced
> 8 medium-size carrots, cut into ¼-inch-thick slices
> ¼ cup water
> Salt and pepper

In a bowl, combine cornstarch, orange peel, orange juice, and mustard; set aside. Melt butter in a wide frying pan over medium heat. Stir in onion and carrots, then add water. Cover pan, bring to a boil, then reduce heat and simmer until carrots are tender-crisp (10 to 12 minutes). Stir cornstarch mixture, pour into pan, and cook, stirring, until sauce boils and thickens. Season to taste with salt and pepper. Makes 6 servings.

Curried Cauliflower

> 3 tablespoons salad oil
> 1½ teaspoons curry powder
> ¾ teaspoon salt
> ½ teaspoon *each* ground ginger and cumin
> 1 head cauliflower, trimmed and broken into flowerets
> ¾ cup water

Heat oil in a wide frying pan over medium heat. Stir in curry powder, salt, ginger, and cumin and cook for 1 minute. Add cauliflower and stir to coat. Add water and bring to a boil. Cover and simmer until cauliflower is crisp-tender (6 to 8 minutes). Drain. Makes 4 to 6 servings.

Crusty Baked Eggplant

> 1 eggplant (1 to 1¼ lbs.)
> 1 teaspoon salt
> 1 egg
> 2 tablespoons grated Parmesan cheese
> ¼ cup fine dry bread crumbs
> 1 tablespoon finely chopped parsley
> About ¼ cup all-purpose flour
> 2 tablespoons butter or margarine, melted

Peel eggplant, if you wish; cut into ½-inch slices. Sprinkle salt on both sides of slices. Let stand for 30 minutes; rinse with water and pat dry.

In a pie pan, beat egg slightly. In another pan, combine cheese, bread crumbs, and parsley. Dust each eggplant slice with flour, dip in egg to coat all over, and dredge in crumb mixture.

Brush butter over bottom of a shallow, rimmed baking pan. Arrange eggplant slices in butter in a single layer. Bake, uncovered, in a 400° oven for 25 minutes, turning once to brown both sides. Makes 4 servings.

Mushroom Sauté

> 1 pound mushrooms
> 2 tablespoons butter or margarine
> 1 medium-size onion, thinly sliced
> 1 teaspoon sugar
> 2 tablespoons *each* dry white wine and soy sauce
> Dash *each* of salt and pepper

Rinse mushrooms *briefly* in cold water. If stem ends are gritty, slice them off. Cut mushrooms lengthwise through caps and stems into thick slices. Melt butter in a wide frying pan over medium heat. Add onion and cook until soft (about 5 minutes). Add mushrooms, sugar, wine, soy, salt, and pepper. Stir to blend. Cook, stirring, over high heat until liquid is nearly gone (about 5 minutes). Serve hot. Makes 4 servings.

Preparing Artichokes with Sour Cream-Ham Dip (Recipe on page 136)

1 Using a sharp stainless steel knife (not carbon steel—it turns artichokes black), cut stem even with base; then cut off top ⅓ of artichoke. Remove coarse outer leaves.

2 Cut off thorny tips of remaining leaves, then immediately immerse cut artichoke in vinegar water to prevent discoloring. When all are trimmed, cook until fork-tender.

3 Remove small inside leaves and choke by reaching into center of artichoke with a spoon. Gently ease spoon under fuzzy choke, separating it from heart; lift choke out and discard.

4 For an elegant first course, fan out leaves from heart in petal fashion. Spoon sour cream mixture into center. Use leaves as scoopers; eat heart with a fork.

...Seasonal parade of vegetables

Sherried Peas & Mushrooms

2½ **pounds unshelled peas or 2 packages (10 oz. each) frozen tiny peas, thawed**
2 **tablespoons butter or margarine**
½ **pound mushrooms, sliced**
¼ **teaspoon marjoram leaves**
⅛ **teaspoon ground nutmeg**
2 **tablespoons dry sherry**
Salt

Prepare and boil or steam fresh peas (see chart, page 129). Melt butter in a wide frying pan over medium-high heat. Add mushrooms and cook until their juices have evaporated. Stir in drained peas (or thawed peas), marjoram, nutmeg, and sherry. Cook until juices are boiling and peas are heated through. Season to taste with salt. Makes 6 to 8 servings.

Peas with Lettuce

2½ **pounds unshelled peas or 2 packages (10 oz. each) frozen tiny peas, thawed**
4 **tablespoons butter or margarine**
3 **cups shredded iceberg lettuce**
¼ **cup minced parsley**
½ **teaspoon sugar**
⅛ **teaspoon ground nutmeg**
Salt

Prepare and boil or steam fresh peas (see chart, page 129). Melt butter in a wide frying pan over high heat. Add lettuce and cook, stirring, until wilted (2 to 3 minutes). Immediately stir in drained peas (or thawed peas), parsley, sugar, and nutmeg. Cook until juices are boiling and peas are heated through; drain. Season to taste with salt. Makes 6 to 8 servings.

Stuffed Baked Potatoes

4 **large baking potatoes**
4 **tablespoons butter or margarine**
½ **cup half-and-half (light cream)**
½ **cup shredded Cheddar cheese**
2 **tablespoons minced green onion**
Salt
Paprika

Prepare and bake potatoes (see chart, page 129). While potatoes are still warm, cut a thick slice off top of each potato. Using a spoon, scoop out pulp into a bowl, leaving potato shells ¼ inch thick. Using an electric mixer or a potato masher, beat potatoes until they're in fine lumps. Add butter and half-and-half and continue beating until smooth. Stir in cheese, onion, and salt to taste.

Mound mixture into potato shells; sprinkle lightly with paprika. Place stuffed potatoes on a rimmed baking sheet. If made ahead, cover and refrigerate for up to 24 hours. Bake, uncovered, in a 375° oven for 20 to 30 minutes or until tops are golden brown and potatoes are piping hot. Makes 4 servings.

Baked Potato Sticks

4 **medium-size baking potatoes**
3 **tablespoons butter or margarine, melted**
¼ **teaspoon ground cumin**
4 **dashes liquid hot pepper seasoning**

Scrub potatoes, but do not peel. Cut lengthwise into quarters. In a small container, combine butter, cumin, and hot pepper seasoning; brush over cut surfaces of potatoes. Arrange potato quarters, skin side down, in a shallow pan. Bake, uncovered, in a 400° oven for 1 hour or until potatoes are fork-tender. Makes 4 servings.

Rosemary Roasted Potatoes

2 **pounds small, red, thin-skinned potatoes (1 to 2 inches in diameter)**
1 **small red onion, finely chopped**
1 **tablespoon lemon juice**
1 **teaspoon dry rosemary**
Olive oil
Salt

Scrub potatoes, but do not peel; cut in half if larger than 1 inch in diameter. Arrange in a single layer in a shallow pan. Sprinkle onion, lemon juice, and rosemary over potatoes. Pour olive oil into pan to a depth of ⅛ inch. Turn potatoes over in oil. Bake, uncovered, in a 400° oven, shaking pan occasionally to rotate potatoes in oil, until largest potatoes are fork-tender (25 to 40 minutes). Season to taste with salt. Makes 6 servings.

A PROFILE OF POTATOES

Though there are many varieties of potatoes, from a cook's point of view they actually fall into only two categories: baking potatoes and thin-skinned potatoes (see photo 1, page 142).

When buying potatoes from either category, choose those that are smooth and firm. Reject those with cracks, green-tinged skins, and sprouting eyes.

Baking potatoes. You can recognize these by their thick, brown skins. The smaller and medium-size ones are frequently sold in 5 and 10-pound bags. Larger ones are sold individually under various names, such as russet, Idaho, or Burbank potatoes —or in some cases, they're simply called all-purpose potatoes. They have a dry, mealy texture that makes them the best choice for baking. They may also be fried, boiled, or mashed.

Thin-skinned potatoes. These potatoes come in two varieties—red-skinned and white-skinned. They range from ping-pong ball size (often called new potatoes) to half pounders. Because of their waxy texture, they hold their shape well and are perfect for boiling and steaming. These are the potatoes to use for potato salad.

Mashed Potatoes

> 3 pounds baking potatoes
> ¼ cup milk
> 3 tablespoons butter or margarine
> Salt and pepper

Prepare and boil quartered potatoes (see chart, page 129); drain. Using an electric mixer or a potato masher, beat hot potatoes until they're in fine lumps. Add milk and butter and continue beating until smooth. Season to taste with salt and pepper. Serve immediately. Makes 4 to 6 servings.

Mashed Potato Casserole

(Pictured on page 142)

> 1 package (3 oz.) cream cheese, softened
> 1 teaspoon garlic salt
> ¼ teaspoon pepper
> ½ cup sour cream
> 2½ to 3 pounds baking potatoes
> 2 tablespoons butter or margarine
> Paprika
> Parsley sprigs (optional)

In a bowl, stir together cream cheese, garlic salt, pepper, and sour cream until smooth; set aside. Prepare and boil quartered potatoes (see chart, page 129); drain. Using an electric mixer or a potato masher, beat hot potatoes until they're in fine lumps. Add sour cream mixture and continue beating until fluffy and smooth. Spoon potatoes into a well-buttered shallow 2-quart casserole; dot with butter and sprinkle with paprika. If made ahead, cover and refrigerate until next day.

Bake, covered, in a 400° oven for 25 minutes (50 minutes, if refrigerated); uncover and bake for 10 more minutes or until top is golden brown. Garnish with parsley sprigs, if desired. Makes 6 servings.

Creamed Spinach

> 2 bunches (1½ lbs. *total*) spinach or 2 packages (10 oz. *each*) frozen chopped spinach
> 2 tablespoons butter or margarine
> 2 tablespoons all-purpose flour
> 1 cup half-and-half (light cream)
> ½ teaspoon *each* salt and Worcestershire
> Dash *each* of dry mustard and pepper
> 4 strips bacon, crisply cooked, drained, and crumbled (optional)

Prepare and boil spinach (see chart, page 130); drain well, then coarsely chop. Or cook frozen spinach according to package directions; drain.

Melt butter in a 2-quart pan over medium heat. Add flour and cook, stirring, until bubbly (about 2 minutes). Remove pan from heat. Stirring constantly, pour in half-and-half. Return to heat and cook, stirring, until sauce boils and thickens. Stir in salt, Worcestershire, mustard, and pepper. Add chopped spinach and heat through. Stir in bacon, if used. Makes 4 to 6 servings.

Preparing Mashed Potato Casserole (Recipe on page 141)

1 Baking potatoes (at top) also make good mashed potatoes; they have a dry, mealy texture. Thin-skinned potatoes (at bottom) have a smooth, waxy texture and retain shape after boiling.

2 Potatoes are ready for mashing when a fork can easily pierce them—they will break in two.

3 With an electric mixer, slowly begin to mash potatoes until they are in fine lumps.

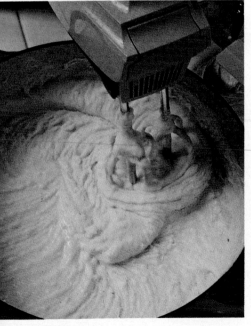

4 After adding sour cream mixture, continue beating until potato mixture is fluffy and smooth.

5 This creamy, golden brown Mashed Potato Casserole is a most fitting companion for roast turkey, chicken, or beef. Garnish with parsley, if desired.

...Seasonal parade of vegetables

Succotash

    4   strips bacon, diced
    1   package (10 oz.) frozen baby lima beans
    ¾   cup water
        About 2 cups creamy uncooked corn (see
        photo, page 126), cut from 4 ears of corn
    2   tablespoons butter or margarine
        Salt and pepper

In a 3-quart pan over medium heat, cook bacon until crisp. With a slotted spoon, remove bacon; drain on paper towels and set aside. Discard all but 1 tablespoon drippings. Add lima beans and water; cover and bring to a boil. Reduce heat and simmer until beans are tender (10 to 12 minutes). Add corn and cook, uncovered, over medium-high heat, stirring occasionally, until corn is tender and most of liquid is absorbed (about 5 minutes). Stir in bacon and butter; season to taste with salt and pepper. Makes 6 servings.

Garlicky Baked Tomatoes

    6   to 8 medium size tomatoes
    2   tablespoons olive oil or salad oil
    2   tablespoons *each* finely chopped garlic
        (about 7 cloves), chopped parsley, and fine
        dry bread crumbs
        Dash of pepper
        Salt

Core tomatoes and cut in half horizontally. Gently squeeze out juice and seeds (see photo, page 126). Arrange tomatoes, cut side up, in a 9 by 13-inch baking dish. Drizzle with oil. Bake, uncovered, in a 400° oven for 10 minutes.

  Meanwhile, combine garlic, parsley, bread crumbs, and pepper in small bowl. Sprinkle mixture over tomatoes and continue baking, uncovered, for 15 more minutes. Season to taste with salt. Makes 6 to 8 servings.

Candied Yams

    6   medium-size yams or sweet potatoes
    4   tablespoons butter or margarine
        Salt
    ⅓   cup firmly packed brown sugar
    3   tablespoons rum or orange juice

Prepare and boil whole yams or sweet potatoes (see chart, page 130); drain. Let yams cool, then peel and cut into ¼-inch-thick slices. Arrange slices, overlapping, in a buttered shallow casserole. Dot with butter, sprinkle lightly with salt, then sprinkle evenly with brown sugar. Drizzle with rum or orange juice. Bake, uncovered, in a 350° oven for 30 minutes or until bubbly and glazed. Makes 6 servings.

Winter Squash with Apples

    4   tablespoons butter or margarine
    1   pound butternut or banana squash, peeled
        and cut into 1-inch cubes
    ¼   cup water
    1   large tart apple, cored, peeled, and cut into
        ½-inch cubes
    2   teaspoons lemon juice
    ¼   cup firmly packed brown sugar
    ¼   teaspoon ground cinnamon
    ⅛   teaspoon ground nutmeg
        Salt

Melt butter in a wide frying pan over medium-high heat. Add squash, water, apple, and lemon juice. Cover and cook, stirring occasionally, until squash is just tender and liquid is absorbed (4 to 5 minutes). Stir in brown sugar, cinnamon, nutmeg, and salt to taste. Heat for 1 minute to melt brown sugar. Makes 4 servings.

Zucchini with Corn & Peppers

    3   tablespoons butter or margarine
    1½ pounds zucchini, cut into ½-inch cubes
    1½ cups uncooked corn, cut from 3 ears, or
        1 package (10 oz.) frozen corn, thawed
    1   red or green bell pepper, seeded and
        chopped
    1   medium-size onion, chopped
    1   clove garlic, minced or pressed
        Salt and pepper

Melt butter in a wide frying pan over medium-high heat. Add zucchini, corn, bell pepper, onion, and garlic. Cook, stirring frequently, until most of vegetable liquid has evaporated and vegetables are crisp-tender (about 5 minutes). Add salt and pepper to taste. Makes 6 servings.

BREADS

It's not hard to enjoy the baker's sweet smell of success. Scones, French toast, waffles—their aromas lure everyone into the kitchen. And who can resist the tug of home-baked goodness arising from yeast bread or popovers baking in the oven?

It's easiest to start with quick breads. They use baking powder or baking soda instead of yeast for leavening, and they're fast to assemble, stirred only briefly, and baked immediately.

Yeast breads, on the other hand, have the reputation of being chancy and difficult—there's the extra work of kneading the dough, the extra hour or two of letting it rise. But once you've given it a try, you'll find it's easy and rewarding.

Chemical leavenings & what they do

Leavenings produce the carbon dioxide gas that lightens doughs and batters. Baking powder and baking soda are chemical leavenings (unlike yeast, which is a biological leavening).

Baking powder is sold in three forms, all activated when combined with liquid. *Tartrate* acts instantly. *Phosphate* is activated partially by liquid, partially by heat. *Double-acting* is activated mainly by heat, releasing most of its carbon dioxide in the baking process. *(Recipes in this book were tested with double-acting baking powder.)*

Baking soda releases gas only when mixed with an acid agent, such as buttermilk, sour milk, or lemon juice.

BAKING BREAD IN HIGH COUNTRY

Baking high in the mountains—above 3000 feet—requires some adjustment of recipes. Baking powder and baking soda are the ingredients affected. At high elevations, they produce gases at a greatly accelerated rate. In the early stages of baking this can create too great a volume; the gas cells burst, causing your quick bread to collapse. Specialists in high elevation cooking sometimes suggest that the baking powder and baking soda in standard, sea level recipes for biscuits, muffins, and quick breads be decreased by one-fourth the amount specified.

Yeast breads are affected even more by high elevations. Yeast bread dough rises more rapidly in high country, so you must punch it down after the first rising and let it rise again until fully doubled in bulk before continuing with the recipe. Use slightly less yeast, too, unless you're in a hurry. But you may need to use a little more liquid in the dough because liquid evaporates faster at high elevations and ingredients dry out more quickly.

Popovers even pop faster at high elevations, so use an extra egg in standard recipes—this will strengthen the popovers' hollowed shells.

Baking powder biscuits

For tender, flaky biscuits with just enough moisture, be sure to measure ingredients precisely, and knead the dough for as long as the recipe recommends. Sift dry ingredients together for a more even distribution of the baking powder; otherwise tiny yellow and brown spots will appear on the surface of the baked biscuits. Once liquid is added to the dry ingredients, stir only until the flour is moist. Overzealous mixing or kneading may result in heavy biscuits that fail to rise completely. Biscuits made from rolled-out dough should, when baked, have straight sides and level tops toasted to a golden hue.

> 2 **cups all-purpose flour**
> 4 **teaspoons baking powder**
> ½ **teaspoon salt**
> 5 **tablespoons solid shortening**
> ¾ **cup milk**

Preheat oven to 450°. In a bowl, sift together flour, baking powder, and salt. Using a pastry blender or 2 knives, cut shortening into flour mixture until it resembles coarse cornmeal; make a well in center. Pour in milk all at once and stir with a fork until dough cleans sides of bowl.

With your hands, gather dough into a ball; turn out onto a lightly floured board (use about 1 tablespoon flour). Knead (see page 159) about 10 times (dough will feel light and soft, but not sticky). Roll out or pat dough into a ½-inch-thick circle. Using a floured 2-inch cutter, cut biscuit rounds as close together as possible, since rerolling toughens dough. Fit leftover bits of dough together, pat smooth, and cut. (Grandma baked the odd bits of dough without rerolling, and called them "puppy-dogs' tails.") Place biscuits close together (for soft sides) or 1 inch apart (for crispy sides) on an ungreased baking sheet.

Bake for 15 to 20 minutes or until tops are lightly browned. Makes 10 to 12 biscuits.

BUTTERMILK BISCUITS

Prepare **Baking Powder Biscuits,** but reduce baking powder to 2½ teaspoons, and add ½ teaspoon **baking soda** and 1 tablespoon **sugar** to dry ingredients. Use ¾ cup **buttermilk** instead of sweet milk.

DROP BISCUITS

Prepare **Baking Powder Biscuits,** but increase **milk** to 1 cup. Drop by tablespoons onto a greased baking sheet.

Old-fashioned Cream Scones

Scones are the Scottish cousins of biscuits, but noticeably richer because they include eggs and cream.

> 2 **cups all-purpose flour**
> 3 **teaspoons baking powder**
> 2 **tablespoons sugar**
> ½ **teaspoon salt**
> 4 **tablespoons butter or margarine**
> 2 **eggs**
> ⅓ **cup whipping cream**
> 2 **teaspoons sugar**

Preheat oven to 400°. In a bowl, sift together flour, baking powder, the 2 tablespoons sugar, and salt. Using a pastry blender or 2 knives, cut butter into flour mixture until it resembles coarse cornmeal; make a well in center. Separate 1 of the eggs; reserve egg white. Stir together egg yolk and remaining whole egg, then stir in cream. Pour into well and stir with a fork until dough cleans sides of bowl.

Sprinkle a board with about 1 tablespoon flour. With your hands, gather dough into a ball. Turn dough out onto board and knead (see page 159) about 10 times. Divide into 2 parts. Roll out each part into a 1-inch-thick circle about 6 inches in diameter. With a knife, cut each circle into 4 wedges and arrange on an ungreased baking sheet about 1 inch apart. Brush tops with reserved egg white and sprinkle with the 2 teaspoons sugar.

Bake for 15 minutes or until golden brown. Serve warm. Makes 8 scones.

ORANGE CREAM SCONES

Prepare **Old-fashioned Cream Scones,** but add 2 to 3 teaspoons grated **orange peel** and ¼ teaspoon **vanilla** when you add liquid.

Muffins

Baking magnificent muffins is not only rewarding, but surprisingly easy as well. The keys to perfection are careful measuring and just the right mixing technique. Follow directions precisely, and you won't experience the classic pitfalls of muffin-making—tunnels, coarse texture, and toughness.

The following basic recipe creates a slightly sweet muffin that is tender but a bit coarse, with a pebbly, browned surface and a fairly even shape.

  2   cups all-purpose flour
  3   tablespoons sugar
  3   teaspoons baking powder
  ½   teaspoon salt
  1   cup milk
  1   egg
  4   tablespoons butter or margarine, melted and cooled

Preheat oven to 425°. Grease a muffin pan with 2½-inch-diameter cups, or line them with paper baking cup liners; set aside.

In a bowl, sift together flour, sugar, baking powder, and salt; make a well in center. Pour milk into a 2-cup glass measure and add egg and butter; blend well. Pour liquid all at once into flour well. (This method allows you to mix the batter with fewer strokes, avoiding overstirring.) Making 12 to 15 full circular strokes that scrape bottom of bowl, stir just until dry ingredients are moistened. Batter should be lumpy. Fill each prepared muffin cup 2/3 full with batter.

Bake for 20 to 25 minutes or until tops are lightly browned. Remove muffins from pan immediately (otherwise moisture condenses on bottom of cups and muffins become soggy). Makes 12 muffins.

CREATING THE PERFECT MUFFIN

 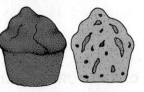

Well-made muffins have pebbly tops and a golden crust. When muffin is cut, inside texture shows even cell structure.

Overstirred muffins have peaked tops usually sloping to one side. When muffin is cut, inside texture shows tunnels—elongated air cells.

BLUEBERRY MUFFINS
(Pictured on facing page)

Prepare **Muffins,** but increase **sugar** to ½ cup and stir ¾ cup fresh or frozen (unthawed) **blueberries** into flour mixture before making the well.

CHEESE MUFFINS

Prepare **Muffins,** but reduce sugar to 1 tablespoon and stir ½ to ¾ cup shredded **Cheddar cheese** into flour mixture before making the well.

CORNMEAL MUFFINS

Prepare **Muffins,** but substitute 1 cup **yellow cornmeal** for 1 cup of the flour.

JAM MUFFINS

Prepare **Muffins,** but just before baking, place ½ teaspoon of your favorite **jam** in center of batter in each muffin cup.

ORANGE MUFFINS

Prepare **Muffins,** but increase **sugar** to ½ cup and add 1 tablespoon grated **orange peel;** substitute ¼ cup **orange juice** for ¼ cup of the milk (you'll need 1 medium-size orange.)

NUT MUFFINS

Prepare **Muffins,** but increase **sugar** to ½ cup and stir ½ cup chopped **nuts** into flour mixture before making the well.

RAISIN MUFFINS

Prepare **Muffins,** but stir ¾ cup **raisins** into flour mixture before making the well.

WHOLE WHEAT MUFFINS

Prepare **Muffins,** but substitute 1 cup **whole wheat flour** for 1 cup of the flour.

How to make Blueberry Muffins (Recipe on facing page)

1 Make a well in center of flour mixture (push mixture up sides of bowl) and pour combined liquid ingredients all at once into well. This step is essential to light, tender muffins.

2 About one more stir and it's ready—you stir just to moisten flour mixture. Count strokes—12 to 15 circular stirs will blend batter. It should look lumpy, not smooth and liquid.

3 Served hot from the oven, these golden, pebbly-topped Blueberry Muffins make an irresistible morning treat.

Quick breads

These effortless breads require no rising time—they are extremely versatile, too. You can lace them with fruit, nuts, spices—even chiles and cheese.

Banana Bread

    3   large ripe bananas
    1   cup sugar
    1   egg
    4   tablespoons butter or margarine, melted and
        cooled
 1½   cups all-purpose flour
    1   teaspoon *each* salt and baking soda

Preheat oven to 325°. Lightly grease a 9 by 5-inch loaf pan; set aside.

In a bowl, mash bananas; you should have 1 cup. Beat in sugar, then egg and butter. In another bowl, stir together flour, salt, and baking soda; add to banana mixture and stir just until all flour is moistened. Pour batter into prepared pan.

Bake for 55 to 60 minutes (see doneness test below). Makes 1 loaf.

Apricot Nut Loaf

    ¾   cup dried apricots
        Lukewarm water
    1   orange
    ½   cup raisins
        Boiling water
    ⅔   cup sugar
    2   tablespoons butter or margarine, melted
    1   egg
    2   cups all-purpose flour
    2   teaspoons baking powder
    1   teaspoon *each* salt and baking soda
    ½   cup chopped walnuts
    1   teaspoon vanilla

Preheat oven to 350°. Lightly grease a 9 by 5-inch loaf pan; set aside.

In a bowl, cover apricots with lukewarm water and let stand for 30 minutes; drain. Using a vegetable peeler, remove zest (thin, colored part of peel) from only half the orange. Cut orange in half and squeeze all juice from both halves. Force apricots, orange zest, and raisins through a food grinder or finely chop with a knife.

Add enough boiling water to orange juice to make 1 cup and pour into a bowl along with ground fruit. Stir in sugar and butter; beat in egg. In a separate bowl, stir together flour, baking powder, salt, baking soda, and walnuts; add to fruit mixture along with vanilla and stir just until all flour is moistened. Pour into prepared pan.

Bake for 55 to 60 minutes (see doneness test below). Makes 1 loaf.

Pineapple-Zucchini Bread

    3   eggs
    2   cups sugar
    1   cup salad oil
    2   teaspoons vanilla
    2   cups coarsely shredded, unpeeled zucchini
    1   can (8¼ oz.) crushed pineapple, drained well
    3   cups all-purpose flour
    2   teaspoons baking soda
    1   teaspoon salt
    ½   teaspoon baking powder
 1½   teaspoons ground cinnamon
    ¾   teaspoon ground nutmeg
    1   cup finely chopped walnuts

Preheat oven to 350°. Lightly grease two 9 by 5-inch loaf pans; set aside.

In a bowl, beat eggs with an electric beater until frothy; beat in sugar, oil, and vanilla and continue beating until mixture is thick and foamy.

QUICK BREAD: THE FINISHED PRODUCT

When a quick bread has baked just long enough, it begins to pull away from the sides of its pan; a wooden pick inserted in the center of the loaf should come out clean. A crack down the center of the loaf is characteristic of this kind of bread and cannot be prevented. Let the loaf cool in its pan on a wire rack for 10 minutes, then turn out onto the rack to cool completely. If you wait a day before slicing, the bread will be easier to slice and more flavorful. If made ahead, wrap the cooled loaf tightly in foil or plastic wrap and store in the refrigerator, or freeze for longer storage.

Stir in zucchini and pineapple. In another bowl, stir together flour, baking soda, salt, baking powder, cinnamon, nutmeg, and nuts; add to zucchini mixture and stir just until all flour is moistened. Spoon batter into prepared pans.

Bake for 50 to 60 minutes (see doneness test on facing page). Makes 2 loaves.

Quick Coffee Cake

        Cinnamon-nut topping (recipe follows)
 1¼ cups all-purpose flour
 ½ cup sugar
  2 teaspoons baking powder
 ½ teaspoon salt
 ½ cup milk
  1 egg
  3 tablespoons butter or margarine, melted and cooled

Preheat oven to 375°. Prepare topping; set aside. Lightly grease an 8-inch square or round baking pan; set aside.

In a bowl, stir together flour, sugar, baking powder, and salt. Pour milk into a 1-cup glass measure; stir in egg and butter. Pour all at once into dry ingredients and stir just until flour is moistened. Pour batter into prepared pan. Sprinkle cinnamon-nut topping evenly over batter. Bake for 20 to 25 minutes or until a wooden pick inserted in center comes out clean. Makes about 8 servings.

Cinnamon-nut topping. In a bowl, stir together ¼ cup *each* firmly packed **brown sugar** and **chopped nuts,** 1 tablespoon **all-purpose flour,** 1 tablespoon softened **butter** or margarine, and 2 teaspoons **ground cinnamon.**

Spoon Bread

Similar to a soufflé, this moist, tender spoon bread is more stable and will not deflate.

 ¾ cup yellow cornmeal
 2¼ cups milk
 ¼ cup sugar
 ½ teaspoon salt
 ½ cup (¼ lb.) butter or margarine, cut into chunks
  3 eggs

Preheat oven to 375°. Generously grease a 1½-quart soufflé dish and set aside. In a bowl, combine cornmeal with 1 cup of the milk; let stand for 5 minutes. In a 2-quart pan, bring remaining 1¼ cups milk to a boil, then stir in cornmeal mixture. Cook, stirring, until thick (about 5 minutes). Remove from heat and stir in sugar, salt, and butter until butter melts.

While cornmeal mixture cools, carefully separate eggs; beat 1 yolk at a time into cornmeal mixture.

In a large bowl, beat egg whites just until stiff, moist peaks form. Carefully fold a third of the beaten whites into cornmeal mixture; then pour mixture back into egg whites and gently fold together. Spoon into prepared soufflé dish.

Bake for 30 to 35 minutes or until set (does not jiggle when gently shaken) and top is golden brown. Spoon out servings immediately. Makes about 6 servings.

Mexican Cornbread

Some chiles are sizzling hot and others aren't. Because their potency varies, it's wise to sample a bit of each one to determine how many you want to use.

  2 eggs
 ¼ cup salad oil
  1 to 4 canned green chiles, seeded and chopped
  1 small can (about 9 oz.) cream-style corn
 ½ cup sour cream
  1 cup yellow cornmeal
 ½ teaspoon salt
  2 teaspoons baking powder
  2 cups (8 oz.) shredded sharp Cheddar cheese

Preheat oven to 350°. Grease an 8 or 9-inch round or square pan; set aside. In a bowl, beat eggs and oil until well blended. Add chiles, corn, sour cream, cornmeal, salt, baking powder, and 1½ cups of the cheese; stir until thoroughly blended. Pour batter into prepared pan and sprinkle the remaining ½ cup cheese over the top.

Bake for 1 hour or until crust is lightly browned and a wooden pick inserted in center comes out clean. Makes 6 to 8 servings.

How to make Popovers (Recipe on facing page)

1 Popover batter should have consistency of whipping cream. Fill well greased custard cups half full. Placing cups on a tray makes it easy to transport them to the oven.

2 In 10 minutes, shells begin to form and popovers start to rise.

3 Shown after 25 minutes at 375°, popovers are literally popping out of cups; a draft now would make them fall. Note varying shapes of popovers—no two are ever the same.

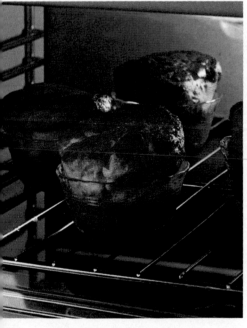

4 At full size, and nearing end of cooking time, popovers raise the roof in one final push.

5 Inside crisp popover, thin, eggy walls form pockets for melted butter, jam, or honey. Or you can fill them with your favorite creamed meat or seafood.

Popovers (Pictured on facing page)

These fragile shells are nothing but crisp golden crusts and tasty air. The egg batter puffs as it bakes, forming hollows that you can fill with butter or preserves, or something creamy and savory.

For all their smashing good looks, popovers are easy to make. Measure the few ingredients accurately and avoid overbeating the batter, or the popovers won't rise as high. Once they're in the oven, resist the temptation to peek. Popovers will collapse if a draft of air reaches them just as they're swelling above the cup.

You can bake popovers in your choice of containers: shiny, lightweight metal muffin pans; dark, heavy cast-iron popover pans; or ovenproof glass custard cups.

> 1 **cup all-purpose flour**
> ¼ **teaspoon salt**
> 1 **teaspoon sugar (optional)**
> 1 **tablespoon butter or margarine, melted and cooled, or salad oil**
> 1 **cup milk**
> 2 **eggs**

Preheat oven (see temperatures below). Grease containers (see choices above). In a bowl, stir together flour, salt, and sugar (if used) until thoroughly blended. Add butter, milk, and eggs. With an electric mixer, beat until very smooth (about 2½ minutes), scraping bowl frequently with a rubber spatula. Pour into greased containers, filling each about half full. In ovenproof cups of ⅓-cup size, batter will yield 12 popovers; ½-cup size, 10 popovers; 6-ounce size, 6 or 7 popovers.

For a richly browned shell with fairly moist interior, bake on center rack in a preheated 400° oven for about 40 minutes or until well browned and firm to touch. For a lighter-colored popover, drier inside, bake in a preheated 375° oven for 50 to 55 minutes. Remove from pans and serve hot. Makes 6 to 12 popovers.

FOR DRY POPOVERS

If you like your popovers especially dry inside, loosen them from pan but leave them sitting at an angle in cups; prick sides of each popover with a wooden pick and let stand in turned-off oven, door slightly ajar, for 8 to 10 minutes.

CHEESE POPOVERS

Prepare **Popovers,** but omit sugar, and stir ½ cup finely shredded sharp Cheddar or Parmesan **cheese** into batter.

ORANGE-SPICE POPOVERS

Prepare **Popovers,** but add the 1 teaspoon **sugar** to batter along with ½ teaspoon grated **orange peel** and ¼ teaspoon ground **nutmeg.**

SAVORY HERB POPOVERS

Prepare **Popovers,** but omit sugar and add 1 small clove **garlic,** finely minced or pressed, and ¼ teaspoon **dry rosemary** or oregano leaves to batter.

Yorkshire Pudding

Yorkshire pudding is simply popover batter baked to a crisp golden puff in flavorful roast beef drippings. It's more moist and tastes eggier than the hollow-shelled popovers shown at left—thus the name "pudding." You bake this side dish while the roast stands waiting to be carved, and you start carving the roast 5 minutes before the golden puff is done.

> 1 **cooked beef roast (page 47)**
> 1 **cup all-purpose flour**
> ½ **teaspoon salt**
> 1 **cup milk**
> 2 **eggs**

Remove roast from oven and turn oven up to 450°. Pour pan drippings into a measuring cup; tent roast with foil and set aside. Measure out ¼ cup of the pan drippings and pour into a 9-inch square baking pan. Place pan in oven to keep warm while you prepare batter.

In a bowl, stir together flour and salt until blended. Add milk and eggs. With an electric mixer, beat until very smooth (about 2½ minutes), scraping bowl frequently with a rubber spatula. Remove pan from oven and pour in batter. Bake, uncovered, for 20 to 25 minutes or until puffy and well browned. Cut into squares and serve immediately. Makes 6 servings.

Pancakes, waffles & French toast

These breakfast favorites share one requirement: they all need to begin cooking at just the right temperature, and there's a simple test for determining it. Preheat your griddle or frying pan over medium heat, then sprinkle a few drops of water over the surface. When the drops begin to sizzle and jump about, the heat is just right. (If the water evaporates instantly, though, the griddle is too hot.) Use the same test with a preheated waffle iron.

For lightness, cook pancakes for only 2 to 3 minutes on the first side, even less on the second (which won't be as golden brown); turn them only once, or they'll become flat. For crispness, leave waffles in the closed iron for a minute or so after it has stopped steaming. As for French toast—it's not the least bit fussy.

Pancakes

> 1½ cups all-purpose flour
> 3 teaspoons baking powder
> ½ teaspoon salt
> 2 tablespoons sugar
> 1 to 1¼ cups milk
> 1 egg
> 3 tablespoons butter or margarine, melted

Preheat a griddle or large frying pan over medium heat. Grease lightly—just enough to prevent pancakes from sticking.

In a medium-sized bowl, stir together flour, baking powder, salt, and sugar. Pour milk (use 1 cup for thick pancakes and 1¼ cups for thinner pancakes) into a 2-cup glass measure and stir in egg and butter; blend well. Pour liquid all at once into dry ingredients; stir together just until all flour is moistened.

Pour batter, about ¼ cup for each pancake, onto hot griddle; spread batter out to make a 5-inch circle. Cook until bubbles form and just start to pop on top surface, and edges appear dry

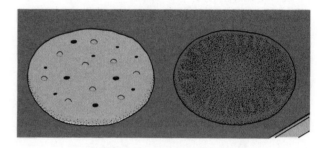

(left); turn pancake with a wide spatula to lightly brown other side (right). (Turn pancakes only once.) Makes 8 or 9 pancakes.

BLUEBERRY PANCAKES

Prepare **Pancakes,** but stir ½ to ¾ cup fresh or frozen (unthawed) **blueberries** into batter.

BUTTERMILK PANCAKES

Prepare **Pancakes,** but substitute 1½ cups **buttermilk** or sour milk (see page 13) in place of sweet milk, reduce baking powder to 1½ teaspoons, and add ½ teaspoon **baking soda.**

NUT PANCAKES

Prepare **Pancakes,** but stir ⅓ cup finely chopped **nuts** into batter.

HOMEMADE MAPLE-FLAVORED SYRUP

After cooking, our syrup will have a watery appearance. It thickens after cooling, but it's thinner than commercially prepared syrup. Don't try to double the recipe—the chemical magic just won't work. The syrup, which should be refrigerated, keeps for as long as a month. If crystals form, place the open jar in a pan of hot water; this will melt the crystallized sugar.

In a small pan, combine 2 cups **sugar,** 1 cup **water,** and 3 tablespoons **light corn syrup.** Bring to a boil, uncovered, over medium-high heat; boil for exactly 3 minutes. Remove from heat and stir in ½ to ¾ teaspoon **imitation maple flavoring.** Let cool, then pour into a glass jar; cover and refrigerate. Makes about 1½ cups.

Old-fashioned Oatmeal Pancakes

You start the batter for these cakelike pancakes the night before.

2 cups *each* regular rolled oats and buttermilk
2 eggs, lightly beaten
4 tablespoons butter or margarine, melted and cooled
½ cup raisins (optional)
½ cup all-purpose flour
2 tablespoons sugar
1 teaspoon *each* baking powder and baking soda
½ teaspoon ground cinnamon
¼ teaspoon salt

In a bowl, combine oats and buttermilk; stir to blend well. Cover and refrigerate until next day.

Preheat a griddle or large frying pan over medium heat; grease lightly. Just before cooking, add eggs, butter, and raisins (if used) to batter; stir just to blend. In another bowl, stir together flour, sugar, baking powder, baking soda, cinnamon, and salt; add to oat mixture and stir just until moistened. If batter seems too thick, add more buttermilk (up to 3 tablespoons).

Spoon batter, about ⅓ cup for each pancake, onto griddle; spread batter out to make 4-inch circles. Cook until tops are bubbly and appear dry (2 to 3 minutes); turn and cook until lightly browned. Makes about 1½ dozen pancakes.

Waffles

1⅓ cups all-purpose flour
2 teaspoons baking powder
½ teaspoon salt
1 tablespoon sugar
2 eggs, separated
1¼ cups milk
3 tablespoons salad oil

In a medium-size bowl, combine flour, baking powder, salt, and sugar; set aside.

In a medium-size bowl, beat egg whites just until stiff, moist peaks form. In another bowl, beat yolks lightly, stir in milk and oil, and blend well. Pour liquid all at once into dry ingredients; beat until smooth. Fold in beaten whites.

Bake in a preheated waffle iron according to manufacturer's directions. Makes about ten 4-inch-square waffles.

BACON WAFFLES

Prepare **Waffles,** but add to batter 6 to 8 strips **bacon,** cooked, drained, and crumbled.

BLUEBERRY WAFFLES

Prepare **Waffles,** but stir into batter ½ to ¾ cup fresh or frozen (unthawed) **blueberries.**

French Toast

4 eggs
1 cup milk
2 tablespoons sugar
1 teaspoon vanilla (optional)
¼ teaspoon ground nutmeg (optional)
8 slices day-old bread
Butter or margarine

In a bowl, beat together eggs, milk, sugar, vanilla (if used), and nutmeg (if used). Place bread slices on a rimmed baking sheet. Pour egg mixture over bread and let stand for a few minutes. Turn slices over and let stand until all egg mixture is absorbed. Melt butter on a griddle or in a frying pan over medium heat. Add a few bread slices at a time and cook until browned; turn and brown other side. Place cooked toast on a serving plate and keep warm in a 150° oven. (If you preheat oven to 150°, then turn it off, oven will retain enough heat to keep your toast warm without overbaking.) Repeat with remaining slices. Makes 4 servings of 2 slices each.

FREEZER FRENCH TOAST

Prepare **French Toast,** but once egg mixture is absorbed by bread slices, freeze them on baking sheet, uncovered, until firm; then package airtight and return to freezer. To serve, place desired number of frozen slices on a lightly greased baking sheet. Brush each slice with melted **butter.** Bake in a preheated 500° oven for 5 minutes. Turn slices over, brush with melted butter, and bake for 5 more minutes or until nicely browned.

Crêpes (French pancakes) (Pictured on facing page)

Delectable wraparounds for sweet or savory fillings, crêpes are nothing more than wafer-thin pancakes. Convenient and versatile, they make elegant fare for brunch, lunch, late supper, or dessert.

Though crêpe-making is a little time consuming, you can make your crêpes days or even months ahead, and freeze them until they're needed. To prevent tearing, let the frozen crêpes come to room temperature before unwrapping and separating them.

> 1½ cups milk
> 3 eggs
> 1 cup all-purpose flour
> 1 tablespoon salad oil
>   About 4 teaspoons butter or margarine

In a blender or food processor, whirl milk, eggs, flour, and oil until smooth. (Or blend eggs and milk with an electric mixer or a wire whisk; add flour and oil and mix until smooth.) Let batter rest at room temperature for 1 hour. Or cover and refrigerate batter overnight.

Heat a 6 to 7-inch crêpe pan or other flat-bottomed frying pan over medium heat until a drop of water sizzles and jumps about the pan. (If water evaporates instantly, pan is too hot; remove it from heat and let it cool slightly.) Grease lightly with about ¼ teaspoon of the butter. Stir batter, then pour 2 to 3 tablespoons of batter all at once into center of pan, swiftly tilting pan in all directions so batter flows quickly over entire flat surface. If you've poured in too much batter, pour excess back into bowl.

If heat is correct and pan hot enough, crêpe will set at once and form tiny bubbles. (If batter makes a smooth layer, pan is too cool. If there are a few small holes, don't worry; no two crêpes look alike.) Cook until edge of crêpe is lightly browned and surface looks dry (30 to 40 seconds). Run a small spatula around edge to loosen. Pick up crêpe with finger tips and flip over. Cook other side for about 20 seconds (this side doesn't brown). Turn crêpe out of pan onto a plate.

Repeat to make each crêpe, stirring batter occasionally. Stack crêpes and use within a few hours. If made ahead, let each crêpe cool, then stack with wax paper. Package airtight and refrigerate for 2 to 3 days. Freeze for longer storage. Allow crêpes to come to room temperature before separating; they will tear if cold.

You can spread a crêpe with butter and jam to eat as is, or use it to enclose a filling (see facing page and page 156). When filling crêpes, always place filling on side that isn't browned. Makes 16 to 18 crêpes.

Glazed Peach Crêpes
(Pictured on facing page)

If you use frozen fruit, look for bags of slices that are unsweetened and individually frozen. You could use sliced apples, nectarines, apricots, or pears in place of peaches.

> 8 crêpes
> 2 tablespoons butter or margarine
> 6 medium-size peaches, peeled and sliced ½ inch thick, or 6 cups unsweetened frozen peach slices, partially defrosted
> 1 teaspoon grated lemon peel
> 1 tablespoon lemon juice
> ⅛ teaspoon ground nutmeg
> ½ cup sugar
> 2 tablespoons brandy or apricot liqueur
> ½ cup sour cream (optional)

Prepare crêpes, or bring to room temperature if refrigerated or frozen. Melt butter in a wide frying pan over medium heat. Add peaches, lemon peel, lemon juice, and nutmeg. Cook, gently turning occasionally with a wide spatula, until peaches begin to soften and look translucent (about 7 minutes). Gradually sprinkle in sugar and cook, stirring gently, for 2 more minutes. Sprinkle brandy over peaches; continue cooking until liquid is thickened. Remove from heat and let cool slightly.

Spoon about 3 tablespoons filling across lower third of each crêpe and roll to enclose; save a few slices of fruit for garnish. Place filled crêpes, seam side down, in a lightly buttered baking dish.

Cover with foil and bake in a 325° oven for 25 minutes or until crêpes are heated through. Before serving, top each crêpe with reserved fruit and a spoonful of sour cream, if desired. Makes 8 crêpes.

How to make Crêpes (Recipe on facing page)

1 Pour about 3 tablespoons batter into center of hot buttered 7-inch pan.

2 With your other hand, immediately tilt pan so batter flows over entire flat surface. Crêpe should start to form tiny bubbles about 5 seconds after coating pan bottom.

3 Cook crêpe until lightly browned (about 30 seconds). Run knife around edge to loosen. With fingers, quickly pick up crêpe and turn over for a few seconds to brown other side.

4 Place filling down center of crêpe's light side. Fold one side over filling, then roll to enclose. Place seam side down in baking dish; bake briefly to heat.

5 To serve Glazed Peach Crêpes, place two warm filled crêpes on a plate and spoon some of the reserved peaches on top.

...Crêpes

Mushroom Crêpes

Make your own convenience foods—you can freeze these filled crêpes, then bake as many as you need, without thawing.

12 to 16 crêpes (page 154)
3 pounds mushrooms
4 tablespoons butter or margarine
1 large onion, chopped
2 cloves garlic, minced or pressed
¾ teaspoon marjoram leaves
¼ cup all-purpose flour
¾ cup milk
3 tablespoons dry sherry
½ cup grated Parmesan cheese
¼ cup chopped parsley
Salt and pepper
2 cups (8 oz.) shredded Swiss cheese

Prepare crêpes, or bring to room temperature if refrigerated or frozen. Remove stems from mushrooms and chop; slice caps and set aside. In a wide frying pan over medium heat, melt 2 tablespoons of the butter. Add mushroom stems, onion, and garlic; cook, stirring, until onion is soft. Add remaining 2 tablespoons butter, sliced mushroom caps, and marjoram; cook, stirring, until mushrooms are soft and juices have evaporated. Sprinkle flour over mushrooms and cook, stirring, until bubbly. Gradually pour in milk and continue cooking and stirring until sauce boils and thickens. Remove from heat. Add sherry, Parmesan cheese, and parsley. Let cool; then season to taste with salt and pepper.

Spoon about 3 heaping tablespoons filling across lower third of each crêpe; roll to enclose. (At this point you may place filled crêpes, seam side down and not touching, on greased baking sheets, then cover and refrigerate; or freeze, uncovered, until firm, then individually package airtight and return to freezer for as long as 2 weeks.)

To heat, arrange desired number of filled crêpes in a lightly greased shallow casserole dish or in individual ramekins. Cover with foil and bake in a 375° oven for 15 to 20 minutes (20 to 25 minutes, if refrigerated; 25 to 30 minutes, if frozen) or until heated through. Remove foil, sprinkle each crêpe with about 2 tablespoons Swiss cheese, and bake for 5 more minutes or until cheese is melted. Makes 6 to 8 servings of 2 crêpes each.

Meat & Spinach Crêpes

12 to 16 crêpes (page 154)
1 package (10 or 12 oz.) frozen chopped spinach, thawed
1 tablespoon salad oil
1 clove garlic, minced or pressed
1 small onion, chopped
½ pound lean ground beef
¼ pound bulk pork sausage
½ teaspoon *each* salt and oregano leaves
¼ teaspoon pepper
2 cans (8 oz. *each*) tomato sauce
2 cups (8 oz.) jack cheese

Prepare crêpes, or bring to room temperature if refrigerated or frozen. With your hands, squeeze as much moisture as possible from spinach. Heat oil in a wide frying pan over medium-high heat. Add garlic and onion; cook, stirring, until onion is soft but not browned (about 4 minutes). Crumble in beef and sausage. Cook, stirring occasionally and breaking up large pieces, until meat is browned; pour off excess fat. Add spinach, salt, oregano, and pepper. Cook over medium-high heat for 3 minutes or until all liquid has evaporated.

Spoon equal amount of filling down center of each crêpe; roll to enclose. Arrange crêpes, side by side, seam side down, in a lightly greased 9 by 13-inch baking dish. (At this point you may cover and refrigerate for as long as 3 days, or freeze for longer storage.)

To heat, pour tomato sauce over crêpes. Sprinkle with cheese and bake, uncovered, in a 350° oven for 30 minutes (35 minutes, if refrigerated; 40 to 45 minutes, if frozen) or until hot and bubbly. Makes 6 to 8 servings of 2 crêpes each.

Yeast bread

Home-baked yeast bread satisfies in every way—it's almost as much fun to make as it is to eat. Six basic ingredients interact to create this age-old food: yeast, liquid, sugar, salt, fat, and flour.

When yeast (a microscopic plant and therefore a biological, not chemical, leavening) is activated by warm water, it gives off bubbles of carbon dioxide. It is this gas that leavens the dough and makes it rise, just as baking powder and baking soda leaven quick breads. You will need at least ¼ cup of warm (110°) water to dissolve 1 package (1 tablespoon) of active dry yeast granules. Here, temperature is crucial—if the water is too cool, the yeast action will be sluggish; if the water is too hot, it will destroy the yeast and the dough will fail to rise. Use a candy thermometer until you learn to feel the right temperature with your hand.

Sugar provides food for the yeast, enabling it to grow; salt slows the action. The two together keep the dough on just the right leavening schedule for good texture and flavor. Fats make the bread tender, moist, and palatable. Flour provides structure and strength. There is no need to sift flour—on the other hand, you should never pack it in the cup or shake it down.

Three steps to a perfect loaf

The secret to a shapely, springy loaf of bread is the care and thoroughness given to mixing and kneading the dough. These steps develop the gluten in the flour. (Gluten is a protein that gives dough its elasticity and helps bread retain its shape when baked.)

Mixing. Dissolve the yeast first, then mix in other ingredients, and add flour last of all. A 4-quart bowl will hold the ingredients for most yeast breads. Yeast reacts well to a warm kitchen; in a cool kitchen, dough takes a bit longer to rise. The main thing is to keep dough away from drafts.

When adding the flour, sprinkle it, 1 cup at a time, over the yeast mixture, stirring with a wooden spoon until evenly moistened. When enough flour has been stirred in to form a thick batter (usually ⅔ of the total amount the recipe calls for), beat the batter very well with a wooden spoon or with a heavy-duty electric mixer on medium speed. After 5 minutes you can see the gluten developing—the batter becomes glossy and elastic, stretching with the motion of the spoon.

Kneading. Spread about ½ to ¾ cup flour on a board, heavily coating the center area. Turn the dough out onto this area and sprinkle it lightly with flour. Now the dough is ready for kneading, which will complete the gluten formation.

As you knead, make sure the dough is never without a light coating of flour. Your object is to shape it into a ball, keeping the underside smooth and unbroken. Pace yourself; frequency, rhythm, and a gentle touch do a better job than brute force. (To knead, follow step-by-step instructions on pages 158 and 159.)

Overkneading is virtually impossible; the longer you spend at it (perhaps 20 or 30 minutes), the higher and fluffier your finished loaf is likely to be. It's best to judge by feel. When dough is smooth and no longer sticky, and its surface is faintly pebbled with air bubbles, hold it to your cheek. If it has a firm bounce and velvety touch, you have probably kneaded it long enough.

Letting it rise. After the dough has been thoroughly kneaded, it almost takes care of itself. Your job is simply to provide a warm (about 80°) draft-free place for the rising (sometimes called "proofing"). Most yeast breads rise twice: the first time until doubled in bulk, the second time until almost doubled.

Like so many aspects of bread making, rising times are variable, depending mostly on temperature but also on the heaviness of the dough (whole grain breads rise more slowly than white breads).

...IN A WARM PLACE

The most convenient warm place in which dough can rise is the inside of a switched-off oven with the light on. If your oven feels cool, turn it to the lowest setting for a minute or two, then switch it off before putting the bread inside. You can also place a pan of hot water on the shelf below the bowl. Or place the bowl near a radiator, but not on it.

How to make yeast bread (Recipe on facing page)

1 Dissolve yeast and sugar in warm water. After about 15 minutes, mixture will have a distinct light, bubbly layer on top—this means that the yeast is good and active.

2 Dough is ready to knead when it is stiff enough to pull away from sides of the bowl with a wooden spoon.

3 Turn dough out onto floured board. Sprinkle dough with flour and start kneading by folding dough toward you with your fingers; push away with heel of your hand.

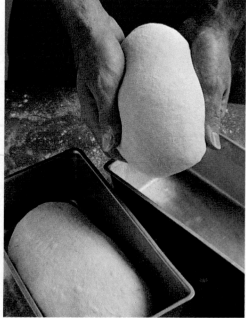

4 Rotate dough a quarter-turn and repeat folding-pushing motion, adding flour as you knead. Kneading is finished when dough is nonsticky, smooth, satiny.

5 Form each dough half into a loaf by gently pulling top surface toward underside to make top smooth; pinch seam and turn ends under. Put loaves, seam side down, in greased pans.

6 Raised loaves in pans are now ready to bake. After baking, loaves are nicely browned. Let stand in pans for 10 minutes, then turn out onto rack to cool completely.

Basic White Bread

(Pictured on facing page)

Here is a step-by-step illustrated lesson in the simple art of bread making. On these two pages you'll learn what to expect and what to do at each stage to make a beautiful loaf. Once you've practiced a bit, try your hand at some of the variations that follow our basic recipe.

- ¼ **cup warm water (about 110°)**
- 1 **package active dry yeast**
- 2 **tablespoons granulated sugar**
- 2 **cups warm milk (about 110°)**
- 2 **tablespoons salad oil (or butter or margarine, melted and cooled)**
- 2 **teaspoons salt**
- 6 **to 6½ cups all-purpose flour**

Pour water into a measuring cup; add yeast and 1 tablespoon of the sugar; stir until dissolved. Let stand in a warm place (80°) until light-colored and bubbly (about 15 minutes); this tells you that yeast is active and has not been destroyed by excessively hot water.

Pour milk into a large bowl (about 4-quart size); stir in oil, salt, the remaining 1 tablespoon sugar, and yeast mixture. Sprinkle in 3 cups of the flour, 1 cup at a time, stirring until flour is evenly moistened. Add 4th cup of flour and, with a wooden spoon or heavy-duty mixer, beat until dough is smooth and elastic (about 5 minutes—rest when you get tired). Mix in 5th cup of flour to make dough stiff enough to pull up on wooden spoon.

Measure out 6th cup of flour and sprinkle about ¾ cup onto a board; turn dough out onto heavily floured area. Sprinkle dough lightly with some of the remaining flour and begin to knead.

To knead, reach over the ball of dough and grasp the edge farthest from you. Pull it toward you in a rolling motion (but not enough to tear the surface) and fold dough almost in half. Then, with the heel of your palm, gently roll the ball away from you to lightly seal the fold. When fold line is returned to the top center of dough, rotate dough a quarter turn and continue this folding-rolling motion, making a quarter turn each time.

Work quickly, adding remaining flour as needed; dough grows sticky if allowed to stand. If tears occur on the surface, try to fold them in rather than add more flour to cover them. If dough sticks to board, lift dough, scrape board clean, re-

flour, and continue. Five minutes of kneading may be long enough, but the longer you spend at it (as long as 20 to 30 minutes) the lighter the loaf will be. When dough is nonsticky, smooth, and satiny, kneading is finished.

Put dough in greased bowl; turn dough over to grease top. Cover bowl loosely with clear plastic wrap or a damp cloth. Let rise in a warm place (80°) until doubled (45 minutes to 1½ hours). Test by pushing 2 fingers into dough—if indentations remain (see *Illustration 1*), dough is ready to shape.

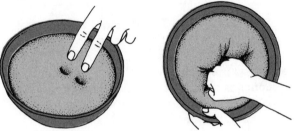

Illustration 1   Illustration 2

After dough has risen, punch it down with your fist (see *Illustration 2*) to release air bubbles, then turn dough out onto a lightly floured board. Knead dough briefly and shape into a smooth oval.

With a sharp knife, divide dough in half for 2 loaves. Form each half into a loaf by gently pulling top surface toward underside to make top smooth. Turn each loaf over and pinch a seam down center; then turn ends under, and pinch to seal.

Put shaped loaves, seam side down, in greased 9 by 5-inch loaf pans. Cover; let rise in a warm place until almost doubled (about 45 minutes). Loaves should come just to top of pans—when baked, they will rise above top of pans.

Bake in a 375° oven (350° for glass pans) for 35 to 45 minutes or until loaves are nicely browned and sound hollow when tapped. Remove from oven. Let loaves cool in pans on a wire rack for 10 minutes, then turn loaves out onto rack to cool completely. Makes 2 loaves.

OATMEAL BREAD

Prepare **Basic White Bread,** but use 4 cups **unbleached white flour** and 2 cups **oat flour** (both unsifted). Oat flour is sold in health food stores—or you can make your own by whirling rolled oats in an electric blender until fine.

...Yeast breads

HERB BREAD

Prepare **Basic White Bread** (page 159), but before kneading, divide dough into 2 parts, add **one** of the following herbs to each part, and knead into dough: 1 tablespoon **dill weed**, 1 tablespoon **savory**, 1½ teaspoons **dry basil**, 1½ teaspoons **oregano leaves**, 1½ teaspoons **thyme leaves**, or 2¼ teaspoons **marjoram leaves**. Knead each part separately.

CINNAMON SWIRL LOAF

Prepare **Basic White Bread** (page 159), but after dividing dough in half, roll out dough for each loaf into a rectangle about 6 by 16 inches. Mix 4 tablespoons **sugar** with 4 tablespoon **ground cinnamon**; sprinkle half of mixture evenly onto each rectangle. Beginning with narrow side, roll each rectangle tightly into a cylinder; seal ends and bottom by pinching together to make seam. Place loaves, seam side down, in 2 greased 9 by 5-inch pans and let rise. Bake in a 375° oven (350° for glass pans) for 30 to 35 minutes or until nicely browned.

DARK MIXED-GRAIN BREAD

Prepare **Basic White Bread** (page 159), but omit sugar; reduce milk to 1½ cups and add ½ cup **dark molasses**. Instead of all-purpose flour, use ½ cup each **wheat germ** and **buckwheat flour** (found in health food stores), 1 cup **rye flour**, and 4 cups **whole wheat flour** (all unsifted).

YEAST FOCACCIA

Prepare **Basic White Bread** (page 159). After punching dough down, divide in half.

Preheat oven to 450°. Lightly grease two 10 by 15-inch baking sheets and place a dough half on each; stretch out to almost fit sheet. Brush top surfaces with **olive oil** and sprinkle with **garlic powder** and (if desired) chopped **green onions**. Bake for about 15 minutes or until surfaces are lightly browned.

For pizza, just remove focaccia from oven, spread with your favorite **flavored tomato sauce**, and top with grated Cheddar, jack, or mozzarella **cheese**. Return to oven until cheese has melted.

EGG BRAID

Prepare **Basic White Bread** (page 159), but instead of the 2 cups milk, break 2 **eggs** into a 2-cup measure and beat in enough warm **milk** (110°) to equal 2 cups. After dividing dough in half, separate each half into 3 parts (you will have 6 pieces of dough). Roll each piece into a strand; braid 3 strands together, pinching ends to seal. Place each braid on a lightly greased baking sheet, cover loosely with a towel, and let rise. Bake for 30 to 35 minutes or until lightly browned.

POPPY SEED BUBBLE LOAF

Prepare **Basic White Bread** (page 159), but after punching dough down, pinch off pieces of dough and shape into smooth 1-inch balls; set aside. Lightly grease a 10-inch tube pan. Melt 4 tablespoons **butter** or margarine and let cool slightly. Place ¼ cup **poppy seeds** in a dish. Dip top of each ball into butter and then into poppy seeds; pile balls, seed side up, in prepared pan. Cover and let rise. Bake for 50 to 55 minutes or until lightly browned.

Super Simple Refrigerator Bread

This tender white loaf couldn't be easier—even when you're pressed for time. There's no kneading, and it waits in the refrigerator for as long as 24 hours.

- ⅓ cup each sugar and solid shortening
- 1 tablespoon salt
- 2 cups boiling water
- 2 packages active dry yeast
- 1 teaspoon sugar
- ¼ cup warm water (about 110°)
- 2 eggs, well beaten
- 7½ to 8 cups all-purpose flour

In a large bowl, combine the ⅓ cup sugar with shortening, salt, and boiling water; let cool to lukewarm. Dissolve yeast and the 1 teaspoon sugar in the ¼ cup warm water; let stand in a warm place (80°) until bubbly (about 15 minutes).

Combine yeast mixture with sugar mixture; stir in eggs. Stir in 4 cups of the flour; then gradually stir in as much of the remaining flour as dough will absorb, mixing well. Place in a greased bowl; cover and chill for at least 3 hours or up to 24 hours.

To bake, divide dough in half. With greased hands, shape each half into a smooth loaf. Place each in a greased 9 by 5-inch loaf pan; cover and let rise in a warm place (80°) until almost doubled (about 2 hours).

Bake in a 350° oven for 30 to 35 minutes or until loaves sound hollow when tapped. Remove from oven. Let loaves cool in pans on a wire rack for 10 minutes, then turn loaves out onto rack to cool completely.

Three Wheat Batter Bread

  1 package active dry yeast
  ½ cup warm water (about 110°)
  ⅛ teaspoon ground ginger
  3 tablespoons honey
  1 large can (13 oz.) evaporated milk
  1 teaspoon salt
  2 tablespoons salad oil
  2½ cups all-purpose flour
  1¼ cups whole wheat flour
  ½ cup wheat germ
  ¼ cup cracked wheat

Thoroughly grease two 1-pound coffee cans and their plastic lids, or one 2-pound coffee can and its lid. In a large bowl, combine yeast, water, ginger, and 1 tablespoon of the honey; let stand in a warm place (80°) until bubbly (about 15 minutes). Stir in the remaining 2 tablespoons honey, along with milk, salt, and oil. In another bowl, stir together all-purpose flour, whole wheat flour, wheat germ, and cracked wheat; add to liquid ingredients, 1 cup at a time, beating after each addition until well blended.

Spoon batter evenly into greased cans; cover with lids. Let rise in a warm place (80°) until lids pop off (55 to 60 minutes for 1-pound cans, 1 to 1½ hours for 2-pound cans).

Bake, uncovered, in a 350° oven for about 45 minutes (about 60 minutes for a 2-pound can) or until bread sounds hollow when tapped. Let cool in cans on a rack for 10 minutes; then loosen crust around edge of can with a thin knife, slide bread out onto rack in an upright position, and let cool completely. Makes 1 large or 2 small loaves.

FLOUR & OTHER GRAIN PRODUCTS

Wheat has always been the main ingredient of yeast bread because of its gluten content, which makes bread dough elastic enough to rise when leavened. But other grains blend happily with wheat in many recipes.

All-purpose flour (regular white flour) is a blend of refined wheat flours ground without the bran and wheat germ. It is available bleached or unbleached; the latter creates a better texture. Because it makes a relatively light dough, all-purpose flour is often combined with heavier whole grain flours to improve texture.

Whole wheat flour, ground from the entire wheat kernel, is heavier, richer in nutrients, and more perishable than all-purpose flour. Unless you use it up quickly, you should store it in the refrigerator to prevent its wheat germ from becoming rancid. Many people prefer stone ground whole wheat to regularly milled whole wheat because the stone ground is slightly coarser and has a heartier flavor.

Unprocessed bran and wheat germ are portions of the wheat kernel sometimes added to breads in small quantities for nutritional enrichment, heartiness, and special flavors. Both are much coarser than flour. Bran contributes roughage; wheat germ is rich in food value (B and E vitamins, certain proteins, iron, and fat).

Cracked wheat, also much coarser than flour, results when wheat kernels are cut into angular fragments. In small additions, it gives whole grain breads a nutty flavor and crunchy texture.

Cornmeal and oatmeal come, respectively, from coarsely ground white or yellow corn and from rolled or steel-cut oats. In some recipes, one or the other is combined in small quantities with wheat flour to create distinctive flavors and textures. Corn and oat flours, less widely available than the meals, can sometimes be found in health food stores.

...Yeast breads

Buttery Pan Rolls

> 2 packages active dry yeast
> ½ cup warm water (about 110°)
> 4½ cups all-purpose flour, unsifted
> ¼ cup sugar
> 1 teaspoon salt
> 1 cup (½ lb.) plus 2 tablespoons butter or margarine, melted and cooled
> 1 egg
> 1 cup warm milk (about 110°)

In a large bowl, dissolve yeast in water; let stand until bubbly (about 15 minutes). Stir together 2 cups of the flour, sugar, and salt until well mixed. Add 6 tablespoons of the melted butter, along with egg, yeast mixture, and milk; beat for 5 minutes to blend well. Gradually beat in the remaining 2½ cups flour. Cover bowl and let batter rise in a warm place (80°) until doubled (about 45 minutes).

Pour half of the remaining melted butter into a 9 by 13-inch baking pan, tilting pan to coat bottom. Beat down batter and drop by spoonfuls into buttered pan, making about 15 rolls. Drizzle remaining butter over dough. Cover lightly and let rise in a warm place (80°) until almost doubled (about 30 minutes).

Bake in a 425° oven for 12 to 17 minutes or until lightly browned. Serve hot. Makes about 15 rolls.

To bake in muffin cups, make batter as directed, but spoon about 1 teaspoon melted butter into each muffin cup. Fill cups about half full; let batter rise until almost doubled. Bake as directed.

FREEZING & REHEATING BREADS

To freeze baked bread, let it cool completely, wrap each loaf airtight in foil, package in a plastic bag, label, and place in the freezer for up to 3 months.

To serve, unwrap but leave partially covered; let thaw completely at room temperature before serving or reheating.

To reheat, place thawed bread on a baking sheet in a 350° oven. Heat rolls and small loaves for about 10 minutes, large loaves for 15 minutes. If bread has a soft crust, protect it during reheating with a loose wrapping of foil; if bread is crusty, reheat it uncovered.

Sticky Pecan Rolls

(Pictured on facing page)

Only one rising is required for these sweet breakfast treats. Be sure they cool for at least 10 minutes before you touch them—the caramel-pecan topping will be hot enough to burn your fingers.

> ¼ teaspoon baking soda
> ¼ cup granulated sugar
> 1 teaspoon salt
> 1 package active dry yeast
> 3 cups all-purpose flour
> 1 cup buttermilk
> 3 tablespoons salad oil
> 4 tablespoons water
> 6 tablespoons butter or margarine, melted and cooled
> ¾ cup *each* firmly packed brown sugar and pecan pieces
> 1 teaspoon ground cinnamon

In a large bowl, combine baking soda, granulated sugar, salt, yeast, and 1 cup of the flour. Place buttermilk and oil in a pan over medium-low heat until warm (about 120°); add to flour mixture and beat with an electric mixer, on high, for about 2 minutes. Stir in 1½ cups of the remaining flour and beat with a wooden spoon until smooth. Sprinkle some of the remaining ½ cup flour on a board. Turn dough out onto floured board and knead (see page 159) until smooth and elastic (8 to 10 minutes), adding more flour as needed. Let dough rest on board while preparing pans.

In a small bowl, combine water, 4 tablespoons of the melted butter, and ½ cup of the brown sugar. Distribute mixture equally among twelve 2½-inch muffin cups; top mixture with pecans.

Roll dough into a 12 by 15-inch rectangle. Brush surface with the remaining 2 tablespoons butter. Combine cinnamon with the remaining ¼ cup brown sugar and sprinkle evenly over buttered dough. Starting with narrow end, roll rectangle into a cylinder, cut into 12 equal slices, and place, cut side down, in muffin cups. Let rise, uncovered, in a warm place (80°) until doubled (about 1½ hours).

Bake in a 350° oven for about 25 minutes or until tops are golden. Invert immediately onto a serving plate; let pan remain briefly on rolls so syrup can drizzle over them. Let cool for 10 minutes before serving. Makes 1 dozen rolls.

How to make Sticky Pecan Rolls (Recipe on facing page)

1 Sprinkle brown sugar and cinnamon mixture over butter-brushed dough. Starting at narrow end, use palms of hands to roll dough into a cylinder.

2 Cut rolled-up dough into 12 equal slices and place, cut side down, in muffin cups atop brown sugar-pecan mixture.

3 Let rolls rise, uncovered, in a warm place until doubled (about 1½ hours). They are now ready to bake.

4 After baking, immediately place serving plate over pan and invert; let pan rest briefly on rolls so syrup can drizzle over them. Allow rolls to cool for 10 minutes before touching.

DESSERTS

Sometimes rich and creamy, sometimes light and refreshing, dessert gives any meal a happy ending. You'll want to plan the dessert to fit the meal —it makes sense, for example, to serve a light dessert after a meal that's heavy or robust, a rich dessert after a light entrée.

This chapter offers spectacular cakes, cookies, and pies... creamy custards and Bavarians ... light and refreshing ways to serve fresh fruits... desserts, in short, for every type of meal and occasion. Most are simple to make, and many can go together hours or even days in advance.

• Start each batch of cookies on a cold baking sheet; otherwise the cookies will begin to spread and cook before they reach the oven. To make another batch on the same baking sheet, wash it, then regrease if the recipe specifies.

• Each of our cake recipes has been carefully developed. If you follow the directions exactly, you should have success every time. To ensure a light and tender cake, be sure to use cake flour if the recipe calls for it. Measure ingredients accurately, combine them in the order given, and beat for the precise length of time indicated.

• Pan size is also very important. In too large a pan, cakes bake too quickly and turn out pale and flat. If the pan is too small, the batter may overflow, the center is likely to shrink, and the texture will be heavy and compact.

• The natural sweetness of fresh fruits makes them an ideal finale to any meal. To prevent fruit like apples, apricots, bananas, peaches, and pears from turning dark when exposed to the air, sprinkle all cut surfaces with lemon, lime, or orange juice.

Cookies

Cookies bring joy to the young-of-appetite. Here are two of the easiest—bar and drop cookies. Both survive traveling and freezing well.

You'll appreciate the speed and simplicity of bar cookies—you just make the dough, spread it in a pan, and bake. Child's play—right? Absolutely. Bar cookies are sometimes cakelike, sometimes chewy, usually moist. But watch out for overbaking, which turns them dry, crumbly, and difficult to cut neatly.

Just as their name indicates, drop cookies drop from a spoon, forming little mounds on the prepared baking sheets. These cookies are done when they're slightly brown around the edges and an imprint remains when they're gently touched in their centers. If they look too brown, reduce the baking time for the next batch.

For even distribution of heat, use shiny pans when baking cookies. Place the baking sheet in the center of the oven, leaving at least an inch of space between the sheet and the oven wall. Bake only one panful of cookies at a time—if you place one baking sheet on a rack above another, the cookies will bake unevenly.

Oatmeal Chip Cookies

- 1 cup (½ lb.) butter or margarine, softened
- 1½ cups firmly packed brown sugar
- 2 eggs
- 1 teaspoon vanilla
- 1½ cups all-purpose flour or whole wheat flour
- 2⅓ cups regular or quick-cooking rolled oats
- 2 teaspoons baking soda
- 1 teaspoon salt
- 1 large package (12 oz.) semisweet chocolate chips
- 1 cup chopped nuts

Preheat oven to 350°. Lightly grease a baking sheet and set aside.

In a large bowl, cream butter and sugar until light and fluffy. Beat in eggs and vanilla. Stir in flour, oats, baking soda, and salt; mix well. Stir in chocolate chips and nuts. Drop dough, about 1 level tablespoon for each cooky, 1½ inches apart onto prepared baking sheet.

Bake for 10 to 12 minutes or until edges are lightly browned. Transfer cookies to wire racks to cool completely. Makes about 3½ dozen cookies.

OATMEAL RAISIN COOKIES

Prepare **Oatmeal Chip Cookies,** but add 1 teaspoon **ground cinnamon** and ½ teaspoon **ground nutmeg** with the flour. Omit chocolate chips; instead use 1½ cups **raisins.**

Fudge Brownies

- 10 tablespoons (¼ lb. plus 2 tablespoons) butter or margarine
- 4 ounces unsweetened chocolate
- 2 cups sugar
- ½ teaspoon salt
- 1½ teaspoons vanilla
- 4 eggs, at room temperature
- 1 cup all-purpose flour
- ½ to 1 cup coarsely chopped walnuts

Preheat oven to 350°. Generously grease a 9 by 13-inch baking pan; set aside.

In a 2-quart pan, melt butter and chocolate over medium-low heat; stir until well blended. Remove from heat and stir in sugar, salt, and vanilla. Add eggs, one at a time, beating well after each addition. Stir in flour, then nuts. Pour into prepared pan.

Bake for 20 to 25 minutes or until top springs back when lightly touched. Transfer pan to a wire rack. Let cool completely before cutting—otherwise brownies will fall apart. Cut into 2-inch squares to serve. Makes about 2 dozen squares.

Shortbread

- 1 cup (½ lb.) butter or margarine, softened
- ½ cup sifted powdered sugar
- 2 cups all-purpose flour

Preheat oven to 325°. Lightly grease a 9-inch square baking pan; set aside.

In a bowl, cream butter and sugar until light and fluffy. Stir in flour and blend well. With your hands, gather up dough and press it evenly over bottom of prepared pan. Bake for 40 to 50 minutes or until pale golden brown. Transfer pan to wire rack and cut into small squares; let cool in pan. Makes 25 squares.

BUTTERY LEMON SQUARES

Prepare **Shortbread,** but press into a 9 by 13-inch pan; bake in a 350° oven for only 20 minutes.

Meanwhile, in a bowl, beat 4 **eggs** until light and frothy. Gradually add 2 cups **granulated sugar,** beating until thick. Add 1 teaspoon grated **lemon peel,** 6 tablespoons **lemon juice,** ⅓ cup all-purpose **flour,** and 1 teaspoon **baking powder;** beat until blended. Pour over hot baked crust, return to oven, and bake for 15 to 20 minutes or until pale golden. Remove from oven; sprinkle evenly with 3 tablespoons **powdered sugar;** let cool in pan. Cut into 2-inch squares. Makes 2 dozen squares.

COOLING & STORING COOKIES

Let cookies cool on a wire rack—in a single layer, never stacked or overlapped. Cool them completely before stacking them on a plate or storing them. To keep cookies fresh, store them in an airtight container, but do not store moist cookies in the same container with crisp cookies.

Making Flaky Pastry (Recipe on facing page)

1 With a pastry blender, cut shortening into flour until particles are about the size of small peas.

2 Place chilled dough round on a lightly floured board. Place rolling pin in center of dough and start rolling from center to edge in an even, light stroke. Work quickly. Handle as little as possible.

3 After unrolling dough from pin (as in photo 4), ease pastry into ungreased pan; don't stretch dough. Work out from center, using finger tips to fit dough gently into pan sides. Trim, leaving ½-inch overhang.

4 Roll out second dough round to same size circle as first; wrap loosely around rolling pin and gently unroll to cover filling. Trim, leaving 1-inch overhang.

5 Fold top pastry under bottom pastry. With index finger on outside edge, and thumb and other index finger on inside edge, pinch pastry around outside finger to flute edge. Cut slits.

6 Golden-crusted Apple Pie (recipe on page 168) tastes so marvelous, it won't last long. Serve in wedges, warm or cold, topped with a scoop of your favorite ice cream.

Pastry

The secret to blue-ribbon pie crust is careful measuring, mixing, and handling. Too much flour or too much handling toughens pastry. Too little liquid results in crumbly, unmanageable dough, and too much liquid makes it soggy and sticky.

There are two types of pie crust—flaky pastry and butter pastry. Flaky pastry, the usual choice for a double-crust pie (especially a fruit pie), is made with solid shortening or lard; it can tolerate only minimal handling, and it must be rolled out. Butter pastry, ideal for quiches or tarts or any time you want a richer crust, is made with butter and egg; because it can take a little more handling without becoming tough, you can either roll it out or simply press it into the pan.

Lift the rolling pin as it comes to the edge of the dough—otherwise the edge will be thinner than the middle. Lift and turn the dough a quarter-turn after each roll, but avoid excessive handling and rolling. Ideal pastry dough is about ⅛ inch thick, though you may like it slightly thicker for the bottom crust of a fruit pie. Bake in a *preheated* oven.

Baking a pastry shell without a filling is called "baking blind." This can be done with both Flaky Pastry and Butter Pastry.

Flaky Pastry

(Pictured on facing page)

This recipe makes enough for one double-crust 9-inch pie or two single-crust 9-inch pies or pastry shells. To make just one, refrigerate the extra dough and use it within 2 days. Or freeze it for as long as 3 months, then thaw and roll out while it's still chilled.

  2¼ **cups all-purpose flour**
  ½ **teaspoon salt**
  ¾ **cup (12 tablespoons) solid shortening or lard**
  4 **to 5 tablespoons cold water**

In a bowl, stir together flour and salt. With a pastry blender or two table knives, cut shortening into flour until particles are about the size of small peas.

Pour water into a cup. While stirring lightly and quickly with a fork, sprinkle water over mixture, 1 tablespoon at a time (up to 4 tablespoons), just until all flour is moistened. If mixture seems dry and crumbly, sprinkle with another tablespoon of water; mixture should not be wet or sticky. Stir with fork until dough forms a ball and almost cleans sides of bowl.

With your hands, gather up mixture into a ball. Divide ball in half and flatten each half into a 4-inch round. Wrap each with plastic wrap and refrigerate for 1 hour to allow dough to rest. (This tenderizes dough and makes it easier to handle.)

Roll out as directed in photo 2, until dough is about ⅛ inch thick and 2 inches larger in diameter than pie pan. Wrap rolled-out dough loosely around rolling pin (as shown with a top crust in photo 4), then unroll onto pie pan. Fit pastry into pan, as shown in photo 3.

For a single-crust pie or baked pastry shell. Leaving about a 1-inch overhang, trim edge of pastry with scissors. Fold edge under so it's even with rim. Flute edge as shown in photo 5. Prick bottom and sides of shell thoroughly with a fork and bake in a preheated 450° oven for 10 minutes or until lightly browned. Let cool before filling.

For a double-crust pie. Trim bottom pastry as shown in photo 3; fill. Roll out, place, and trim top pastry (see photo 4). Fold edge of top pastry around and under edge of bottom pastry, and flute (see photo 5). Cut several small slashes in top to allow steam to escape.

Butter Pastry

(Pictured on page 110)

  1 **cup all-purpose flour**
  ¼ **teaspoon salt**
  6 **tablespoons firm butter, cut into chunks**
  1 **egg**

In a bowl, stir together flour and salt. Add butter chunks and stir to coat them. With a pastry blender or two table knives, cut butter into flour until you have fine particles. Stir in egg with a fork until dough holds together. With your hands, shape into a ball; wrap in plastic wrap and refrigerate for 1 hour.

Roll out pastry, fit into pan, and flute edge as shown in photo 5. Or press in dough (see photos, page 110).

To bake blind—without a filling—see page 110. Bake in a preheated 450° oven for 10 minutes, then lift off foil and beans. Bake empty shell for 5 minutes. Makes one single-crust pie.

Fruit pies

Homemade fruit pie...its filling is tangy and sweet, its crust wonderfully tender. What could be more irresistible?

Apple Pie

(Pictured on page 166)

>   Flaky Pastry (page 167)
>   8   cups peeled, cored, and thinly sliced apples (Gravenstein, Jonathan, Pippin, or Granny Smith)
>   1   tablespoon lemon juice
>   1   cup sugar
>   3   tablespoons cornstarch or tapioca
>   1½ teaspoons ground cinnamon
>   ¼   teaspoon ground ginger
>   2   tablespoons butter or margarine
>   Milk

Preheat oven to 425°. Prepare pastry and refrigerate while making filling. Place apple slices in a large bowl. Sprinkle apples with lemon juice, sugar, cornstarch, cinnamon, and ginger; stir to blend well; set aside.

Roll out pastry for bottom crust (see page 166). Place apples in pastry shell, mounding them a little in center. Pour in any remaining juice from bowl, then dot with butter. Roll out top crust, place over filling, and flute edge to seal (see photo 5, page 166). Brush top lightly with milk. To prevent excess browning of rim, wrap edge with a 2 to 3-inch-wide strip of foil. Set pie on a rimmed baking sheet and bake on lowest rack of oven.

Bake for 30 minutes. Remove foil and continue to bake for 20 to 30 more minutes or until apples are fork-tender. Let cool on a rack. Serve warm or at room temperature; or refrigerate and serve cold. To reheat, warm pie, uncovered, in a 350° oven for 10 to 15 minutes. Makes 6 to 8 servings.

SINGLE-CRUST APPLE PIE

Bake a 9-inch **Flaky Pastry shell** (page 167). Following directions for **Apple Pie,** combine 6 cups sliced **apples,** 1 tablespoon **lemon juice,** ¾ cup **sugar,** 2 tablespoons **cornstarch** or tapioca, 1½ teaspoons **ground cinnamon,** and ¼ teaspoon **ground ginger.** Place in baked shell. Sprinkle with **streusel topping** (recipe follows), if desired. Bake in a preheated 375° oven for 60 minutes,

checking pie after 15 to 20 minutes; if it's browning too fast, cover loosely with foil.

Streusel topping. In a bowl, combine 1 cup **all-purpose flour,** ½ cup firmly packed **brown sugar,** and ½ teaspoon **ground cinnamon.** With your fingers, work 6 tablespoons **butter** or margarine into flour until butter lumps are no longer distinguishable. Stir in ½ cup **chopped nuts,** if desired. Makes enough topping for a 9-inch pie.

Berry Pie

>   Flaky Pastry (page 167)
>   6   cups whole berries (blue, black, boysen, logan, or olallie)
>   1½ cups sugar
>   4   tablespoons cornstarch or tapioca
>   1   tablespoon lemon juice (for blueberry only)
>   2   tablespoons butter or margarine
>   Milk

Preheat oven to 425°. Prepare pastry and refrigerate while making filling. Place berries in a large bowl and sprinkle with sugar and cornstarch (and lemon juice, if making blueberry pie). Gently stir to blend well; set aside.

Roll out pastry for bottom crust (see page 166). Place berries and their juices in pastry shell and dot with butter. Roll out top crust, place over filling, and flute edge to seal (see page 166). Brush top lightly with milk. To prevent excess browning of rim, wrap edge with a 2 to 3-inch-wide strip of foil. Set pie on a rimmed baking sheet and bake on lowest rack of oven.

Bake for 30 to 35 minutes. Remove foil and continue to bake for 25 to 30 more minutes. Let cool on a rack. Serve warm or at room temperature; or refrigerate and serve cold. To reheat, warm pie, uncovered, in a 350° oven for 10 to 15 minutes. Makes 6 to 8 servings.

SINGLE-CRUST BERRY PIE

Bake a 9-inch **Flaky Pastry shell** (page 167). Prepare filling for **Berry Pie** and place in baked shell, but omit butter. Sprinkle with **streusel topping** (recipe above), if desired. Bake in a preheated 375° oven for 55 minutes (425° for 1¼ to 1½ hours, for blueberry pie). Check pie after 15 to 20 minutes; if it's browning too fast, cover loosely with foil.

Fresh fruit tarts

A fruit tart consists of a pastry shell, a little filling, and often a dusting of sugar or a light glaze of jelly. Whether bite-size or party-size, tarts are attractive, seasonal, and a snap to assemble if you keep baked tart shells in your freezer.

Tarts invite creativity—you can use one fruit or a colorful combination. Pick your favorites from strawberries, raspberries, blueberries, loganberries, sectioned oranges, and sliced plums, figs, and kiwis. Peaches, nectarines, apricots, apples, and pears also make marvelous tarts, but these fruits darken when cut, so dip slices in lemon juice before arranging them over the filling.

Short Paste for Tarts

Unlike pie dough, this pastry actually benefits from plenty of handling. If you use only egg yolks, you'll have a more golden dough.

- **2 cups all-purpose flour**
- **¼ cup sugar**
- **¾ cup (12 tablespoons) butter or margarine, cut into chunks**
- **2 egg yolks or 1 whole egg**

Preheat oven to 300°. Stir together flour and sugar; add butter. With your fingers, work butter into flour mixture until well blended. With a fork, stir in egg yolks or whole egg. Stir until dough holds together. (Or whirl flour, sugar, and butter in a food processor until mixture resembles fine crumbs; add yolks or whole egg and whirl until dough holds together.)

With your hands, press dough firmly into a smooth shiny ball (the warmth of your hands will help to blend dough). If made ahead, wrap with plastic wrap and refrigerate for at least 1 hour or up to 1 week; let come to room temperature before using. Makes 2 cups dough.

Measure pan size (see page 7). Use about 1 cup dough for an 11-inch pan, 2 cups for a 12-inch pan. (To serve tart outside of pan, use a pan with removable bottom.) For small tarts, allow about 2 teaspoons dough for tiny pans, 2 to 3 tablespoons for 3 to 5-inch pans, and ¼ to ½ cup for 6 to 7-inch pans.

To shape, press measured amount of pastry into pan, pushing dough firmly into bottom and sides to make an even layer; edge should be flush with pan rim. Bake, uncovered, for 30 to 40 min-

utes or until lightly browned. Let cool in pan.

Invert small pans and tap lightly to free shells; then turn them cup side up. Leave large tart shell in pan. At this point you may wrap shells airtight and store at room temperature for up to 4 days or freeze for longer storage.

UNCOOKED PASTRY CREAM

Place 1 small package (3 oz.) **cream cheese** (softened) in a deep bowl and, with an electric mixer at high speed, beat until smooth. Beating constantly, pour in ½ pint (1 cup) **whipping cream** in a steady stream. (Mixture should have consistency of stiffly whipped cream at all times; if it looks soft, stop adding cream until mixture thickens. *Do not overbeat* or sauce will break down.)

Stir in ½ cup sifted **powdered sugar**, ½ teaspoon *each* **vanilla** and **grated lemon peel**, and 1 teaspoon **lemon juice**.

If made ahead, cover and refrigerate until next day. Makes about 2½ cups.

FILLING TART SHELLS

Since a tart has no top crust, the filling serves to hold the fruit in place. Only the shell is baked, not the fruit or filling.

To assemble a tart, fill baked tart shells with your choice of filling, then top filling with a layer of fruit. You can leave the fruit plain, sprinkle it with a little granulated or powdered sugar, or brush it with a glaze of 1 to 1½ cups currant, apricot, or strawberry jelly, melted over low heat and cooled slightly.

Choices of filling include **Uncooked Pastry Cream** (above), cooked **French Pastry Cream** (page 170), and **Lemon Butter Filling** (page 180). For an 11 to 12-inch tart, you'll use a full recipe of filling; for an 8 or 9-inch tart, about half of the filling; and for a 6 to 7-inch tart, about a third.

Individual tarts can take a proportionately more generous amount of filling than large ones that must be cut. Allow ¼ to ⅓ cup filling for each 3 to 5-inch tart, 2 to 3 tablespoons for each 2-inch tart.

Cream puffs & éclairs

The batter for these versatile morsels is known as *choux* paste—a simple mixture of butter, flour, and eggs. Shape into éclairs or cream puffs for dessert, or cocktail-size puffs for hors d'oeuvres. Fill them with pastry cream, sweetened whipped cream, ice cream, or tuna or chicken salad.

The baked puff should have a hollow, moist interior, and a crisp outer shell with a lightly browned, somewhat pebbly surface and irregular shape. Like popovers, these delicate puffs collapse if they're underbaked.

Choux Paste

(Pictured on facing page)

> 1 **cup water**
> ½ **cup (¼ lb.) butter or margarine**
> ¼ **teaspoon salt**
> 1 **teaspoon sugar (use only for dessert puffs)**
> 1 **cup all-purpose flour**
> 4 **eggs**

Preheat oven to 425°. Lightly grease a baking sheet and set aside.

In a 3-quart pan over medium-high heat, bring water, butter, salt, and sugar (if used) to a boil. When butter melts, remove pan from heat, add flour all at once, and beat with a wooden spoon until well blended. Reduce heat to medium. Return pan to heat and stir vigorously with a wooden spoon until mixture forms a ball and leaves sides of pan. Remove pan from heat and let mixture cool for 5 minutes. Add eggs, one at a time, beating mixture after each addition until smooth. (After each egg is added, mixture breaks apart into clumps and is slippery, but will return to a smooth paste after vigorous beating.) Let batter cool for 10 minutes before shaping.

Shaping and baking cream puffs. You need two spoons to shape cream puffs. With one spoon, scoop up about 2 tablespoons batter for a large puff, 1 tablespoon for medium-size, or 1½ teaspoons for cocktail-size. With other spoon, push batter off first spoon and drop in a mound onto prepared baking sheet. Place mounds about 2 inches apart.

In a small dish or cup, beat 1 **egg** with 1 teaspoon **water.** Brush egg glaze over tops of puffs, being sure it doesn't drip down sides and onto baking sheet (preventing proper rising of puffs).

Bake in upper third of preheated 425° oven for 15 minutes. Reduce heat to 375°.

Cut a slash in lower side of each puff and continue baking until puffs are firm, dry to touch, and golden brown (5 to 10 more minutes). Let cool on wire racks. Use within 24 hours; or wrap airtight and freeze. Makes about 2 dozen large puffs, 3 dozen medium-size puffs, or 5 to 6 dozen cocktail-size puffs.

Shaping and baking éclairs. Onto prepared baking sheet, drop about ¼ cup batter for each éclair, placing mounds 2 to 3 inches apart. (Or put batter into a pastry bag and pipe out.) Using a small metal spatula, spread each mound into a strip 4½ inches long and 1 inch wide. Brush tops with **egg glaze** and bake as for cream puffs. Makes about 12 éclairs.

Serving dessert cream puffs and éclairs. With a knife, carefully cut the top (upper third) from each puff and scoop out moist, doughy interior. Just before serving, fill with French Pastry Cream (recipe follows) or whipped cream (see page 171) sweetened with powdered sugar; replace tops and dust with powdered sugar. Or fill puffs with ice cream. Replace tops, and drizzle with Chocolate Glaze (recipe follows).

FRENCH PASTRY CREAM

In top pan of a double boiler, stir together ¾ cup **sugar,** ½ cup all-purpose **flour,** dash of **salt,** and 4 beaten **egg yolks.** Beating constantly with a spoon, to keep mixture smooth, gradually pour in 2 cups **scalded milk** (heated until small bubbles appear). Pour hot water into bottom of double boiler, being sure water will not touch bottom of top pan. Bring water to a boil; then reduce to a simmer. Put top of double boiler in place over simmering water. Stir vigorously with a wire whisk or a spoon for 4 to 5 minutes or until mixture boils and thickens. Stir in 1 tablespoon **butter** and 1 teaspoon **vanilla.** Let cool before using. Makes 3 cups (fills 12 large cream puffs or 12 éclairs).

CHOCOLATE GLAZE

In a small pan, place 4 ounces **semisweet chocolate** (coarsely chopped) and 6 tablespoons **whipping cream.** Cook, stirring constantly, over medium heat, until chocolate is melted and well blended with cream. Makes about ½ cup.

Making Choux Paste (Recipe on facing page)

Whipping cream

1 Stir vigorously with a wooden spoon until flour-butter mixture forms a ball and leaves sides of pan. Remove from heat; let cool for 5 minutes.

2 As you beat in each egg, mixture separates into clumps and becomes slippery, but smooths out again after each egg is completely incorporated into mixture.

1 Whip cream just before using. With chilled bowl and beaters, beat cream until soft peaks form. Cream doubles in volume during beating—1 cup whipping cream produces 2 cups whipped cream.

3 After all eggs are beaten in, paste will be creamy, smooth, shiny, and very thick. Let it cool before shaping into cream puffs or éclairs.

4 Form cream puff mounds by dropping batter from one spoon while pushing it off with the other spoon. Mounds puff up into irregularly shaped crisp golden shells during baking.

2 Slightly overbeaten cream is lumpy—still usable, but hard to incorporate with other ingredients. (Extremely overbeaten cream will eventually clump and make butter.)

Cheesecakes, Bavarians & creams

Most of us watch out for calories these days, but now and then a splurge cheers the soul and highlights a special occasion. Presented here are several rich, luscious, and elegant desserts that are also quick and easy. Each can be made at least a day in advance, and our Chocolate Cream can even be frozen.

Easy Cheesecake Pie

- 1 crumb crust of your choice (recipes at right)
- 4 small packages (3 oz. *each*) cream cheese, softened
- ⅔ cup sugar
- 2 eggs, at room temperature
- ½ pint (1 cup) sour cream
- 2 teaspoons vanilla

Preheat oven to 350°. Prepare and bake crumb crust; set aside.

In a large bowl, stir together cream cheese and sugar until soft and creamy; then beat in eggs, one at a time. Stir in sour cream and vanilla; blend well. Pour into baked crust.

Bake for 20 to 25 minutes or until center jiggles slightly when pan is gently shaken (center will set upon standing). Transfer pan to a wire rack. Let cool completely, then cover with wax paper and refrigerate for at least 8 hours or until next day. Cut into wedges to serve. Cover and refrigerate any remaining pie. Makes 8 to 10 servings.

Elegant Cheesecake

- 1 graham cracker crust (recipe at right)
- 3 large packages (8 oz. *each*) cream cheese, softened
- ½ teaspoon salt
- 1 tablespoon vanilla
- 4 eggs, at room temperature
- 1 cup sugar
- 1 pint (2 cups) sour cream
- 2 tablespoons sugar

Preheat oven to 350°. Prepare graham cracker crust, but press mixture firmly over bottom and 2 inches up sides of a 9-inch spring-form pan. Bake crust, then set aside.

In a large bowl, stir together cream cheese, salt, and vanilla until soft and creamy. Add eggs one at a time, beating well after each addition. Gradually beat in the 1 cup sugar until it is all incorporated. Pour into prepared pan.

Bake for 30 to 35 minutes or until center jiggles slightly when pan is gently shaken (center will set upon standing). Remove cake from oven; let stand for 10 minutes. Increase oven temperature to 450°. In a small bowl, stir together sour cream and the 2 tablespoons sugar; spread over top of cake. Return cake to oven and bake for 5 more minutes or until cream is set. Transfer pan to a wire rack. Let cool completely before removing sides from pan. Then cover and refrigerate for at least 24 hours. Cut into wedges to serve. Cover and refrigerate any remaining cake. Makes 12 servings.

CRUMB CRUSTS

Crushed graham crackers, chocolate and vanilla wafers, gingersnap cookies, and nuts can become quick, delicious crusts for cheesecakes or cream fillings. Simply break the crackers or cookies into pieces, place them in a plastic bag, and crush with a rolling pin. Or put pieces into a food processor and whirl to make fine crumbs.

Graham cracker crust. Preheat oven to 350°. In a bowl, combine 1½ cups fine **graham cracker crumbs** (about 24 cracker squares), ⅓ cup **butter** or margarine, melted, and ¼ cup **sugar**. Press mixture firmly over bottom and up sides of a 9-inch pie pan. Bake for 10 minutes.

Chocolate, gingersnap, or vanilla crust. Follow recipe for **Graham cracker crust,** but instead of graham crackers, use 27 2½-inch **chocolate wafers** or gingersnap cookies, or 36 2-inch vanilla wafers; omit the ¼ cup sugar.

Crumb and nut crusts. Follow recipe for **Graham cracker crust** (or chocolate, gingersnap, or vanilla crust), but use only 1 cup of crumbs and add ½ cup finely chopped **nuts;** omit the ¼ cup sugar.

Strawberry Bavarian

  2 cups sliced hulled strawberries
  ½ cup sugar
  1 envelope (1 tablespoon) unflavored gelatin
  ¾ cup cold water
  2 egg whites
  1 cup whipping cream

Place berries and sugar in a bowl. Partially crush berries with a fork or potato masher (there should be some berry chunks); set aside.

In a 1-quart pan, stir together gelatin and water; let stand for 5 minutes or until gelatin has softened. Stir in strawberry mixture. Bring just to a boil, stirring constantly. Pour into a large bowl and let cool thoroughly until mixture is thick but not set. In another bowl, beat egg whites until soft peaks form (see page 30). Fold beaten egg whites into strawberry mixture. In same bowl, whip cream; fold into strawberry mixture. Pour into 6 to 8 dessert glasses. Cover and refrigerate for at least 4 hours or until next day. Makes 6 to 8 servings.

Kaffee Bavarian

  1 envelope (1 tablespoon) unflavored gelatin
  ½ cup cold water
  6 egg yolks
  1 cup sugar
  ⅓ cup coffee-flavored liqueur, rum, or cream sherry
  1 pint (2 cups) whipping cream, whipped

In a small pan, stir together gelatin and water; let stand for 5 minutes or until gelatin has softened. Bring just to a boil, stirring constantly. Remove pan from heat and set aside.

Place yolks in a large bowl and beat with an electric mixer on high speed until thick and lemon colored. Gradually beat in sugar, 2 tablespoons at a time, and continue beating until mixture forms a ribbon (see page 174). With mixer on medium speed, pour hot gelatin into egg yolk mixture; beat until blended. Beat in liqueur, then fold in whipped cream. Pour into 6 to 8 dessert glasses. Cover and refrigerate for at least 4 hours or until next day. Makes 6 to 8 servings.

Chocolate Cream

  1 cup (½ lb.) butter or margarine (preferably unsalted), softened
  ¾ cup sugar
  8 ounces semisweet chocolate or 1½ cups semisweet chocolate chips, melted
  6 eggs
  3 tablespoons rum or brandy, or 2 tablespoons orange-flavored liqueur (optional)
     Sweetened whipped cream (optional)

With an electric mixer, beat butter and sugar at high speed until well blended. Slowly pour in melted chocolate and continue beating until blended. Still at high speed, beat in eggs, one at a time, until thoroughly blended. Mix in rum, if desired.

Spoon into 8 to 10 small dessert glasses. Cover and refrigerate for at least 4 hours or up to 3 days. Freeze for longer storage; let stand at room temperature for 20 minutes before serving.

Just before serving, garnish each portion with a dollop of whipped cream, if desired. Makes 8 to 10 servings.

Russian Cream

  ¾ cup sugar
  1 envelope (1 tablespoon) unflavored gelatin
  ½ cup cold water
  ½ pint (1 cup) whipping cream or half-and-half (light cream)
 1½ cups sour cream
  1 teaspoon vanilla
     Raspberry or strawberry sauce (page 185) or sliced strawberries (optional)

In a small pan, stir together sugar and gelatin. Stir in water and let stand for 5 minutes or until gelatin has softened. Stirring constantly, bring to a full rolling boil over high heat. Remove pan from heat and stir in whipping cream. In a bowl, stir together sour cream and vanilla; gradually beat into hot gelatin mixture until smooth.

Pour into 8 dessert glasses or into a 4 to 5-cup serving bowl. Cover and refrigerate for at least 4 hours or until next day. Accompany each serving with berry sauce or strawberries, if you wish. Makes 8 servings.

Making Stirred Custard (Recipe on facing page)

Beating egg yolks

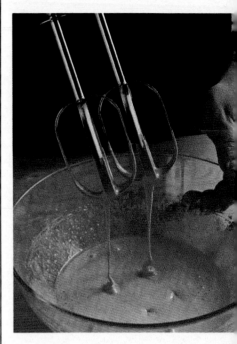

1 While constantly stirring with a wire whisk, gradually pour lightly beaten egg yolks into warm milk-sugar mixture.

2 Bring water in bottom of double boiler to a boil, then reduce heat so water simmers; set top of boiler with milk-egg mixture over water (water should not touch bottom of top pan).

1 These egg yolks have been beaten until light and lemon colored.

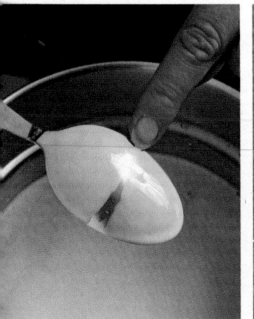

3 Stir constantly until custard coats a metal spoon—about 10 minutes. A finger drawn across spoon should leave a clean path, and consistency should be smooth and creamy. Cool immediately.

4 Stirred custard doesn't set up and gel as baked custard does, but remains fluid even when cool. Pour over fresh strawberries for an elegant dessert.

2 Gradually beat in sugar, scraping bowl often, until mixture falls in a thick ribbon. This stage is important for leavening sponge cakes on pages 179–180.

Custards

Exquisitely simple, custards are nothing more than egg and milk mixtures sweetened and flavored, then stirred over heat or baked.

Baked custard should be tender, smooth, and creamy—baked just until the mixture gels or sets to a firm yet still jiggly consistency. If it is completely firm before it's removed from the oven, it is overcooked and will shrink and become tough.

Stirred custard, is soft, fluid, and smooth. It should be cooked only until the mixture coagulates—the point at which it evenly coats a metal spoon. Stirred custard doesn't gel. It will thicken slightly as it cools but will remain fluid enough to pour.

For a smoother custard, baked or stirred, you can substitute egg yolks for whole eggs, but the custard will need a slightly longer cooking time. (Two yolks are equal to one whole egg in thickening power.)

Soft Stirred Custard

(Pictured on facing page)

Cook this custard sauce in a 1½-quart heavy-bottomed pan over low heat, or in the top of a double boiler. In a double boiler, there's less chance that the custard will curdle from too much heat. Either way, constant stirring is a must.

- 2 **cups milk**
- ⅓ **cup sugar**
- 4 **or 5 egg yolks, lightly beaten**
- 1 **teaspoon vanilla**

In the top of a double boiler placed directly over medium heat, scald milk (heat until small bubbles appear); remove from heat and stir in sugar until dissolved. Gradually add yolks to milk mixture while stirring constantly.

Pour hot water into bottom of double boiler, being sure water will not touch bottom of top pan. Bring water to a boil over high heat, then reduce heat so water only simmers.

Put top of double boiler in place over simmering water. Stir milk mixture constantly (to prevent lumping) until custard has thickened and coats a metal spoon (about 10 minutes); a finger drawn across spoon should leave a clean path. (Overcooking results in a grainy, curdled custard. If custard is slightly curdled, strain it into a bowl and beat with an electric mixer, or whirl in a blender or food processor for 1 minute until smooth. Excessively curdled custard cannot be corrected.) Stir in vanilla, then cool as directed below. Makes about 2½ cups.

Baked Custard

- 2 **cups milk**
- ¼ **cup sugar**
- 3 **whole eggs or 6 egg yolks**
- ½ **teaspoon vanilla**
  Ground nutmeg or ground cinnamon

In a pan over medium heat, scald milk (heat until small bubbles appear); remove from heat and stir in sugar until dissolved. In a small bowl, beat eggs slightly. While constantly stirring, gradually pour milk mixture into eggs, then stir in vanilla. Pour into five or six 6-ounce custard cups (or into a 1-quart round baking dish). Sprinkle with nutmeg or cinnamon. Place cups or baking dish in a 9 by 13-inch baking pan and pour hot water into pan to a depth of 1 inch.

Bake in a 350° oven for 25 to 30 minutes (50 to 60 minutes for 1-quart dish) or until a knife inserted just off center of custard comes out clean. Custard should jiggle slightly in center when gently shaken—it will set up upon cooling. Remove custard from hot water immediately; cool as directed below. Makes 5 or 6 servings.

COOLING BAKED & STIRRED CUSTARDS

It's important to cool both baked and stirred custards immediately after the gelling or coagulation point has been reached, in order to stop the cooking action. As soon as you remove baked custard from the oven, remove from the water; place on rack to cool.

When stirred (soft) custard evenly coats a spoon, immediately remove it from heat and place the pan in a bowl of ice water, or pour the custard into a cold bowl. To release steam and aid the cooling process, stir the soft custard often until it has cooled to room temperature.

Once cooled, all custards should be loosely covered with wax paper and refrigerated.

Shortening cakes

Traditionally known as "butter cakes," these moist, rich delicacies were once made exclusively with butter, but margarine or solid shortening (except lard) will do nicely. Cake flour gives a light and tender texture. Have all ingredients at room temperature before you start. Frost with Fluffy Butter Frosting (page 181).

Yellow Cake

> 2¼ cups sifted cake flour
> 3 teaspoons baking powder
> 1¼ cups sugar
> 1 teaspoon salt
> ½ cup (¼ lb.) butter or margarine, softened
> 1 cup milk
> 2 eggs
> 1 teaspoon vanilla

Preheat oven to 375° and prepare pan(s) as directed below.

Sift flour, baking powder, sugar, and salt into

LAYERS, SHEET CAKE, OR CUPCAKES:
PAN PREPARATION & BAKING TIMES

The basic recipe for Yellow Cake can produce several different shapes and sizes. Oven temperature is the same for all—a preheated 375°; only the time varies. You can bake the batter in three 8-inch or two 9-inch round baking pans (for 20 to 25 minutes), or in one 7 by 11-inch baking pan (for 30 to 35 minutes), or in 24 muffin cups (for 18 to 20 minutes). Pans should always be greased and flour-dusted, though muffin pans can be lined with paper baking cups instead.

Cake is done if the top springs back when lightly touched and the cake begins to pull away from the sides of the pan. The same test applies for cupcakes. Immediately after baking, remove cupcakes from the pan and let them cool on wire racks. A sheet cake can cool in its pan on a rack. Layers should cool in the pans on racks for 10 minutes, then be turned out onto racks. They all should be allowed to cool completely before being frosted.

---

a medium-size mixing bowl; add butter and ⅔ cup of the milk. With an electric mixer at medium speed, beat for 2 minutes, scraping bowl often with a rubber spatula. Add eggs, vanilla, and remaining ⅓ cup milk; continue beating for 2 more minutes. Pour batter into prepared pan(s). Bake and let cool as directed below left. Makes a three-layer 8-inch cake, a two-layer 9-inch cake, a 7 by 11-inch sheet cake, or 24 cupcakes.

WHITE CAKE

Prepare **Yellow Cake,** but substitute 4 **egg whites** for the 2 whole eggs.

Carrot Cake

Use the cream cheese frosting if you bake the cake in a rectangular pan, the orange glaze if you use a bundt pan.

> 2 cups sugar
> 1 cup salad oil
> 4 eggs
> 1 teaspoon vanilla
> 2 cups all-purpose flour
> 2 teaspoons *each* baking powder and ground cinnamon
> 1½ teaspoons baking soda
> 2 cups lightly packed shredded carrots
> 1 can (8 oz.) crushed pineapple, well drained
> ½ cup chopped walnuts
> Cream cheese frosting or orange glaze (recipes follow)

Preheat oven to 350°. Grease and flour-dust a 9 by 13-inch baking pan or a 10-inch bundt pan; set aside.

In a medium-size bowl, stir together sugar and oil. Beat in eggs, one at a time, then stir in vanilla. Stir in flour, baking powder, cinnamon, and baking soda. Add carrots, pineapple, and nuts; stir just to blend. Pour batter into prepared pan.

Bake for 45 minutes if using a rectangular pan, 55 minutes if using a bundt pan, or until a wooden pick inserted in center comes out clean and cake starts to pull away from sides of pan. Place pan on a wire rack to cool; or, if using a bundt pan, let cake cool in pan for 15 minutes, then turn out of pan and finish cooling on wire rack. Let cake cool completely before frosting or glazing. Makes 12 to 15 servings.

Cream cheese frosting. In a small bowl, blend until smooth 2 packages (3 oz. *each*) **cream cheese,** softened; 6 tablespoons **butter** or margarine, softened; 1 teaspoon grated **orange peel** (optional); 1 teaspoon **vanilla;** and 2 cups sifted **powdered sugar.** Makes enough to frost a 9 by 13-inch cake.

Orange glaze. In a small bowl, stir together 2 cups sifted **powdered sugar,** 3 tablespoons **orange juice,** 1 teaspoon grated **orange peel,** and 1 teaspoon **vanilla.** Drizzle over cooled bundt cake.

Powdered Sugar Pound Cake

This old-fashioned favorite takes its name from its original proportions: a pound each of butter, sugar, eggs, and flour. Through the years, that simple formula has undergone numerous refinements and variations. But even today, we still use pure butter to assure a distinctive, rich flavor.

Our basic recipe yields either one large tube cake or two loaf cakes. To store, wrap the completely cooled cake airtight and refrigerate for as long as a week—or freeze for longer storage.

Pound cake is meant to be served without icing. Cut the cake into slices and embellish it with fresh fruit slices, whipped cream, or soft custard.

> 1½ cups (¾ lb.) butter, softened
> 1 box (1 lb.) powdered sugar, sifted
> 6 eggs, at room temperature
> 1 teaspoon vanilla
> 2¾ cups sifted cake flour

Preheat oven to 325°. Grease and flour-dust a 10-inch tube pan or two 9 by 5-inch loaf pans; set aside.

In a large bowl, cream butter and sugar with an electric mixer until light and fluffy. Add eggs, one at a time, beating well after each addition; then beat in vanilla. Turn mixer to lowest speed and gradually beat in flour, scraping bowl often, until all flour has been incorporated. Spoon batter into prepared pan; if using loaf pans, divide batter evenly.

Bake for 1 hour or until a wooden pick inserted in center comes out clean. Let cake cool in pan on a wire rack for 5 minutes, then turn out onto rack to cool completely. Makes 14 to 16 servings.

BAKING CAKES AT HIGH ELEVATIONS

Cake, with its delicate structure, is more affected by high elevation than almost any other baked food. Above 3,000 feet, a cake is likely to fall and become coarse-textured unless you alter the recipe. Because each cake recipe differs in the proportions of its ingredients, there can be no set rules for modifying sea-level cake recipes to suit high elevations. You'll have to experiment.

With angel food cakes, the trick is to beat egg whites just to the soft-peak stage (see page 30) and reduce the total amount of sugar by 1 tablespoon for each 1,000 feet of elevation above 3,000 feet.

For cakes that use shortening, increase the baking temperature by 25° and follow these general guidelines:

- *At 3,000 to 5,000 feet,* reduce each teaspoon of baking powder by ⅛ teaspoon, reduce each cup of sugar by up to 3 teaspoons, and increase each cup of liquid by up to 2 tablespoons.
- *At 5,000 to 7,000 feet,* reduce each teaspoon of baking powder by ⅛ to ¼ teaspoon, reduce each cup of sugar by up to 2 tablespoons, and increase each cup of liquid by 2 to 4 tablespoons.
- *At 7,000 to 10,000 feet,* reduce each teaspoon of baking powder by ¼ teaspoon, reduce each cup of sugar by 1 to 3 tablespoons, and increase each cup of liquid by 3 to 4 tablespoons.
- *Above 10,000 feet,* reduce each teaspoon of baking powder by ¼ to ½ teaspoon, reduce each cup of sugar by 2 to 3 tablespoons, increase each cup of liquid by 3 to 4 tablespoons, add an extra egg to the batter, and increase each cup of flour by 1 to 2 tablespoons.

Because cakes tend to stick to their baking pans at high elevations, be generous in greasing and flour-dusting pans (unless you're making a sponge-type cake).

Though pastry is not usually affected by altitude, you may need to use slightly more liquid at high elevations because liquids evaporate so quickly there.

...Shortening cakes

Chocolate Brownie Cake

1 cup water
10 tablespoons (¼ lb. plus 2 tablespoons) butter or margarine
2 cups *each* sugar and all-purpose flour
1 teaspoon baking soda
4 tablespoons unsweetened cocoa
½ cup buttermilk
2 eggs
Chocolate Butter Frosting recipe (page 181)

Preheat oven to 350°. Grease a 10 by 15-inch rimmed baking pan; set aside. In a small pan, heat water and butter to boiling; remove from heat and let cool slightly.

In a large bowl, sift together sugar, flour, soda, and cocoa; add water mixture and beat until well combined. Beat in buttermilk; then add eggs, one at a time, beating well after each addition.

Pour batter into prepared pan. Bake for 25 minutes or until cake springs back when lightly touched. Let cool for 15 to 20 minutes. Then prepare frosting; spread on slightly cooled cake. Let cool, then cut into 2½ to 3-inch squares. Makes 14 to 16 servings.

Gingerbread

The gingery flavor permeates as the cake cools, and is most pronounced when the cake is served at room temperature.

1 cup sugar
¼ teaspoon salt
1 teaspoon ground ginger
½ teaspoon *each* ground cinnamon and ground cloves
1 cup *each* salad oil and molasses
2 teaspoons baking soda
1 cup boiling water
2½ cups all-purpose flour
2 eggs, well beaten

Preheat oven to 350°. Lightly grease a 9 by 13-inch baking pan; set aside.

In a medium-size bowl, combine sugar, salt, ginger, cinnamon, and cloves. Stir in salad oil, then molasses; blend well. Combine baking soda and boiling water and immediately stir into molasses mixture. Stir flour into liquid mixture gradually to prevent lumping. Stir in eggs, then pour into prepared pan.

Bake for 40 to 45 minutes or until a wooden pick inserted in center comes out clean and cake starts to pull away from sides of pan. Remove pan to wire rack and let cool. Makes 12 servings.

Date Cake

1 cup water
½ teaspoon baking soda
1 cup pitted dates, chopped
1½ cups all-purpose flour
1 teaspoon baking powder
½ teaspoon ground cinnamon
¼ teaspoon salt
½ cup (¼ lb.) butter or margarine
1 cup sugar
2 eggs
1 teaspoon vanilla
Date frosting (recipe follows)

Preheat oven to 350°. Grease a 9-inch square baking pan and set aside. In a 2-quart pan, bring water to a boil. Add baking soda and stir until dissolved, then add dates and set aside to cool. Sift together flour, baking powder, cinnamon, and salt; set aside.

In a bowl, cream together butter and sugar. Add eggs, one at a time, beating well after each addition. Pour off water from dates into butter mixture; beat until blended. Stir in flour mixture. Stir in dates and vanilla. Pour batter into prepared pan. Bake for 40 minutes or until a wooden pick inserted in center comes out clean. Transfer pan to a wire rack and let cool completely before frosting. Makes 9 to 12 servings.

Date frosting. In a 2-quart pan, bring 1 cup **water** and ½ cup *each* firmly packed **brown sugar** and **granulated sugar** to a boil. Reduce heat to medium-low and cook, stirring occasionally, for 10 minutes. Stir in ½ cup *each* finely cut **dates** and chopped **walnuts**, and ½ cup (¼ lb.) **butter** or margarine. Continue cooking, stirring until frosting thickens slightly and drips slowly off a spoon. Pour over cake; frosting will be slightly runny, but will set upon cooling. Let frosting cool completely before cutting cake.

Sponge cakes

Leavened by beaten egg whites, sponge cake is characteristically light and fluffy. Its main ingredients are eggs, sugar, and flour—sponge cakes never contain shortening.

If you make a sponge cake with whole eggs or egg yolks, you'll create a yellow sponge cake; if you use only the egg whites, you'll make an angel food cake. Either way, the air and liquid incorporated into the beaten eggs create steam during baking and make the cake rise. Sometimes baking powder is added to give an extra boost to the leavening process.

Separate eggs when they're cold, because it's easier. Cover the bowl of yolks to prevent their drying out, and let the yolks and whites come to room temperature before you beat them—that way they'll achieve greatest volume.

We always add a little cream of tartar to the egg whites for angel food cakes. This increases tenderness and gives angel food its snowy white color. Remember: never grease the pan for an angel food cake; the fragile batter needs to cling to the pan sides for support. A grease-free pan is also necessary to prevent the cake from falling out of the pan when it's inverted to cool. In fact, it's important that everything—bowl, beaters, and pan—be totally grease-free.

Yellow sponge cakes should be golden, light, and delicate, with a velvety crumb and a slightly sweet flavor. The butter frostings on page 181 and any of the fillings on this page and page 180 will taste marvelous with either the yellow sponge or angel food cake.

Chocolate Cake Roll

- ¾ **cup all-purpose flour**
- ¼ **cup unsweetened cocoa**
- 1 **teaspoon baking powder**
- ¼ **teaspoon salt**
- ½ **teaspoon ground cinnamon**
- 3 **eggs**
- ½ **cup *each* firmly packed brown sugar and granulated sugar**
- ⅓ **cup water**
- 1 **teaspoon *each* vanilla and grated orange peel**
- **Powdered sugar**
- **Creamy chocolate chip filling (recipe follows)**
- **Fresh orange slices (optional)**

Preheat oven to 375°. Lightly grease a 10 by 15-inch rimmed baking pan, line it with wax paper, then grease paper; set aside. Sift together flour, cocoa, baking powder, salt, and cinnamon; set aside.

In a medium-size bowl, beat eggs with an electric mixer at high speed until eggs are thick and lemon colored. Force brown sugar through a strainer to get rid of hard lumps. Gradually add brown sugar and granulated sugar to eggs, while beating egg mixture on high speed. Continue beating, scraping bowl often, until mixture is light and fluffy and falls in a thick ribbon (see page 174). With a rubber spatula, mix in water, vanilla, and orange peel.

Sprinkle about a third of flour mixture over eggs and carefully fold together. Add another third of flour mixture and fold together. Repeat with final third of flour mixture, folding together until ingredients are well blended. Pour batter into prepared pan and spread evenly.

Bake for 12 minutes or until top springs back when gently touched. Immediately invert cake onto a clean dish towel sprinkled with about ⅓ cup powdered sugar. Remove wax paper and immediately roll cake and towel into a cylinder (see *Illustration 1*); let cool completely on a wire rack.

Illustration 1   *Illustration 2*

Unroll cake, spread with filling, then reroll (see *Illustration 2*). If made ahead, wrap in plastic wrap and refrigerate for as long as 24 hours. To serve, let cake warm to room temperature. If desired, sift additional powdered sugar over cake top and garnish with orange slices. Makes 10 servings.

Creamy chocolate chip filling. In a bowl, beat 1 cup **whipping cream** with 3 tablespoons **sugar** until soft peaks form. Add ½ teaspoon **ground cinnamon** and ¾ teaspoon **instant coffee** granules; beat until stiff. Fold in ¾ cup **tiny chocolate chips.**

...Sponge cakes

Yellow Sponge Cake

    4   eggs, separated
    ¾   cup sugar
    1   teaspoon vanilla
    ¾   teaspoon baking powder
    ¼   teaspoon salt
    ¾   cup sifted cake flour
        Powdered sugar
    1   cup warm jam, or Strawberry filling (recipe
        follows), or Lemon butter filling (recipe
        follows)

Preheat oven to 375°. Lightly grease a 10 by 15-inch rimmed baking pan, line it with wax paper, then grease paper; set aside.

In a medium-size bowl, beat egg·yolks with an electric mixer at high speed until yolks are thick and lemon colored. Gradually beat in ½ cup of the sugar, scraping bowl often, until mixture is light and fluffy and falls in a thick ribbon (see page 174). Stir in vanilla. Stir together baking powder, salt, and flour. Using a rubber spatula, gradually fold flour mixture into yolk mixture; set aside.

In another bowl, using clean, dry beaters, beat egg whites until soft peaks form, then gradually beat in the remaining ¼ cup sugar, a tablespoon at a time, until glossy peaks form; fold in yolk mixture just until blended. Pour batter into prepared pan and spread evenly.

Bake for 10 to 12 minutes or until top springs back when gently touched. Immediately invert cake onto a clean dish towel sprinkled with about ⅓ cup powdered sugar. Remove wax paper and immediately roll cake and towel into a cylinder (see *Illustration 1*, page 179); let cool completely on a wire rack.

Unroll cake, spread with warm jam or one of the suggested fillings, then reroll (see *Illustration 2*, page 179). If made ahead, wrap filled cake in plastic wrap and refrigerate for as long as 24 hours. Sift additional powdered sugar over top, if desired. Makes 10 servings.

Strawberry filling. In a small bowl, beat 1 **egg white** until soft peaks form (see page 30). Gradually beat in ¼ cup **sugar** until stiff peaks form. Whip ½ cup **whipping cream** (see page 171) and fold into whites, along with ½ cup mashed **strawberries,** and 1 teaspoon **vanilla.**

Lemon butter filling. In top of a double boiler placed directly over low heat, melt ½ cup (¼ lb.) **butter** or margarine. Remove from heat and add 1 teaspoon grated **lemon peel,** ½ cup **lemon juice,** 1¼ cups **sugar,** and 4 **eggs;** stir to blend well. Pour hot water into bottom of double boiler, being sure water will not touch bottom of top pan. Bring water to a boil over high heat, then reduce heat so water only simmers. Put top of double boiler in place over simmering water and cook, beating with a wire whisk, until thickened and smooth (about 20 minutes). Let cool. Cover and refrigerate until cold. Keeps for 2 weeks. Makes 2 cups.

Angel Food Cake

    1   cup sifted cake flour
    1¼   cups sugar
    1½   cups (about 12) egg whites
    ½   teaspoon salt
    2   teaspoons cream of tartar
    1½   teaspoons vanilla or almond extract

Preheat oven to 375°. Sift together flour and ½ cup of the sugar; sift again and set aside. In a large bowl, beat egg whites with an electric mixer until frothy (see page 30). Add salt and cream of tartar and continue beating until soft peaks form. Add the remaining ¾ cup sugar, 2 tablespoons at a time, beating well after each addition; continue beating until stiff peaks form.

With a rubber spatula, fold in vanilla. Sprinkle flour mixture, about ¼ cup at a time, over stiff whites, each time gently folding in just until blended. Pour batter into an ungreased 10-inch tube pan and gently smooth top. Slide rubber spatula into batter and run it around pan to eliminate large air bubbles.

Bake for 30 to 35 minutes or until crust looks golden and top springs back when gently touched. Remove pan from oven and immediately turn upside down over a funnel or soda pop bottle. (This

prevents cake from shrinking and falling.) Leave cake in this position until completely cooled. Remove from pan and frost if desired. Makes about 12 servings.

Frostings—the final touch

A crowning touch on any homemade cake, butter cream frosting is simple to make, yet deliciously rich. The recipe below will make enough to frost a three-layer 8-inch cake, a two-layer 9-inch cake, two 7 by 11-inch sheet cakes, or two dozen cupcakes.

Fluffy Butter Frosting

- 1 box (1 lb.) powdered sugar
- ½ cup (¼ lb.) butter or margarine, melted and cooled
- 4 to 6 tablespoons milk
- 1 teaspoon vanilla, almond, lemon, orange, or rum extract

Sift powdered sugar into a medium-size bowl. Add melted butter, 4 tablespoons milk, and extract of your choice; stir to blend. Beat with an electric mixer on high speed for 4 to 5 minutes or until frosting is light and fluffy and of spreading consistency. If it seems a little thick, beat in 1 or 2 more tablespoons milk. Makes about 2¼ cups.

CHOCOLATE BUTTER FROSTING

Prepare **Fluffy Butter Frosting,** but sift ¼ cup **unsweetened cocoa** into powdered sugar.

MOCHA BUTTER FROSTING

Prepare **Fluffy Butter Frosting,** but sift ¼ cup **unsweetened cocoa** into powdered sugar, and stir 1 teaspoon **instant coffee** granules into melted butter.

ORANGE BUTTER FROSTING

Prepare **Fluffy Butter Frosting,** but use ¼ cup **orange juice** instead of milk, and stir in 1 teaspoon grated **orange peel** with the powdered sugar.

FROSTING A LAYER CAKE

Completely cool cake layers before frosting them, and brush off all loose crumbs from the sides and bottom of each layer. To keep your cake plate clean, lay four narrow strips of wax paper around the plate's edge to form a square (the ends should overlap and extend beyond the plate). You'll pull the strips away after the entire cake is frosted.

Center the first cake layer, top side down, on the plate. Spoon about ⅓ cup frosting onto the center of the cake layer. Using a metal spatula, evenly spread frosting to the cake's edge. Place the second layer, top side up, on the frosted layer. (When frosting a three-layer cake, place the second layer top side down and the third layer top side up.)

Next frost the sides. With a metal spatula held vertically, spread a thin layer of frosting around the sides of the cake to seal in fine loose crumbs. Then finish the sides with more frosting. Spoon the remaining frosting on top of the cake and spread it evenly from the center to the edges.

Buttercream Frosting

- ½ cup sugar
- 2 tablespoons water
- 2 egg yolks
- ¾ cup (¼ lb. plus 4 tablespoons) butter, softened
  Milk

In a small pan over medium-high heat, bring sugar and water to a boil, then continue to boil without stirring for 1½ minutes.

Meanwhile, place egg yolks in a bowl and beat with an electric mixer until light and lemon colored (see page 174). With beaters going, pour hot syrup into eggs in one steady stream. ***Do not scrape syrup from pan.*** Continue to beat, scraping bowl often, for 5 minutes or until mixture feels cool to the touch. Beat in butter, a tablespoon at a time, until light and fluffy. Stir in milk until mixture reaches desired spreading consistency. Makes about 1½ cups.

Fruits

Offering better nutrition than any other dessert, fruit also presents a nearly endless variety. Brimming with vitamins and minerals, fruits contain very little fat, a minuscule amount of protein, and lots of water. Their carbohydrates come from natural sugars—a good source of energy.

Thanks to modern transportation and storage, perishable fruits now travel the year around to most parts of the country. But for best value in flavor, texture, and price, buy fruits when they're in season. At almost any time of year you'll find many varieties of apples and pears, as well as oranges, grapefruit, bananas, pineapple, papaya, and kiwi.

Summer, of course, brings the fruit cornucopia—apricots, cherries, Gravenstein apples, Bartlett pears, grapes, peaches, nectarines, and plums; watermelon and cantaloupe, as well as casaba, crenshaw, honeydew, and Persian melons; and a bounty of berries from blue to black, plus raspberries, gooseberries, and many others in various parts of the country.

In autumn you'll see more melons and grapes and some continuing stone fruits, along with Bosc and Anjou pears, red and golden Delicious apples, persimmons, and pomegranates.

With the winter months come tangerines, mandarins, oranges, and grapefruit. Then spring opens the show once again, as strawberries reappear among the apples, pears, and citrus that kept us through the wintertime.

Choosing & storing fresh fruit

Fruit quality shows in degree of ripeness, color, firmness, and of course, freedom from decay. Exceptionally large fruits are a risky choice—they may lack flavor and juice. The least expensive varieties may not prove to be bargains after all, if they're priced low because of bruises, pithy texture, or bitter flavor.

Since fruit quality varies throughout a season and depends on the location of the harvest, only experience can guide you to wise choices. But a few general rules will help you select fruit of high quality. Choose loose fruit rather than fruit wrapped in cellophane. Then store it in plastic bags in the refrigerator.

Bananas and pineapples, picked when still green, ripen to sweetness after harvesting. Slightly green bananas will ripen at room temperature—but ripe or not, they should never be refrigerated. Select a pineapple that's faintly yellow orange, heavy for its size, and deliciously fragrant, with a fresh green top. Refrigerate it when you get home, if it's perfectly ripe; if not, let it finish ripening at room temperature.

Apricots, peaches, figs, grapes, and plums, if purchased green or even slightly green, will never reach their ultimate sweetness and flavor. Choose orange yellow apricots and peaches that are firm but yield slightly to touch. Figs and plums should have uniform color and be firm, yielding slightly to touch. If stone fruits are firm to touch and you want to soften them up a bit, put them in a brown paper bag, close it tightly, and leave it at room temperature for a day or two.

Grapes should be plump and firmly attached to the stem. Look for melons that are well rounded and heavy for their size; avoid melons that have flat surfaces or peaked ends. Select watermelons with a yellowish streak on one side. Once ripe, melons should be refrigerated.

Berries are usually expensive, so it pays to be choosy when purchasing them. When you take them home, pick through them, discarding any bruised, decayed, moldy fruit—but don't wash them yet. Refrigerate and use within a day or two.

Choose smooth-skinned citrus fruit that's fairly round, compact, and heavy for its size. In summer, refrigerate it if it's not to be eaten soon.

Apples taste best when firm and crisp. In winter, Rome Beauty is the best candidate for baking whole; red Delicious and Jonathan make the best eating. Summer Gravenstein tastes wonderful either raw or baked. You can keep apples at room temperature for a few days, but they stay crisp longer in the refrigerator.

Cheese with fruit

A natural dessert, fruit and cheese complement each other beautifully. Pass a basket of choice whole fruit with a tray of cheese wedges, and provide cheese cutters and small, sharp knives for informal feasting. Suggested below are some winning cheese and fruit partnerships—there are no rules, though, so experiment freely.

Try blue, Gorgonzola, and Roquefort with apples and pears; Brie with berries, papaya, mangoes, apples, and pears; Cheddar with pears and red-skinned apples; Jarlsberg and Gouda with apples, pears, and apricots; provolone with pineapple; Swiss and Emmentaler with pears; and jack or teleme with apricots, melons, and plums.

HOW TO MAKE PINEAPPLE SHELLS

1 Cut pineapple in half lengthwise. With curved grapefruit knife, cut around fruit on inside of each half, ¼ inch from edge.

2 With straight knife at 45° angle to pineapple, cut out wedge by slicing through core and fruit, but not through shell.

3 Slice core off each wedge and discard; cut wedges into 1-inch cubes.

4 Pile cubes back into pineapple, or mix with other fruit and pile back into shell. If made ahead, cover and refrigerate.

Pineapple Fruit Refresher

Looking like a boat brimming with delicious cargo, our fruit-filled pineapple shells make a stunning display. If you prefer not to use the pineapple shells, you can serve the fruit medley in individual dishes. Feel free to vary the fruit according to your taste and what looks best at the market.

  1 **medium-size pineapple**
  2 **bananas**
  2 **peaches or nectarines**
    Lemon juice
  1 **cup hulled strawberries**
  1 **cup honeydew or casaba melon cubes**
  2 **tablespoons honey**
  1 **tablespoon creamy peanut butter**
  1 **cup unflavored yogurt**
    Topping (optional): chopped peanuts, granola, or toasted shredded coconut

Cut pineapple in half lengthwise. Leaving a ¼-inch-thick shell, cut out fruit from each half, then cut fruit into cubes (see illustrations at left); place fruit in a bowl and set shells aside.

Peel bananas and cut into ½-inch-thick diagonal slices. Peel, pit, and slice peaches (no need to peel nectarines, if used). Sprinkle bananas and peaches with lemon juice, then add to pineapple along with strawberries and melon; pile into pineapple shells. Cover and refrigerate for at least 2 hours.

In a small bowl, stir together honey and peanut butter; stir in yogurt until well blended. Cover and chill until needed. Serve fruit from pineapple shells; pass yogurt sauce to spoon over individual servings. Offer your choice of topping, if desired, in individual bowls. Makes 4 to 6 servings.

Orange Ambrosia

  2 **large oranges**
  1 **large banana**
  1 **cup red or green grapes**
  2 **teaspoons lemon juice**
  ¼ **to ⅓ cup sugar**
  ¼ **cup flaked coconut**

Peel and segment oranges (see illustrations below); place segments in a bowl. Peel bananas and cut into ½-inch-thick slices. Add to bowl along with grapes and lemon juice; toss. Sprinkle sugar and coconut over fruit; cover and refrigerate for at least 2 hours. Makes 4 servings.

SEGMENTING CITRUS FRUITS

1 Slice off ends of fruit. Using a paring knife, remove peel, cutting deeply enough to remove all of white pith as well.

2 Working over a bowl, cut toward center of fruit on one side of white membrane—slide fruit segment off, leaving membrane intact.

...Fruits

Peaches with Raspberries

When fresh peaches are out of season, substitute one large canned peach half, drained.

> ½ cup whipping cream
> 1½ tablespoons powdered sugar
> ½ teaspoon almond extract
> 4 large peaches or nectarines
>   Lemon juice
> ¼ cup sliced almonds
> 1 package (10 oz.) frozen sweetened raspberries, thawed

In a small bowl, whip cream with powdered sugar and almond extract; set aside. Peel, halve, and pit peaches (you need not peel nectarines); coat with lemon juice.

Place peach halves, hollow side up, in small individual bowls. Fill each hollow with 1 teaspoon of the almonds, then evenly distribute raspberries and their liquid over almond-filled peach halves. Top each with 2 to 3 tablespoons of the whipped cream. Sprinkle with remaining almonds. Makes 8 servings.

Minted Poached Pears

> 4 medium-size firm pears (Anjou, Bosc, or winter nelis)
> 1 can (18 oz.) unsweetened pineapple juice
> 4 teaspoons white crème de menthe

Peel pears, using a vegetable peeler; leave stems intact. With melon baller scoop out and discard core and seeds, working from blossom (bottom) end of each pear.

Stand pears, stem up, in a deep 3-quart pan. Pour pineapple juice over pears and bring to a boil; cover, reduce heat, and simmer for 15 to 20 minutes or until just fork-tender (time will vary, depending on variety and ripeness of pears).

With slotted spoon, lift pears from juice to a serving dish; set aside. Increase heat to high and boil juices, uncovered, stirring occasionally, until reduced to about 1 cup. Stir in crème de menthe; pour over pears. Cool, cover, and refrigerate for at least 4 hours or until next day. To serve, spoon some juice over each pear. Makes 4 servings.

Apple Crisp

Nutritious and only lightly sweetened, this dessert is best served on the day you make it. For variety, you can substitute Anjou or Bartlett pears for the apples.

> 1 cup firmly packed brown sugar
> 1 cup all-purpose flour or whole wheat flour
> 2 teaspoons ground cinnamon
> ½ cup (¼ lb.) butter or margarine
> 7 or 8 golden Delicious apples (2 to 2½ lbs. *total*)
> 2 teaspoons lemon juice
> 1 teaspoon grated lemon peel

Preheat oven to 350°. Lightly grease a 9-inch square baking pan; set aside.

In a small bowl, stir together sugar, flour, and 1 teaspoon of the cinnamon. With a pastry blender or your fingers, cut in butter until mixture is crumbly; set aside.

Peel and core apples; slice thinly into prepared baking pan. Sprinkle with the remaining teaspoon of cinnamon, lemon juice, and lemon peel; toss to coat apples, then spread them out in pan. Sprinkle crumb mixture evenly over apples.

Bake, uncovered, for 50 to 60 minutes or until apples are fork-tender and top crust is browned and crisp. Let cool for at least 30 minutes before serving, or let cool completely and serve at room temperature. Makes 6 to 8 servings.

TWO WAYS TO CUT CITRUS ZEST

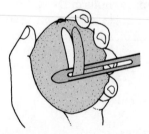 

With a vegetable peeler: Cut off thin colored layer; use a knife to cut into finer shreds or to chop.

With a citrus zester: Place sharper edge on fruit and pull down; fine strands of colored rind will come through.

Sherried Cream with Fresh Fruit

⅓ cup sugar
2 tablespoons cornstarch
⅛ teaspoon salt
2 cups milk
¼ cup cream sherry or apple juice
2 egg yolks, lightly beaten
2 tablespoons butter or margarine
1 teaspoon vanilla
About 1½ cups seedless red or green grapes, or diced fresh pineapple, or sliced fresh nectarines

In a 2-quart pan, stir together sugar, cornstarch, and salt. Gradually add milk and sherry, stirring until well blended. Stirring constantly, bring to a boil over medium heat, then continue to boil for 1 minute. Remove from heat.

Stir part of the hot sauce into beaten yolks, then return all to pan and cook for 30 seconds. Remove from heat and add butter and vanilla, stirring until butter is melted. Cool.

Layer spoonfuls of sherried cream and fruit into 4 stemmed glasses. If you use nectarines, cover top layer with pudding so fruit will not darken. Cover and refrigerate until ready to serve. Makes 4 servings.

Cantaloupe in Strawberry Purée

1 cup sliced hulled strawberries
3 tablespoons sugar
¼ cup cream sherry
1 tablespoon lemon juice
1 large cantaloupe

In a blender or food processor, whirl strawberries to make ½ cup purée. Pour into a bowl; stir in sugar, sherry, and lemon juice. Cut cantaloupe in half, scoop out seeds, remove rind, and cut fruit into bite-size pieces. Add to purée and stir to coat each piece. Cover and refrigerate for 2 hours to blend flavors.

To serve, spoon fruit and purée into 4 stemmed glasses. Makes 4 servings.

FRUIT SAUCES

Versatile and easy, our make-ahead fruit sauces bring bright flavors to quick breads, meats, and desserts. Pancakes perk up with the blueberry, raspberry, or strawberry sauce. Poultry, roast pork, and ham taste delicious with the cranberry-raisin sauce. Or try any one of these sweet sauces drizzled sundae-style over scoops of your favorite ice cream.

Blueberry sauce. In a pan, combine ⅓ cup **sugar** and 1 tablespoon **cornstarch.** Add 2 cups fresh or frozen and thawed **blueberries,** 2 tablespoons **lemon juice,** and ⅓ cup **water.** Cook, stirring, over medium heat until mixture is thickened. Serve warm or cold. Makes about 2 cups.

Cranberry-raisin sauce. (Purchase packages of fresh cranberries when they appear on the market in winter, then freeze for use throughout the year—there's no need to thaw.) In a 2-quart pan, combine 1 package (16 oz.) fresh **cranberries,** 1 cup **water,** 3 cups **sugar,** 1 cup **golden raisins,** 2 tablespoons **lemon juice,** ½ teaspoon each grated **lemon peel** and **ground cinnamon,** and ¼ teaspoon **ground cloves.** Bring to a rolling boil over medium-high heat, stirring constantly; reduce heat and simmer, uncovered, stirring occasionally, for 30 more minutes or until cranberries pop and sauce begins to thicken. Stir in ⅓ cup chopped **walnuts.** Serve warm or cold. Makes about 3 cups.

Raspberry or strawberry sauce. In a small pan, combine 1 package (about 10 oz.) frozen and thawed **sweetened raspberries** or strawberries, ½ teaspoon **cornstarch,** and 1 tablespoon **light corn syrup.** Bring to a rolling boil over medium-high heat; continue to boil, stirring constantly, for 2 minutes. Remove from heat; then cool, cover, and refrigerate. This sauce thickens as it cools. Serve cold. Makes about 1 cup.

Hard meringue shells

Beaten egg whites are lightly sweetened, then transformed into crisp, delicate, baked meringue shells—edible containers for whipped cream or fresh fruit, or for scoops of ice cream drizzled with fresh fruit sauce.

Baked meringues should be white to faint amber in color, crisp and very dry to the touch. Avoid making them on a very humid day because they won't become as crisp. You bake them at a very low temperature, then leave them in the turned-off oven to become crisp and completely dry. Because they absorb moisture readily, they shouldn't be filled until just before serving. If made ahead, store them in an airtight container.

Meringue Shells

> 4 egg whites (about ½ cup), at room temperature
> ½ teaspoon cream of tartar
> 1 cup sugar
> 1 teaspoon vanilla

Preheat oven to 250°. Cover a baking sheet with plain ungreased brown paper (you can cut up a heavy brown paper bag, if you like). Trace eight 3½-inch circles on the brown paper, about 1½ inches apart. Set aside.

Using an electric mixer and a large bowl that holds at least 6 cups below top curve of beaters, combine egg whites and cream of tartar. Beat at highest speed until mixture is just frothy. Continue beating while gradually sprinkling about 1 tablespoon sugar a minute over the beaten whites, and scraping bowl frequently with a rubber spatula.

When all sugar is incorporated, add vanilla and beat for 1 more minute. When beaters are lifted out, whites should hold very stiff, sharp, unbending peaks. Spoon about ½ cup of the beaten egg white mixture onto each circle on prepared

pan. Using the back of the spoon, spread mixture to cover each circle (see *Illustration 1*), then build up a 1½-inch-high rim, creating a hollow in each (see *Illustration 2*). Position baking sheet just below oven center. Bake for 1 hour; turn off heat and leave in closed oven for 3 to 4 hours to dry.

Remove from oven and cool completely; then carefully peel off paper backing. If made ahead, store in an airtight container for as long as 5 days. Makes 8 individual shells.

Meringue Coffee-Cream Torte

> Beaten egg white mixture for Meringue Shells (recipe at left)
> 1 teaspoon instant coffee powder
> 4 tablespoons coffee-flavored liqueur (or 2 additional teaspoons instant coffee powder, 2 tablespoons water, and 1 teaspoon vanilla)
> 1 pint (2 cups) whipping cream
> 1 large bar (about 5 oz.) milk chocolate, coarsely chopped
> Ground sweet chocolate or unsweetened cocoa (optional)

Preheat oven to 250°. Grease two baking sheets and dust with flour; trace an 8-inch circle in flour on each; set sheets aside.

Prepare beaten egg white mixture. Using a pastry bag with plain tip (or a spoon and spatula), pipe or spread half the mixture onto one baking sheet, making a plain disk. Shape remaining meringue in an 8-inch solid disk with a decorative surface of puffs and swirls.

If you have two ovens, position each egg white disk below center in each oven. If you have one oven, position disks just above and below center, then switch their positions halfway through baking. Bake for 1½ hours. Turn off heat and leave in closed oven for 3 to 4 hours to dry; then remove from oven. While pans are still warm, flex them to pop meringues free, but leave meringues in place to cool completely.

In a small cup, blend coffee powder and coffee liqueur. In a bowl, whip cream until stiff, then fold in coffee mixture and chopped chocolate.

Place plain meringue on a flat serving dish; spread all the cream filling evenly over top of meringue only. Place decorative meringue on top of filling. Cover and refrigerate for 8 hours or until next day to mellow for easy cutting. If desired, dust top lightly with ground sweet chocolate. Cut into wedges to serve. Makes 8 to 10 servings.

Illustration 1   *Illustration 2*

INDEX

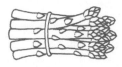

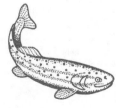
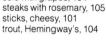